Kanji Alchemy III
A Strategy for Reading Japanese Characters Hyougaiji

Harry Nap

Copyright © 2015 Harry Nap

All rights reserved.

ISBN:- 0-9941964-8-2

ISBN-13:- 978-0994164-8-4

CONTENTS

	Introduction	i
1	Aries	1
2	Taurus	37
3	Gemini	76
4	Cancer	112
5	Leo	146
6	Virgo	177
7	Libra	211
8	Scorpio	243
9	Sagittarius	271
10	Capricorn	300
11	Index & Definitions of Alchemical Symbols	329
12	Index Signature Characters	339
13	Bibliography & Online Resources	361

ACKNOWLEDGMENTS

Jim Breen's Kanjidic compilation of 6,355 kanji as specified in the JIS X0208 1990 standard has been used as the main source for Kanji Alchemy. This publication has included material from the JMdict (EDICT, etc.) dictionary files in accordance with the license provisions of the Electronic Dictionaries Research Group. See http://www.csse.monash.edu.au/~jwb/edict.html and http://www.edrdg.org/.

Kenneth Henshall's "A Guide to Remembering Japanese Characters" has been a major inspiration.

INTRODUCTION

A different approach to kanji is required in order to facilitate reading proficiency:

- Start memorising kanji in groups or **clusters** rather than standalone characters.

- Study in a rational way by focusing on features within kanji that will aid kanji recognition such as **radicals** and an awareness of the etymology of the character.

- Study in a **systematic** way by imposing order and regularity on the multitude of characters. This means abandoning the conventional textbook format.

Hyougaiji refer to kanji that are "outside of the list" of the General Use (Jouyou) characters and Jinmeiyou kanji. Whilst the number of characters covered in Kanji Alchemy III is 3462, the range of these Non General Use (NGU) kanji is vastly more extensive. The Japanese standard work on Chinese characters - Dai Kan-Wa Jiten 大漢和辞典 edited by Morohashi Tetsuji- lists over 50,000 characters and the most comprehensive Chinese dictionary covers more than 85,000 different characters. The third volume of Kanji Alchemy follows the same structure as the previous volumes but with some changes. Whereas with General Use characters treated in Kanji Alchemy I the emphasis was on compound kanji, i.e. emphasising the fact that in texts kanji appear more frequently as words (combinations of more than one kanji) rather than as individual characters, this is with Hyougaiji no longer the case. Given the nature and frequency of these particular characters, often referring to flora & fauna, providing compound characters would seem less useful. (This also applies to the set of Jinmeiyou kanji in Kanji Alchemy II.) Consequently (recall) sentences are no longer a feature in in the last two volumes as there is no reference to compound characters.

Radicals such as 亅 (barb radical) have been allocated within a set of characters where this has been a feature or at least closely resembles the character. In this instance 介 18C has been chosen. This applies as well to other radicals or other kanji with unusual elements.

Japanese characters have a structure that allows for a modicum of understanding. There are recurring features that provide clues and it is clear that there is some kind of consistency in the proliferation of different forms. Characters have their own story to tell and that message can be reinforced when they are grouped together and treated as a set or a cluster. Within each cluster, it is possible to designate one character as a point of reference. 490 of these characters have been selected to act as a chunking device, representing anything from 2 to 14 similar characters in the set. This new allocation of kanji represents a radical departure from the way in which Japanese characters have been studied until now. To focus on approximately 23% of selected General Use characters means a considerable reduction in memorization and learning. The same set of 490 signature characters has also be used in the "Jinmei" series of the second volume and in the "Non General Use" (NGU) characters of the third volume of Kanji Alchemy. The entire range of kanji amounts to 6460 characters. Following is a synopsis of the method.

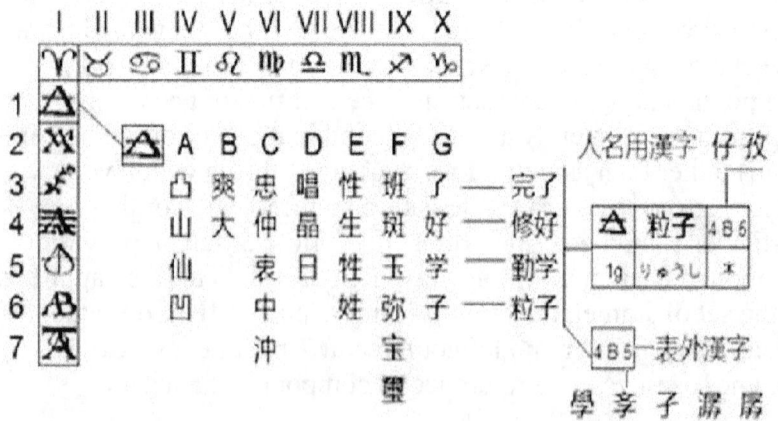

Note that there are ten chapters and that each chapter (named after a star sign) consists of seven weeks. Each week is represented by an alchemical symbol -the first week being AIR- containing seven days (A-G). The example of G shows that there are four characters in the General Use (Jouyou) Kanji range. The symbol in the left corner of the box features the glyph for AIR followed by the "Sight Word" and completed by information showing similar characters in Jinmei Kanji (A = 1, B = 2 etc.) and Non General Use Kanji (5). Learning to read 2136 characters and compounds is a formidable burden on the memory but it is a possible to considerably lessen this strain. Rather than exclusively focusing on memorization and retention, kanji recognition with an analytical focus should become one of the tools for coming to terms with Japanese characters. A case in point are the "semantic-phonetic" characters that represent 85% of all kanji. This category consists of two components: the phonetic component refers to the (long obsolete) pronunciation of the character (on-reading) while the semantic element indicates the meaning or context. An approach that highlights the salient features of kanji will significantly reduce reliance on memorization. A clear understanding of radicals, in particular the ones that function as a semantic or phonetic indicator in the constituent character, will make the learning process much more efficient. Each kanji has one defining radical that is designated as a dictionary index. Kango consists of two (or more) kanji, each character having a reading that approximated the original Chinese at one stage (on-reading). Good knowledge of kango is indispensable for understanding texts. When learning how to read Japanese characters, strong emphasis should therefore be placed on kanji compounds. The key to more efficient study of kanji lies in the reordering of the 2136 general use characters. This is to be achieved through clustering and chunking. Clustering refers to the partitioning of a data set into subsets (clusters), so that the data in all subsets (ideally) share some common trait. Chunking is the practice of grouping units of information into smaller units or chunks in order to facilitate memorization. (signature characters) Just as a string of digits can be regrouped into a smaller number of meaningful units to form a date, Japanese characters can be re-arranged in order to emphasize shared elements that greatly facilitate recognition. Through careful selection 490 signature characters and their clusters represent over 1990 General Use Kanji. Each of these signature characters represents on average 3 to 4 other characters that share the same features; this means that over 90% of the General Use Kanji are related in a meaningful, learner-friendly way. Grouping together characters that share the same elements greatly facilitates the learning process and makes memorization less burdensome. In many cases radicals will make the distinction between characters that have common features. There are about 150 other characters in the 2136 General Use Kanji that are not related and are therefore not directly referenced to the signature characters. (7%) These characters feature of course in kanji compounds but seem to be otherwise singular, unique kanji such as some of the kanji denoting numerals (八 eight 百 hundred) as well as a number of pictographs (月 moon 毛 hair). This aspect changes when Jinmei and NGU kanji are considered: suddenly a great many of these characters become productive and in fact do have their own clusters of kanji with a similar structure. A "productive" non-related character is indicated by an asterisk. The vertical bar or pipe character (|) in the key will sometimes show double or triple vertical bars if more than one of the approximately 150 non related characters have similar forms. Consider 礼 courtesy, salute:

礼	禮	屻	紅	軋
Non Related	Jinmei (Old Form)	Non General Use	Non General Use	Non General Use

The same set of 490 signature kanji is also used for "Jinmei Kanji" (862 kanji that are allocated for writing names) and Non General Use Kanji (more than 3460 kanji that belong neither to the General Use nor the Jinmei category). **Sight words and recall sentences** form an integral part of the learning process. The sight word is a kanji compound (粒子 particle) that refers to a range of similar characters that are grouped (clustered) together and that acts as a chunking device.

Rather than learning one character at a time, a cluster of kanji should be memorized as a group and associated with the relevant signature character in a sight word. Sight words are sometimes used in English reading classes to teach young children high frequency words that are difficult to explain with phonics. (There are various, strongly disagreeing points of view on this subject.) It is part of the whole-word approach that emphasizes visual recognition of a word without analysis of the sub-parts after which the child is able to pronounce the whole word as a single unit. Given the large variety of kanji readings in the Japanese context, a visual approach makes sense because phonological clues are generally not so helpful.

The relevant character that is used in the sight word is a bare or "stripped down" version of the similar kanji it represents, i.e. a character with the least complex radical of the kanji in the cluster or containing no radical at all. When the appropriate radicals are added to the character, the other related kanji in the group will become apparent. This applies not only to the 2136 general use characters but also, often to an even larger extent, to Jinmei and Non General Use characters as well.

A **recall sentence** is a verbal representation of all the characters in the cluster. In the 1G example this would be: **Completed a fine study in small parts**. (Completion 完了, friendship 修好, studying while working 勤学 and particle 粒子) The sentence functions as a mnemonic device incorporating all the compounds of the specific kanji. The recall sentence refers to the other General Use Kanji with a similar structure in the order in which they have been learned making retrieval of relevant information much easier.

The learning process involves the expansion from one character to many: **signature character**; 子 **sight word**; 粒子 **sentence**; 完了/修好/勤学/粒子 **story**; "Notes from the House of Fashion", a short story for practicing kanji that covers a number of the characters featuring in that particular week. (See first week).

It should be noted that, as kanji clusters cover the entire range of General Use Kanji, the conventional order of starting with only "Education Kanji" is no longer the case. Common elements in the structure of kanji can occur anywhere. This means that along with frequent characters – Education Kanji, the first 1006-- less frequent characters in the General Use Kanji range are introduced from the beginning of the series. The use of transliterated Japanese (romaji) should be discouraged. The convention of having katakana for on-reading and hiragana for kun-reading is to be followed. It is less effective to use romaji as it adds an extra step to the learning process. To use kana prepares for future use of Japanese-only materials and maps kanji to pronunciation in the most direct way. A more elaborate overview of kanji and Kanji Alchemy can be found on www.kanjialchemy.com

Chapter 1 Aries

1A 山 AIR

▲	仙術	4A7
1A 並	せんじゅつ	*

Pictograph of a mountain 山
Representation of convexity 凸

山	サン、やま	mountain	1A
汕	サン	fish swimming; fishing with a net	汕
疝	セン、サン	colic; stomach ache	疝
杣	そま	timber; lumber; woodcutter; (kokuji)	杣
岎	タ	fork in a road	岎
岱	タイ	old name for a Chinese mountain; Taishan	岱
圸	まま	steep slope; (kokuji)	圸
岾	やま	used in proper names	岾

1B 大 AIR

▲	大寒	2A1
1B	だいかん	*

Pictograph of a standing person 大

大	ダイ、タイ、おお、おお-きい、おお-いに	big	1B
尢	オウ、だいのまげあし、もっとも	crooked-big radical	尢

1C 中 AIR

◁	中立	5–3
1C	ちゅうりつ	1‖2

Arrow piercing centre of target 中
Pictograph of a standing person 人

中	チュウ、なか	middle, inside, China	1C
沖	チュウ、おき、おきつ、ちゅう.する、わく	offing; open sea; rise high into sky	沖
狆	チュウ、ちん	Pekinese dog; Japanese spaniel	狆
迚	とても	someway or other; very; (kokuji)	迚
人	ジン、ニン、ひと	person	1C
从	ショウ、ジュウ、ジュ、したが.う、したが.える、より	two people	从
仄	ソク、ほの.か、ほの-、ほの.めかす、ほの.めく、かたむ.く	be seen dimly; suggest; intimate; faint; stupid; hint	仄

1D 日 AIR

△	翌日	3B8
1D	よくじつ	*

Pictograph of the sun 日

日	ニチ、ジツ、ひ、か	sun, day	1D
曰	エツ、いわ.く、のたま.う、のたま.わく、ここに、ひらび	say; reason; pretext; history; past; flat sun radical	曰
汨	コツ、イツ、ベキ、しず.む	to sink; name of a Chinese river	汨
衵	ジツ、あこめ	everyday clothing; underwear	衵
娼	ショウ、あそびめ	prostitute	娼
猖	ショウ、くる.う	be insane; severe; violence	猖
倡	ショウ、とな.える、わざおぎ	prostitute; actor	倡
椙	すぎ	Japanese cedar; cryptomeria	椙
榲	まさ	straight grain	榲

1E 生 AIR

△	性分	4A2
1E	しょうぶん	0‖5

Pictograph of a growing plant 生
Mouth and evening, calling out in the dark 名
Variant of talent and child, literal meaning is dam, firmly in place, exist 存

性	セイ、ショウ	nature, sex	1E
徃	オウ、い.く、いにしえ、さき.に、ゆ.く	journey; chase away; let go; going; travel	徃
旌	セイ、ショウ、あら.わす、はた	flag; praise	旌
存	ソン、ゾン	exist, know, think	1E
荐	セン、しきりに	mat; repeatedly	荐
栫	セン、ソン	weir	栫
拵	ソン、こしら.える	make; prepare; arrange	拵
名	メイ、ミョウ、な	name, fame	1E
茗	ミョウ、メイ、ちゃ	tea	茗
酩	メイ、よう	sweet sake	酩

1F 玉 AIR

▲	目玉	6D8
1F	めだま	*

Originally string of beads, jade 玉
Originally device used in spinning, phonetic to press into clay/earth 壐

瑩	エイ	clear	瑩
迩	ジ、ニ、ちか.い	approach; near; close	迩
邇	ジ、ニ、ちか.い	approach; near; close	邇
尓	ジ、ニ、なんじ、しかり、その、のみ	you; that	尓
珎	チン、めずら.しい、たから	precious; valuable; rare	珎
祢	デイ、ネ	ancestral shrine	祢

| 瀰 | ビ | much; many | 瀰 |
| 瀰 | ビ、ミ | copious flow; broad; extensive | 瀰 |

1G 子 AIR

| ⌂ | 粒子 | 4B5 |
| 1G | りゅうし | * |

Infant wrapped in clothes 子

子	シ、ス、こ	child	1G
學	ガク、まな.ぶ	learning; knowledge; school	學
斈	ガク、まな.ぶ	learning; knowledge; school	斈
孑	ケツ、ひとり	mosquito wriggler	孑
潺	セン、サン	sound of flowing water	潺
孱	セン、サン、よわ.い	weak; steep	孱

2A 化 ALEMBIC

| ⚡ | 化け物 | 3A6 |
| 2A | ばけもの | 6‖12 |

Standing person, fallen person, change 化
Cow and variety of streamers, creature, thing 物
Possibly variant of watch tower, high, raised earth 壇

| 化 | カ、ケ、ば-ける、ば-かす | change, bewitch | 2A |

訛	カ、なま.る、なま.り、あやま.る	accent; dialect	訛
鈩	カ、にえ	holmium; pattern on sword blade	鈩
囮	カ、ユウ、おとり	decoy; lure; stoolpigeon	囮
硴	かき	oyster	硴
糀	こうじ	malt	糀
垽	ごみ	garbage; refuse	垽
物	ブツ、モツ、もの	thing	2A
笏	コツ、しゃく	mace; baton; sceptre	笏
惚	ソウ	meaningless; foot race	惚
匆	ソウ、いそが.しい	rush; hurry; be flustered	匆
傯	ソウ、くる.しむ	feel pain; suffer	傯
怱	ソウ、にわか、あわ.てる	rush; hurry; be flustered	怱
葱	ソウ、ねぎ	stone leek; Welsh onion	葱
刎	フン、は.ねる、くびは.ねる	decapitate	刎
壇	ダン、タン	stage, rostrum, podium	2A
羶	セン、なまぐさ.い	smelling like a sheep	羶
顫	セン、ふる.える	shudder	顫
擅	セン、ほしいまま	self-indulgent	擅
氈	セン、もうせん	woolen cloth or rug	氈
亶	タン、セン、あつ.い、ほしいまま	truly; wholly; cordial	亶

2B 丁 ALEMBIC

𝀝	丁寧	7D9
2B	ていねい	0|5

Originally nail (now ngu character + metal) 丁
Formerly roof/house, heart, dish and an element referring to contentment 寧

丁	チョウ、テイ	block, exact	2B
紵	チョ	flax; linen	紵
苧	チョ、お、からんし、からむし	hemp; flax	苧
佇	チョ、たたず.む	stop; linger; appearance; figure; bearing	佇
竚	チョ、たたず.む	stop; linger	竚
廳	チョウ、テイ、やくしょ	government office	廳
甼	チョウ、みち	town; block	甼
叮	テイ	courtesy	叮
疔	テイ、チョウ	carbuncle	疔
酊	テイ、よう	intoxication	酊
寧	ネイ	peace, preferably	2B
獰	ドウ、ネイ、わる.い	bad	獰
聹	ネイ	noisy; earwax	聹
檸	ネイ、ドウ	lemon tree	檸
噂	ネイ、ニョウ	kindness	噂
濘	ネイ、ぬか.る	muddiness	濘

2C 車 ALEMBIC

ᴀᴀ	車庫	5D6
2C	しゃこ	*

Two-wheeled chariot 車

車	シャ、くるま	vehicle, chariot	2C
俥	くるま	jinrikisha; rickshaw; (kokuji)	俥
葷	クン	garlic	葷
轟	コウ、とどろ.かす、とどろ.く	rumble; explosion; blast	轟
嗹	レン、おしゃべり	voluble; garrulous	嗹
鏈	レン、くさり	chain; irons; connection	鏈
縺	レン、もつ.れる	tangle; knot; fasten; fetter	縺

2D 立 ALEMBIC

ᴀᴀ	立場	5A4
2D	たちば	*

Originally person standing on the ground 立

立	リツ、リュウ、た-つ、た-てる	stand, rise, leave	2D
竝	ヘイ、ホウ、な.み、なら.べる、なら.ぶ、なら.びに	line up; be in a row; rank with; rival; equal	竝
莅	リ、レイ、るい、のぞ.む、つ.く	proceed to; assume a post	莅
苙	リュウ、キュウ	type of herb; pigsty	苙
枊	ロウ	bent tree; broken tree	枊

2E 石 ALEMBIC

ꙺ	嫉**妬**	4C4
2E	しっと	*

Cliff and (carved out) rock/boulder 石

石	セキ、シャク、コク、いし	stone, rock	2E
鮖	かじか	bullhead; (kokuji)	鮖
跖	セキ、あしのうら	sole of the foot	跖
鉐	セキ、ジャク	brass	鉐
磊	ライ	many stones	磊

2F 字 ALEMBIC

ꙺ	字幕	2–3
2F	じまく	*

Originally house where children are raised, proliferation, numerous letters 字

字	ジ、あざ	letter, symbol	2F
孛	ハイ、ブツ、ボツ	comet; dark; obscure	孛
悖	ハイ、ボツ、もと.る	be contrary	悖
浡	ボツ、ホツ	place name	浡

2G 目 ALEMBIC

ꙺ	目撃者	4–5
2G	もくげきしゃ	*

Pictograph of an eye 目

目	モク、ボク、め、ま	eye, ordinal, suffix	2G
瞽	コ、めし.い	blind person	瞽
嵋	ビ	place name	嵋
媚	ビ、こ.びる	flatter; humour; flirt	媚
苜	モク、ボク	clover; medic	苜
泪	ルイ、レイ、なみだ	tears; weep; cry	泪

3A 先 ALUM

	指先	2A2
3A	ゆびさき	1|3

Originally foot/stop + person, die, ancestors, precede, tip 先
Originally kneeling at the altar 礼

先	セン、さき	previous, precede, tip	3A
筅	セン、ささら	bamboo whisk for tea-making	筅
跣	セン、はだし	barefooted	跣
礼	レイ、ライ	courtesy, salute, bow	3A
軋	アツ、きし.る、きし.む	squeak; creak; grate	軋
屼	ガイ、たわ、たお	mountain saddle	屼
糺	キュウ、ただ.す、あざな.う	ask; investigate; verify; twist (rope)	糺

Kanji Alchemy III

3B 左 ALUM

🦇	左側	3B7
3B	ひだりがわ	*

Left hand + work upon, auxiliary, assist 左

左	サ、ひだり	left	3B
嵯	サ	high; towering; irregular; rugged	嵯
槎	サ、いかだ、き.る	raft; cut slant wise	槎
搓	サ、サイ、よ.る	braid; cut	搓
嗟	サ、シャ、あ、ああ、なげ.く	be satisfied; grieve; ah	嗟
蹉	サ、つまず.く	stumble	蹉
磋	サ、みが.く	polish	磋
縒	シ、サ、よ.る	twist	縒

3C 十 ALUM

🦇	十字路	4A4
3C	じゅうじろ	*

Sewing needle used as a substitute for more a complex character 十

十	ジュウ、ジッ、とお、と	ten	3C
什	ジュウ、シュウ	utensil; thing; ten	什
瓱	デカグラム	10 grams; (kokuji)	瓱
籵	デカメートル	dekametre; (kokuji)	籵
竍	デカリットル	dekalitre; (kokuji)	竍

3D 足 ALUM

🕊	満足	4A1
3D	まんぞく	0|4

Foot and kneecap, lower leg, able 足
Originally showing a gourd full of water, overflowing 満

足	ソク、あし、た-りる、た-る、た-す	leg, foot, be sufficient	3D
鞜	トウ、くつ	shoes; boots	鞜
満	マン、み-ちる、み-たす	full, fill	3D
滿	マン、バン、み.ちる、み.つ、み.たす	fill; full; satisfied	滿
蹣	マン、ハン、よろ.めく	staggering; tottering	蹣
瞞	マン、モン、バン、ボン、だま.す	deception	瞞
懣	マン、モン、もだ.える	worry; agony; anger	懣

3E 青 ALUM

🕊	青春	7C7
3E	せいしゅん	1||10

Growth around a full well, fresh, green, immature 青
Originally showing exuberant growth of a mulberry plant + sun 春
Hand holding brush, phonetic expressing dark + deep pool, dark deep pool, foreboding 粛

青	セイ、ショウ、あお、あお-い	blue, green, young	3E
猜	サイ、ねた.む	envy; jealousy; doubt	猜

蜻	セイ	dragonfly	蜻
菁	セイ、ショウ	turnip	菁
鯖	セイ、ショウ、さば	mackerel	鯖
瀞	セイ、ショウ、ジュウ、とろ、きよ.い	pure water; clear water; pool in a river	瀞
睛	セイ、ショウ、ひとみ	pupil of the eye	睛
倩	セン、セイ、つらつら、うつく.しい	carefully; attentively; profoundly	倩
春	シュン、はる	spring	3E
惷	シュン	confusion; foolish	惷
蠢	シュン、うご.めく	wriggle	蠢
鰆	シュン、さわら	Spanish mackerel	鰆
粛	シュク	solemn, quiet	3E
渊	エン、カク、コウ、ふち、かた.い、はなわ	edge	渊
渕	エン、カク、コウ、ふち、かた.い、はなわ	edge	渕
肅	シュク、スク、つつし.む	quietly; softly; solemnly	肅
瀟	ショウ	pure; clean	瀟
嘯	ショウ、シツ、うそぶ.く	roar; howl; recite emotionally; feign indifference	嘯
簫	ショウ、ふえ	panpipes; flute	簫
蕭	ショウ、よもぎ	a weed; mugwort; lonely; silent; calm	蕭

3F 貝 ALUM

	魚貝	2–6
3F	ぎょかい	3|2

Originally pictograph of a pointed bivalve 貝
Pictograph of a fish 魚

貝	かい	shellfish	3F
肩	キ	exerting strength (aikido)	肩
闃	ゲキ、ケキ、しずか、ひっそり	quiet; still	闃
鵙	ケキ、ゲキ、もず	shrike	鵙
狽	ケン、バイ、ハイ	wolf; be furried	狽
獺	ダツ、タツ、うそ、かわ、かわうそ	otter	獺
贔	ヒ	strength; power	贔
魚	ギョ、うお、さかな	fish	3F
蘇	ソ、ス、よみがえ.る	be resurrected; resuscitated; revived	蘇
艪	ロ、やぐら、かい	oar; tower	艪

3G 音 ALUM

	発音	7–5
3G	はつおん	1|2

Originally form of speak with addition of tongue 音
Older form is a pictograph of a scorpion 万

音	オン、イン、おと、ね	sound	3G
諳	アン、オン、そら.んじる	memorize; recite from memory	諳
黯	アン、くら.い	black; dark	黯

噫	イ、アイ、オク、ああ、おくび	exclamation; burp; belch	噫
韻	イン、ひびき	rhyme; vowel	韻
檍	オク、い	ilex; holm oak; birdlime tree	檍
万	マン、バン	ten thousand, myriad	3G
卍	バン、マン、まんじ	swastika; gammadion; fylfot	卍
邁	マイ、バイ、ゆ.く	go; excel	邁

4A 七 AMALGAM

![]	七面倒	3–2
4A	しちめんどう	0|2

Vaguely resembling a bent finger under a fist, old way to indicate seven 七
Wood and a variant of odd, phonetic to express slice thinly, thin slice of wood, tag 札

七	シチ、なな、なな-つ、なの	seven	4A
砌	サイ、セイ、みぎり	time; occasion	砌
鴇	ホウ、とき、のがん	wild goose; madam of a brothel; crested ibis	鴇
札	サツ、ふだ	paper money, note	4A
扎	サツ、アツ	pull; tie up; prick; stab	扎
紮	サツ、からげる	tie up	紮

4B 空 AMALGAM

홂	寒空	2A4
4B	さむぞら	*

Hole (open space under roof) + work upon 空

空	クウ、そら、あ-く、あ-ける、から	sky, empty	4B
箜	ク、コウ	type of harp	箜
啌	クウ、コウ	angry voice; gargle; throat	啌
椌	コウ	type of ancient musical instrument; unadorned tool	椌
倥	コウ、ぬか.る	boorish; urgent	倥

4C 耳 AMALGAM

홂	取出す	5H21
4C	とりだす	0|3

Pictograph of a pointed ear 耳
Formerly self and item prominently displayed on table, prominent nose 鼻

耳	ジ、みみ	ear	4C
揖	イツ、ユ、シュウ、ユウ	bow with arms folded; come together; assemble	揖
耺	コウ、ひかり	light	耺
珥	ジ、みみだま	ear bauble; hilt	珥
聢	しか、しかと	certainly; (kokuji)	聢
娵	シュ、シュウ、ス、ソウ、よめ	marry; bride	娵

娵	シュ、めと.る、めあわ.せる	marry; arrange a marriage	娵
楫	シュウ、ショウ、かじ、かい	sculling oar	楫
緝	シュウ、つむ.ぐ	spin thread; bring together; shine	緝
顲	ショウ	temple (of head)	顲
慴	ショウ、おそ.れる	fear	慴
囁	ショウ、ささや.く	whisper; murmur	囁
聶	ショウ、ジョウ、ニョウ、ささや.く	whisper	聶
躡	ジョウ、ふ.む	step on	躡
陬	スウ、シュウ、すみ	corner	陬
鑷	セツ、ジョウ、ニョウ、けぬき	pluck hair; tweezers	鑷
摋	ソウ、シュウ、まも.る、たきぎ、う.つ	night; watch; rake	摋
輒	チョウ、すなわち、わきぎ	promptly; easily; i.e.	輒
輙	チョウ、すなわち、わきぎ	sides of chariot were weapons	輙
鵄	とび	kite (bird)	鵄
揶	ヤ、からか.う	tease; play with	揶
爺	ヤ、じい、じじい、おやじ、じじ、ちち	old man; grandpa	爺
鼻	ビ、はな	nose	4C
嬶	かか、かかあ	wife (vulgar); (kokuji)	嬶
鼾	カン、いびき	snoring	鼾
鼻	ヒ、かかめ、かかあ、はないき	breathing through the nose; snorting; wife;	鼻

17

4D 見 AMALGAM

灬	見易い	4C4
4D	みやすい	*

Eye and (formerly) bent legs, kneeling to stare at something 見

見	ケン、み-る、み-える、み-せる	look, see, show	4D
筧	ケン	water pipe; flume	筧
蜆	ケン、しじみ	fresh-water clam	蜆
俔	ケン、たと.える、うかが.う	compare; spy on	俔
覓	ベキ、エキ、ミャク、もと.める	seek	覓

4E 九 AMALGAM

灬	九折	4B4
4E	きゅうせつ	*

Bent elbow = nine when counting with one arm 九

九	キュウ、ク、ここの、ここの-つ	nine	4E
筑	うつぼ	quiver; arrow holder	筑
馗	キ	road	馗
仇	キュウ、グ、あだ、あた、かたき、つれあい	foe, enemy, revenge	仇
抛	ホウ、なげう.つ	hurl	抛

4F 交 AMALGAM

交	外交	6–13
4F	がいこう	*

Pictograph of person sitting with crossed legs, mix 交

交	コウ、まじ-わる、まじ-える、ま-じる、 ま-ざる、ま-ぜる、か-う、か-わす	mix, exchange	4F
駮	カク、ハク、ぶち、まだら	spots	駮
餃	ギョウ、キョウ、コウ	gyoza	餃
皎	キョウ、コウ、きよ.い、しろ.い	white; shining	皎
佼	キョウ、コウ、こう.す、うつく.しい	beautiful; clever; deceive; sly	佼
纐	コウ	tie-dyeing	纐
鵁	コウ	night heron	鵁
効	コウ、き.く、ききめ、なら.う	result; effect; effectiveness	効
狡	コウ、キョウ、ずる.い、こす.い、わるがしこ.い	cunning; sly; crafty; niggardly	狡
爻	コウ、ギョウ、まじ.わる、めめ、まじわる	to mix with; to associate with; to join; double X radical	爻
蛟	コウ、キョウ、みずち	dragon	蛟
鮫	コウ、さめ、みずち	shark	鮫
傚	コウ、なら.う	imitate; follow; emulate	傚
咬	コウ、ヨウ、か.む	bite; gnaw; chew; dash against	咬

4G 夕 AMALGAM

㐁	夕空	4A2
4G	ゆうぞら	*

Pictograph of a crescent moon 夕

夕	セキ、ゆう	evening	4G
侈	シ、おご.る	luxury; pride	侈
夛	タ、おお.い、まさ.に、まさ.る	much; many; more than; over	夛

5A 六 ANTIMONY

⊕	六角	2-7
5A	ろっかく	*

Originally roof, then used as a substitute for clenched fist; six 六

六	ロク、む、む-つ、むっ-つ、むい	six	5A
宍	ニク、ジク、しし	muscles; meat	宍
楉	ベイ	type of tree	楉
幎	ベキ、とばり	cloth covering	幎
溟	メイ、うみ、くら.い	dark; ocean	溟
瞑	メイ、ベン、ミョウ、ミン、メン、めい.する、つぶ.る、つむ.る、くら.い	sleep; dark; close eyes	瞑
暝	メイ、ミョウ、くら.い	dark	暝
螟	メイ、ミョウ、ずいむし	injurious parasite	螟

5B 正 ANTIMONY

☥	正直	8B8
5B	しょうじき な	0|1

Originally variant of lower leg, straight, proper/correct 正
Formerly boat, hand and a person bending, work, serve, servant's livery? 服

正	セイ、ショウ、ただ-しい、ただ-す、まさ	correct	5B
埊	コウ	mound; used in place names	埊
詔	ジョウ	command; (kokuji)	詔
鉦	セイ、ショウ、かね	bell; gong; chimes	鉦
碇	テイ、いかり	anchor; grapnel	碇
嚔	テイ、くしゃみ、くさめ、くさみ	sneeze	嚔
嚏	テイ、くしゃみ、くさめ、くさみ	sneeze	嚏
掟	トウ、チョウ、ジョウ、テイ、おきて	law; commandments; regulations	掟
歪	ワイ、エ、いが.む、いびつ、ひず.む、ゆが.む	warp; bend; strained; distort	歪
服	フク	clothes, yield, serve	5B
箙	フク、えびら	quiver	箙

5C 分 ANTIMONY

☥	分子	6–9
5C	ぶんし	0||3

Split, sword/cut 分
Tree in confined area, constrained 困
Formerly pictograph of a wheat plant + inverted foot, phonetic expressing sharp, spiky 麦

分	ブン、フン、ブ、わ-ける、わ-かれる、わ-かる、わ-かつ	divide, minute, understand	5C
枌	ショウ、フン、まつ、そぎ	pine tree	枌
瓰	デシグラム	decigram; (kokuji)	瓰
竕	デシリットル	decilitre; (kokuji)	竕
汾	フン	name of a Chinese river	汾
氛	フン	air; atmosphere; weather	氛
忿	フン、いか.る、いかり	be angry	忿
芬	フン、かおり、こうば.しい	perfume	芬
扮	フン、ハン、ヘン、ふん.する、やつ.す、よそお.う	impersonate; dress up; disguise; thin shingles	扮
吩	フン、ふ.く	give an order; sprout forth	吩
麦	バク、むぎ	wheat, barley	5C
麥	バク、むぎ	wheat	麥
困	コン、こま-る	quandary, annoyed	5C
梱	コン、こう.る、こうり、こり、しきみ	pack; tie up; bale	梱
悃	コン、まごころ	sincerity	悃

5D 赤 ANTIMONY

☧	赤面	3–3
5D	せきめん	*

Originally big fire with ruddy glow 赤

赤	セキ、シャク、あか、あか-い、あか-らむ、あか-らめる	red	5D
赫	カク、あかい、あか、かがや.く	suddenly; brighten; illuminate; light up	赫
螫	セキ、カク、さ.す	bee-sting	螫
赧	タン、あから.める	get red	赧

5E 未 ANTIMONY

☧	姉妹	4–1
5E	しまい	3|10

Tree with additional branches at the top, still growing 未
Pictograph of a wheat plant 来

未	ミ	immature, not yet	5E
昧	マイ、バイ、くら.い	dark	昧
来	ライ、く-る、きた-る、きた-す	come	5E
憖	ギン、キン、なまじ.い	thoughtlessly	憖
墻	ショウ、かき	fence; hedge	墻
牆	ショウ、かき	fence; hedge; wall	牆
檣	ショウ、ほばしら	mast	檣
穡	ショク	harvest	穡
嗇	ショク、やぶさ.か、おし.む	miserly; stingy; sparing	嗇

蔷	バ、ショウ、ショク、ソウ、みずたで	a kind of grass	蔷
莱	ライ、あかざ	goosefoot; pigweed	莱
賚	ライ、たま.う、たまもの	gift	賚
艢	ロ、ショウ、ゾウ、とも、ほばしら	bow; stern	艢

5F 今 ANTIMONY

⊕	吟詠	7B9
5F	ぎんえい	1|3

Cover, put in a corner conceal 今
Pictograph of an arm with biceps 力

今	コン、キン、いま	now	5F
頷	ガン、カン、うなず.く、あご	nod approval	頷
菡	ガン、カン、つぼみ	bud (plant)	菡
矜	キン、キョウ、ケイ、あわ.れむ、つつし.む、ほこ.る	pride; respect	矜
衾	キン、ふすま	quilt; bedding	衾
黔	ケン、キン、くろ.い	black	黔
岑	シン、ギン、みね	peak; mountain top	岑
唫	テン、うな.る、うなり	groan; roar	唫
棯	ネン	type of fruit tree	棯
鯰	ネン、なまず	fresh-water catfish; (kokuji)	鯰
力	リョク、リキ、ちから	strength, effort	5F

仂	ドウ、リュク、リキ、ロク、リョク、はたら.く	surplus or excess; remainder	仂
朸	リョク、おおご、おうご	carrying-pole	朸
勒	ロク、くつわ	halter and bit	勒

5G 虫 ANTIMONY

虫 5G	螢雪 けいせつ	6–9 0|4	

Insect 虫
Formerly rain and broom, clearing away what has fallen down, snow 雪

虫	チュウ、むし	insect, worm	5G
螢	ケイ、ほたる	firefly	螢
蠱	コ、ヤ、まじ、まじこ.る	rice worm; lead astray	蠱
蚩	シ	fool; make a fool of	蚩
嗤	シ、わら.う	laugh; ridicule	嗤
虱	シツ、しらみ	lice; vermin	虱
蝨	シツ、しらみ	lice; vermin	蝨
蟲	チュウ、キ、むし	insect; bug; temper	蟲
蠧	ト、きくいむし	worm-eaten	蠧
蠹	ト、きくいむし	moth; insects which eat into cloth	蠹
雪	セツ、ゆき	snow	5G
膌	セツ、そり	used in proper names	膌
鱈	セツ、たら	codfish; (kokuji)	鱈

艜	そり	sled; sleigh	艜
轌	そり	sleigh; sled	轌

6A 土 ARMENIAN BOLE

⍭		土煙	3D3
6A		つちけむり	0|4

Pictograph of a clod of earth on the ground 土
Fire, west and earth meaning embankment/block, fire that blocks, smoke 煙

土	ド、ト、つち	earth	6A
塋	エイ、はか	cemetery	塋
肚	ト、はら	belly; stomach	肚
汢	ヌタ	wetland; marsh	汢
煙	エン、けむ-る、けむり、けむ-い	smoke	6A
湮	イン、エン、しず.む、ふさ.ぐ	sink	湮
垔	イン、ふさ.ぐ	close up; stop up	垔
甄	ケン、シン、すえ	porcelain; make clear; distinguish between	甄
梗	ほくそ	a type of tree	梗

6B 王 ARMENIAN BOLE

⍭		王位	4D16
6B		おうい	*

Originally blade of a large battle axe 王
Originally expressing king and crown 皇

王	オウ	king	6B
汪	オウ	flowing full; expanse of water; wide; deep	汪
枉	オウ、ま.げる、ま.がる、ま.げて	bend; curve; crooked; perverse; lean; forcibly; against one's will	枉
筐	キョウ、かたみ、かご、はこ	bamboo basket	筐
篋	キョウ、かたみ、かご、はこ	bamboo basket	篋
框	キョウ、かまち	framework	框
狂	キョウ、ゴウ	disorder	狂
誑	キョウ、たばか.る、たぶら.かす、た.らす	cheat; coax	誑
皇	コウ、オウ	emperor	6B
遑	カン、コウ、いとま、ひま	leisure	遑
湟	コウ	moat; wetland; name of Chinese river	湟
鍠	コウ	sound of bells and drums	鍠
蝗	コウ、いなご、ばった	locust	蝗
惶	コウ、おそ.れる	fear	惶
徨	コウ、さまよ.う	wandering	徨
篁	コウ、たかむら	bamboo grove	篁
鰉	コウ、ちょうざめ、ひがい	sturgeon	鰉
隍	コウ、ほり	dry moat	隍

6C 園 ARMENIAN BOLE

ⒶⒷ	公園	3B7
6C	こうえん	1|4

Chinese only long robe, phonetic long 園
Pictograph of swirling within an enclosure 回

園	エン、その	garden, park	6C
袁	エン、オン	long kimono	袁
轅	エン、ながえ	shaft	轅
袞	コン	imperial robes	袞
滾	コン、たぎ.る、たぎ.らかす	flow; boil	滾
簑	サ、サイ、みの	a coat, raincoat	簑
簔	サ、サイ、みの	a coat, raincoat	簔
榱	スイ、たるき	rafter	榱
回	カイ、エ、まわ-る、まわ-す	turn, rotate	6C
茴	ウイ、カイ	fennel	茴
廻	カイ、エ	go around	廻
徊	カイ、クワイ、エ、さまよ.う	wandering	徊
蛔	カイ、ユウ、かいちゅう、はらのむし	intestinal worms	蛔

6D 白 ARMENIAN BOLE

ⒶⒷ	告白	6C5
6D	こくはく	*

Literally thumbnail, white 白

| 白 | ハク、ビャク、しろ、 | white | 6D |

	しら、しろ-い		
帕	ハク	dense mountain vegetation	帕
粕	ハク、かす	scrap; waste	粕
狛	ハク、こま	archaic part of Korea; lion-dog shrine guards	狛
怕	ハク、ヒャク、ハ、かしわ、おそ.れる	oak	怕
袙	バツ、ハ、あこめ	warrior's headband	袙

6E 色 ARMENIAN BOLE

ℬ	好色		4E7
6E	こうしょく		*

Person bending over another person 色

色	ショク、シキ、いろ	colour, sensuality	6E
扈	コ、したが.う	follow	扈
滬	コウ、コ	weir; another name for Shanghai	滬
笆	ハ	thorny bamboo; bamboo fence	笆
耙	ハ	forked hoe	耙
爬	ハ、か.く	scratch	爬
葩	ハ、はな	flower; petal	葩
悒	ユウ、ふさ.ぐ、うれ.える	be depressed	悒

6F 同 ARMENIAN BOLE

ÆB	銅像	5A2
6F	どうぞう	*

Possible variant of boat, convey + mouth/say (the same thing?)
同

同	ドウ、おな-じ	same	6F
粡	トウ	unpolished rice	粡
恫	ドウ、トウ、いた.む	painful; fearful	恫

6G 系 ARMENIAN BOLE

ÆB	系統	7A3
6G	けいとう	0|7

Pictogram of skein of yarn, originally doubled 系
Pictograph of a tuft of hair 毛

系	ケイ	lineage, connection	6G
鯀	コン	large mythical fish; proper name	鯀
酳	シン、イン	drunken babbling; offer	酳
幺	ヨウ、ちいさい、いとがしら、ようへん	short thread radical	幺
毛	モウ、け	hair	6G
橇	キョウ、ゼイ、セイ、そり、かんじき	sled; sleigh; snowshoes	橇

毳	ゼイ、セイ、セツ、けば、むくげ	nap; down; fluff	毳
髦	ボウ、モウ、たれがみ	bangs; long hair; excellence	髦
粍	ミリ、ミリメートル	millimetre; (kokuji)	粍
瓱	ミリグラム	milligram; (kokuji)	瓱
竓	ミリリットル	millilitre; (kokuji)	竓
毟	むし.る	pluck; pick; tear; (kokuji)	毟

7A 田 ATHANOR

田		田打ち	4B12
7A		たうち	*

Pictograph of a rice field 田

田	デン、た	rice field	7A
橿	キョウ、かし、もちのき	oak	橿
彊	キョウ、ゴウ、つよ.い	strong	彊
薑	キョウ、コウ、はじかみ	ginger	薑
疆	キョウ、さかい	boundary	疆
僵	キョウ、たお.れる	fall down; collapse	僵
鴫	しぎ	snipe (kokuji)	鴫
沺	デン	vast surging waters	沺
甸	デン、テン、かり	region around the imperial capital; outskirts	甸
畋	デン、テン、かり	till; cultivate; hunting	畋

鈿	デン、テン、かんざし	ornamental hairpiece	鈿
畞	ボウ、ホ、モ、ム、せ、うね	Chinese land measure; fields	畞
畚	ホン、もっこ、ふご	basket; hamper	畚

7B 工 ATHANOR

𝔸	大工	8A8
7B	だいく	*

Carpenter's adze-cum-square 工

工	コウ、ク	work	7B
訌	コウ	get confused	訌
肛	コウ	anus	肛
矼	コウ	stepping stone; hard; serious minded	矼
熕	コウ	cannon	熕
扛	コウ、あ.げる	raise	扛
缸	コウ、かめ	urn	缸
槓	コウ、てこ	lever	槓
杠	コウ、てこ、ゆずりは	carry on the shoulder	杠

7C 明 ATHANOR

𝔸	克明	2B
7C	こくめい	0|2

Sun and moon symbolising light, very bright 明
Bending person + old, literally wearing heavy mask, withstand the weight? 克

克	コク	conquer, overcome	7C
尅	コク、かつ	victory	尅
尅	コク、かつ	subdue; destroy; overcome	尅

7D 寸 ATHANOR

𢦏	一寸	10A8
7D	いっすん	1|9

Originally pulse being one sun (width of finger) from base palm 寸
Originally expressing a hunting dog leaping on a prey 猟

寸	スン	measure, inch	7D
蕁	ジン、タン	a kind of grass	蕁
潯	ジン、ふち	shore; banks	潯
忖	ソン、はか.る	conjecture	忖
對	タイ、ツイ、あいて、こた.える、そろ.い、つれあ.い、なら.ぶ、むか.う	correct; right; facing; opposed	對
紂	チュウ、しりがい	harness strap; window	紂
吋	トウ、ドウ、スン、インチ	inch	吋
埒	レツ、ラツ、ラチ、らち.があく、かこ.い	picket; limits; be settled	埒
埓	レツ、ラツ、ラチ、らち.があく、かこ.い	pale; picket fence; limits;	埓

		come to an end	
猟	リョウ	game-hunting	7D
竄	ザン、サン、かく.れる、のが.れる	flee	竄
鼡	ソ、ショ、ねずみ、ねず	rat; mouse; dark grey	鼡
鼠	ソ、ショ、ねずみ、ねず	rat; mouse; dark grey	鼠
鼬	ユウ、ユ、いたち	weasel; skunk; ermine	鼬
鬣	リョウ、たてがみ	mane	鬣
獵	リョウ、レフ、かり、か.る	hunt; field sports	獵
臘	ロウ	12th lunar month	臘
鑞	ロウ	solder	鑞
蝋	ロウ、みつろう、ろうそく	wax	蝋

7E 己 ATHANOR

𝔸	自己	7B3
7E	じこ	*

Twisted thread, first person pronoun 己

己	コ、キ、おのれ	I, me, you, self	7E
回	カイ、エ、まわ.る、まわ.す、もとお.る、か.える	round	回
杞	コ、キ	river willow	杞
祀	シ、まつ.る、まつり	enshrine; worship	祀

34

7F 合 ATHANOR

𝔄	合唱	6B14
7F	がっしょう	*

Lid, cover, mouth say, cap off remark, reply fittingly 合

合	ゴウ、ガッ、カッ、あ-う、あ-わす、あ-わせる	meet, join, fit	7F
姶	オウ、アイ、あい	good-looking; quiet	姶
峇	コウ	mountain cave	峇
洽	コウ、あまねし、うるお.す	far and wide	洽
袷	コウ、キョウ、あわせ	lined (kimono)	袷
盒	コウ、さら、ふたもの	covered utensil	盒
哈	ゴウ、ハ、ソウ	school of fish; fish's mouth moving; exhaling sound	哈
鴿	コウ、はと、どばと	dove; temple pigeon	鴿
蛤	コウ、はまぐり	clam	蛤
粭	すくも	chaff; rice hulls	粭
拿	ダ、ナ、つか.む、ひ.く	catch; arrest	拿
韜	トウ	rumbling	韜
荅	トウ、あずき、こた.える	adzuki beans; thick	荅
劄	トウ、サツ、チョウ、さ.す	sickle; stay; remain	劄
箚	トウ、サツ、チョウ、さ.す	progress report	箚

7G 北 ATHANOR

𝔄	敗北	2A5

7G	はいぼく	*

Originally two persons sitting back to back, coldest direction 北

北	ホク、きた	north, flee	7G
讌	エン、うたげ	banquet	讌
嚥	エン、の.む	swallow	嚥
臙	エン、のど、べに	rouge	臙
乖	カイ、そむ.く、もとる	oppose; disobey	乖
埀	スイ、た.れる、た.らす、なんなんと.す	let down; suspend; hand down	埀

Chapter 2 Taurus

8A 内 BALM

♉	獄内	2–6
8A	ごくない	0|1

Originally enter + dwelling = inside 内
Two dogs and words, fight, litigation 獄

内	ナイ、ダイ、うち	inside	8A
鞢	ケツ	archer's arm protector	鞢
蚋	ゼイ、ネイ、ゼツ、ネチ、ぶゆ、ぶよ、ぶと、か	gnat; sand fly	蚋
衲	ドウ、ノウ、ころも	mend; priestly vestments; priest	衲
朒	トツ、ジク	new moon	朒
吶	トツ、ども.る	stutter	吶
訥	トツ、ども.る	stutter	訥
獄	ゴク	prison, litigation	8A
嶽	ガク、たけ	peak	嶽

8B 広 BALM

♉	広告	3B9
8B	こうこく	*

Originally spacious building illuminated by flaming arrow 広

広	コウ、ひろ-い、ひろ-まる、ひろ-める、ひろ-がる、ひろ-げる	wide, spacious	8B
擴	カク、コウ、ひろ.がる、ひろ.げる、ひろ.める	broaden; extend; expand; enlarge	擴
絋	コウ	cotton wadding	絋
吰	コウ、あきらか、むな.しい	extensive; wide; broad; empty	吰
曠	コウ、あきらか、むな.しい	wide; worthless	曠
壙	コウ、あな	hole	壙
砿	コウ、あらがね	ore	砿
礦	コウ、あらがね	mine; mineral; ore	礦
鑛	コウ、あらがね	ore	鑛
簧	コウ、した	flute reed	簧

8C 馬 BALM

ꝏ̃ 8C	馬乗り うまのり	6A10 *

Pictograph of a horse 馬

馬	バ、うま、ま	horse	8C
馭	ギョ	driving (horse)	馭
驫	ショウ	many horses	驫
搔	ソウ、か.く	scratch; rake; comb; paddle; behead	搔
蚤	ソウ、のみ、はやい	flea	蚤
隲	チョク、シツ、のぼ.る	stallion; climb; make	隲

闖	チン、うかが.う	inquire about	闖
碼	バ、メ、やあど、やある	number; wharf; agate; yard (91.44 cm)	碼
憑	ヒョウ、つ.く、つか.れる、よ.る、たの.む	depend; rely; evidence; proof; according to; possess; haunt	憑
馮	ヒョウ、フ、フウ、たの.む、よ.る	displeasure; proper name	馮
瑪	メ、バ	agate; onyx	瑪

8D 陽 BALM

☀		太陽		8C11
8D		たいよう		0|4

Chinese only bright and open out, sun rising high and shining down 陽
Originally expressing misty/shady side of the hill 陰
Pictograph of an open mouth 口

湯	トウ、ゆ	hot water	8D
愓	ショウ	be sad; grieve	愓
觴	ショウ、さかずき	cup	觴
場	ジョウ、チ、ウ、ば	open space; field; market	場
殤	ショウ、わかじに	dying at a young age	殤
腸	チョウ、はらわた	guts; bowels; intestines; viscera	腸
盪	トウ、とろ.かす、あら.う、うご.く	melt; be charmed; captivated	盪

盪	トウ、とろ.かす、あら.う、うご.く	to toss about; to swing; to rock	盪
蕩	トウ、とろ.かす、とろ.ける、うご.く	melt; be charmed; captivated	蕩
昜	ヨウ	open; sun	昜
晹	ヨウ	sunrise	晹
煬	ヨウ、あぶ.る、や.く	roast; burn	煬
口	コウ、ク、くち	mouth, opening	8D
釦	コウ、ク、ぼたん	button	釦
叩	コウ、たた.く、はた.く、すぎ	strike; beat; hit; thrash; criticize	叩
扣	コウ、たた.く、ひか.える	knock; strike; rap; tap; button	扣
唧	ショク、ソク、かこ.つ	speak resentfully	唧

8E 首 BALM

𦣻	首肯	4A2
8E	しゅこう	*

Originally eye with exaggerated eyebrow, eye area of face 首 Countenance and phonetic 貌

貌	ボウ、かお、かたち	appearance	8E
藐	ビョウ、バク、かろ.んじる、とお.い	make light of; far away; beautiful	藐
皃	ボウ、バク、かたち、かたどる	countenance; appearance	皃

8F 売 BALM

꩜	売り物	4A9
8F	うりもの	*

Formerly to buy, put out for buying; sell 売

売	バイ、う-る、う-れる	sell	8F
贖	ショク、あがな.う	redeem	贖
續	ゾク、ショク、コウ、キョウ、つづ.く、つづ.ける、つぐ.ない	continue; carry on; succeed	續
覿	テキ、あ.う	meet; see	覿
竇	トウ、トク、あな	hole; doorway; ditch	竇
牘	トク、かきもの、ふだ	letter	牘
黷	トク、けが.す、けが.れる	make dirty; become dirty	黷
犢	トク、こうし	calf	犢
瀆	トク、トウ、けが.す、けが.れ、みぞ	defile; blaspheme; ditch	瀆
讀	ドク、トク、トウ、よ.む	read; study; pronounce	讀

8G 池 BALM

꩜	用水池	3C3
8G	ようすいち	0|1

Twisting creature, snake undulating ground 池
Formerly pictograph of a river with current and ripples 水

池	チ、いけ	pond, lake	8G

鈚	シ	halberd	鈚
葹	シ、おなもみ	cocklebur	葹
髢	テイ、セキ、かもじ	wig	髢
水	スイ、みず	water	8G
汞	コウ、みずがね	mercury	汞

9A 楼 BATH OF VAPOURS

ⅤB	鐘楼	3A22
9A	しょうろう	*

Shamaness chanting whilst holding counting stick 楼

楼	ロウ	tower	9A
鸚	イン、オウ、ヨウ	parrot; parakeet	鸚
嬰	エイ、ふ.れる、みどりご、あかご	sharp (music); baby	嬰
瑛	エイ、ヨウ	a necklace made of precious stones	瑛
纓	エイ、ヨウ	crown string; breast harness	纓
瓔	エイ、ヨウ	jewelled necklace	瓔
嚶	オウ、な.く	chirping; birds singing together	嚶
数	スウ、ス、サク、ソク、シュ、かず、かぞ.える、しばしば、せ.める、わずらわ.しい	number; strength; fate; law; figures	數

薮	ソウ、やぶ	thicket; bush; underbrush; grove	薮
藪	ソウ、やぶ	thicket; bush; underbrush; grove	藪
籔	ソウ、やぶ	thicket; bush; underbrush; grove	籔
屢	ル、しばしば	often; frequently	屢
簍	ル、ロウ	bamboo basket	簍
縷	ル、ロウ、いと	thread	縷
瘻	ル、ロウ、せむし、かさ、できもの	fistula	瘻
鏤	ル、ロウ、ちりば.める	inlay; set; mount	鏤
婁	ル、ロウ、つな.ぐ、ひ.く	frequently; tie	婁
髏	ロ	skull	髏
褸	ロ、ル、ロウ、いと	rags	褸
窶	ロウ、ク、ル、や.つる、や.つれる	emaciated	窶
樓	ロウ、たかどの	tower; turret	樓
僂	ロウ、ル、かが.む	bend over	僂
螻	ロウ、ル、けら	mole cricket	螻

9B 里 BATH OF VAPOURS

𝕭	古里	5E13
9B	ふるさと	2|3

Ground with fields and dividing paths, settlement 里
Originally dancing person, borrowed phonetic to express "not" 無

里	リ、さと	village, league	9B
墅	ショ、ヤ、しもやしき	shed; country house; countryside	墅
糎	センチ、センチメートル	centimetre; (kokuji)	糎
瓱	センチグラム	centigram; (kokuji)	瓱
竰	センチリットル	centilitre; (kokuji)	竰
㙏	テン	fine residence; shop; store	㙏
躔	テン、ふ.む	movement of the sun/moon through the heavens	躔
纏	テン、まつ.わる、まと.う、まと.める、まと.まる	wear; wrap; tie; follow around; collect	纏
廛	テン、みせ、やしき、たな	fine residence; shop; store	廛
霾	バイ、つちふる	wind-blown dust falling like rain	霾
俚	リ、いや.しい	rustic; ill-mannered	俚
釐	リ、おさ.める、さいわ.い、りん	few; 10th of a bu	釐
狸	リ、ライ、たぬき	tanuki; raccoon	狸
貍	リ、ライ、たぬき	a fox-like animal	貍
無	ム、ブ、な-い	not, non, cease to be	9B
憮	ブ、コ、いつくし.む	disappointment	憮
廡	ブ、しげ.る、ひさし	walking under the eaves	廡
嘸	ブ、ム、さぞ、さぞや、さぞかし	how; indeed; I dare say	嘸

9C 黃 BATH OF VAPOURS

VB	黄色	3C
9C	きいろ	*

Original meaning flaming arrow, yellow 黄

9D 家 BATH OF VAPOURS

VB	作家	3A7
9D	さっか	*

Pictograph of a pig 家

家	カ、ケ、いえ、や	house, specialist	9D
糠	すくも	chaff; rice hulls	糠
檬	モウ	lemon tree	檬
濛	モウ、こさめ	dark	濛
艨	モウ、ボウ、いくさぶね	fighting ship	艨
朦	モウ、ボウ、おぼろ	dim; obscure	朦
曚	モウ、ボウ、くら.い	darkness	曚
矇	モウ、ボウ、くら.い、めし.い	blind	矇

9E 原 BATH OF VAPOURS

VB	原子	4–1
9E	げんし	*

Cliff + variant of spring 原

| 原 | ゲン、はら | plain, origin | 9E |

愿	ゲン、つつし.む	respectful; honest	愿

9F 斗 BATH OF VAPOURS

VB	北斗星	3-6
9F	ほくとせい	*

Pictograph of a ladle 斗

斗	ト	dipper, measure	9F
蚪	カ	tadpole	蚪
蔊	カ	type of wisteria	蔊
槲	コク、かしわ	oak	槲
斛	コク、と	measure; 10; unit of volume, about 180 litres	斛
蚪	ト	tadpole	蚪
抖	ト、トウ	shake; jiggle	抖

9G 戸 BATH OF VAPOURS

VB	戸籍	5B5
9G	こせき	*

Pictograph of "half" a door 戸

戸	コ、と	door	9G
綮	ケイ	emblem on banner	綮
鈩	ロ、いろり	hearth; fireplace; furnace	鈩
粐	ロ、コ	rice-bran	粐
艫	ロ、とも、へさき	bow or prow of boat	艫
櫨	ロ、はぜ	wax tree; sumac	櫨

46

10A 申 BISMUTH

ß	申し込む	6E16
10A	もうしこむ	*

Originally forked lightning, 'voice of the gods?' 申

申	シン、もう-す	say, expound	10A
菴	アン、いおり、いお	hermitage	菴
罨	アン、エン、あみ	cover	罨
洩	エイ、セツ、も.らす、の.びる、も.れる	leak; escape	洩
曳	エイ、ひ.く	trail; tow; drag; pull	曳
淹	エン	dip; soak; immerse; stop; linger	淹
閹	エン、アン、おお.う	eunuch	閹
掩	エン、おお.う	cover; conceal	掩
坤	コン、つち、ひつじさる	divination sign; land; earth	坤
呻	シン、うめ.く、うめき	moan; groan	呻
抻	シン、チン	stretch; extend	抻
紲	セツ	tie	紲
鯍	はたはた	sandfish; (kokuji)	鯍
茰	ユ	oleaster; river ginger tree	茰
腴	ユ、あぶら、こえ.る	fat; grease; growing fat	腴
諛	ユ、へつら.う、へつら.い	flatter	諛
臾	ユ、ヨ、ヨウ	a little while; urging	臾

10B 作 BISMUTH

₿	製作	5A9
10B	せいさく	*

Non General Use character adze on wood, make/construct 作

作	サク、サ、つく-る	make	10B
乍	サ、サク、-なが.ら、たちま.ち	though; notwithstanding; while; during; both; all	乍
鮓	サ、すし	sushi; seasoned rice	鮓
咋	サク、サ、か.む、く.う、くら.う	shout; chew; eat	咋
笮	サク、しゃく	bamboo rope	笮
柞	サク、ははそ	type of oak	柞
怎	シン、ソ、いかで、なんぞ	why; how	怎
祚	ソ、くら.い、さいわ.い	imperial throne; happiness	祚
胙	ソ、サク、ひもろぎ	offerings to gods	胙
炸	タク、サ、サク	frying; explosion	炸

10C 弱 BISMUTH

₿	文弱	2B6
10C	ぶんじゃく	*

Doubling of bow, bending and delicate hairs, easily bent 弱

弱	ジャク、よわ-い、よわ-る、よわ-まる、よわ-める	weak	10C
搦	ジャク、ジョク、ダク、ニャク、から.める、-がら.み	bind; tie; approx.	搦

蒻	ジャク、ニャク	a kind of water plant	蒻
鶸	ジャク、ひわ	siskin; greenfinch; light yellow-green	鶸
嫋	ジョウ、ジャク、デキ、なよ.やかな、しなや.か、たお.やか	supple; pliant; delicate; slender	嫋
嵶	たお.やか、たわ.む	mountain pass	嵶
弼	ヒツ、たす.ける、ゆだめ	help	弼

10D 曜 BISMUTH

₿	曜日	3D3
10D	ようび	*

Bird and wings, passing 曜

曜	ヨウ	day of the week	10D
戳	タク	poke; prod	戳
糶	チョウ、せり、うりよね	auction	糶
糴	チョウ、テキ、う.る、せり、かいよね	sell (grain); auction	糴

10E 寺 BISMUTH

₿	侍女	8A5
10E	じじょ	1|5

Growing plant, hand, regular use of hands, clerical work 寺
Pictograph of a kneeling woman 女

寺	ジ、てら	temple	10E
時	ジ、シ	festival grounds	時
恃	ジ、シ、たの.む	depend on	恃
塒	シ、ジ、ねぐら、とや、とぐろ	roost; hencoop; spiral	塒
峙	ジ、そばだ.つ	tower; soar	峙
痔	ヂ、ジ、しもがさ	piles; haemorrhoids	痔
女	ジョ、ニョ、ニョウ、おんな、め	woman	10E
姦	カン、ケン、かん.する、かしま.しい、みだら	wicked; mischief; seduce; rape; noisy	姦
妝	ソウ、ショウ、よそお.う	dress up	妝
嬲	ドウ、ジョウ、なぶ.る	frolic; play with; flirt with	嬲
媽	ボ、モ、はは	mother; mare	媽
婪	ラン、むさぼ.る	covet	婪

10F 語 BISMUTH

B 10F	語調 ごちょう	3C7 *

Words + ngu character I/me (originally two identical reels) 語

語	ゴ、かた-る、かた-らう	tell, speak, talk	10F
唔	ゴ	reading voice	唔

珸	ゴ	jewel	珸
悟	ゴ	go against; be contrary to	悟
齬	ゴ	irregular teeth	齬
晤	ゴ、あきらか	clear	晤
圄	ゴ、ギョ、ひとや	prison; arrest	圄
寤	ゴ、さ.める	awake; understand	寤

10G 方 BISMUTH

ᛒ	見方	12A20
10G	みかた	02|03

Possibly tethered boats in the current, square 方
Originally three tens, thirty years, one generation 世

方	ホウ、かた	side, way, square, direction, person	10G
閼	ア、アツ、エン、ヨ、とど.める、ふさ.ぐ	obstruct; conceal	閼
唹	オ	laugh; smile	唹
淤	オ、ヨ、どろ	mud; silt; clog up; obstruct	淤
鎊	かざり	metal jewellery; (kokuji)	鎊
餝	コウ、シキ、ショク、かざり、かざ.る	decorate; ornament; adorn; embellish	餝
鰌	どじょう	loach; lamprey	鰌
髣	ホウ	dimly	髣
魴	ホウ、かがみたい、おしきうお、	type of seabream	魴

		かがみだい		
彷	ホウ、さまよ.う		stray; wander; loiter	彷
枋	ホウ、ヘイ、ほ		raft; boat	枋
滂	ホウ、ボウ		flowing; vast	滂
膀	ボウ、ホウ		bladder	膀
蒡	ボウ、ホウ		burdock	蒡
榜	ボウ、ホウ、かじ、たてふだ、ふだ		rudder; oar; nameplate	榜
謗	ボウ、ホウ、そし.る		slander; disparage; censure; criticize	謗
旁	ボウ、ホウ、つくり、かたがた、かたわら		right-hand radical of a character; at same time	旁
磅	ボウ、ホウ、ぽんど		become obstructed; pound (sterling, lb)	磅
舫	ホウ、もや.う、もやいぶね		moor; berth	舫
膂	リョ、ロ、せぼね		backbone	膂
楞	リョウ、ロウ、かど		corner; protrusion	楞
世	セイ、セ、よ		world, society, age, generation	10G
丗	セイ、セ、ソウ、よ、さんじゅう		thirty	丗
泄	セツ、エイ、も.れる		leak	泄
紲	セツ、きずな		fetters	紲

11A 仏 BLACK BRIMSTONE

志		仏教	6C13
11A		ぶっきょう	*

Nose, self 仏

仏	ブツ、ほとけ	Buddha, France	11A
泓	オウ、ふか.い	deep clear water	泓
蚣	コウ、ショウ	centipede; grasshopper	蚣
ム	シ、ボウ、ム、わたくし、ござ.る、む	I; myself; katakana mu radical	ム
淞	ショウ	name of a Chinese river	淞
鬆	ショウ、ソウ、シュ	loose; dishevelled; pore; cavity in overboiled daikon	鬆
枩	ショウ、まつ	pine tree; firtree	枩
菘	スウ、シュウ	type of rape plant	菘
舩	セン、ふね、ふな	boat; ship; vessel	舩
狒	ヒ、ひひ	baboon	狒
彿	フツ	dimly	彿
髴	フツ	dimly	髴
怫	フツ、ハイ、ヒ	anger	怫
弗	フツ、ホチ、どる、ず	dollar	弗

11B 才 BLACK BRIMSTONE

ᚼ 11B	天才 てんさい	4–2 6‖8

Originally dam across a stream 才
Pictograph of a tree 木
Originally showing a person with a large head, up, above 天

才	サイ	talent, year of age	11B

犲	サイ、やまいぬ	wolf; cruel; wicked; mean	犲
豺	サイ、やまいぬ	jackal	豺
木	ボク、モク、き、こ	wood	11B
杰	ケツ、ゲチ、すぐ.れる	hero; heroic; outstanding	杰
凩	こがらし	wintry wind; (kokuji)	凩
儿	ジン、ニン、がい、にんにょう、ひとあし	legs radical	儿
禿	トク、ちび.る、かむろ、は.げる、はげ	become bald; bare; wear out; waste away; little girl employed at a brothel	禿
杢	モク	woodworker; (kokuji)	杢
沐	モク、もく.する、あら.う	wash	沐
耒	ライ、ルイ、き、く、すき、らいすき	come; plough; 3-branch tree radical	耒
天	テン、あめ、あま	heaven, sky	11B
无	ブ、ム、なし、ない、むにょう、む、なし	nothing; not exist; crooked heaven radical	无

11C 至 BLACK BRIMSTONE

𠃉	至らない	9B17
11C	いたらない	2‖10

Pictograph of an arrow falling to the ground 至
Birth/life and forehead, phonetically expressing birth/growth 産
Pictograph of a wine jar + liquid 酒
Formerly movement, sheep and big, phonetic expressing pass, easy movement to attain goal 達

至	シ、いた-る	go, reach, peak	11C
齷	アク	grating the teeth; fretful	齷
幄	アク、とばり	curtain	幄
椡	くぬぎ	type of oak; (kokuji)	椡
鵄	シ、とび	kite; horned owl; wine cups	鵄
桎	シツ、あしかせ	fetters	桎
蛭	シツ、チツ、ひる	leech	蛭
縉	シン、さしはさ.む	thin red cloth; high officer	縉
晉	シン、すす.む	advance	晉
臺	ダイ、タイ、うてな、われ、つかさ	stand; counter for vehicles	臺
薹	タイ、とう、あぶらな	seedpod	薹
擡	タイ、もた.げる	lift; raise	擡
軽	チ	low	軽
腟	チツ	vagina	腟
膣	チツ	vagina	膣
垤	テツ、ありづか	anthill; hill	垤
咥	テツ、キ、か.む、くわ.える	laugh; chew; eat	咥
桎	むろ	needle juniper	桎
産	サン、う-む、う-まれる、うぶ	birth, produce	11C
崘	リュ、やまのかたち	shape of a mountain	崘

窿	リュウ	vault (of sky); dome	窿
達	タツ	attain	11C
燵	タツ	footwarmer; (kokuji)	燵
達	タツ、ダ、-たち	arrive at; reach; intelligent	達
闥	タツ、タチ	gate	闥
韃	ダツ、タツ	proper name	韃
撻	タツ、むちうつ	whip; flog; strike	撻
酒	シュ、さけ、さか	alcohol, sake	11C
鰌	シュ、シュウ、どじょう	loach (fish)	鰌
酥	ソ	milk	酥
奠	テン、デン、テイ、さだ.める、まつ.る	decision	奠

11D 止 BLACK BRIMSTONE

⛢	中止	3B13
11D	ちゅうし	*

Foot, stop, planting the foot 止

止	シ、と-まる、と-める	stop	11D
齲	ク、ウ、むしば	decayed tooth; cavity	齲
噛	コウ、ゴウ、か.む、か.じる	chew; bite; gnaw	噛
齪	サク、ソク、セク、シュク、シュウ、せま.る	grating the teeth	齪
址	シ、あと	ruins	址
阯	シ、あと	foundation; site; address	阯

趾	シ、あと、はや.い	footprint; remains	趾
沚	シ、なぎさ	shore; shoal	沚
齒	シ、よわい、は、よわ.い、よわい.する	tooth; cog	齒
齣	シャク、シュツ、セキ、こま	a paragraph; section	齣
澀	ジュウ、シュウ、しぶ、しぶ.い、しぶ.る	astringent; harsh; uneven; rough	澀
齔	シン、ソン、トン、かけば	losing baby teeth; child	齔
蕊	ズイ、しべ	pistil; stamen	蕊
恥	チ、は.じる、はじ、は.じらう、は.ずかしい	shame; humiliation; ashamed	恥

11E 心 BLACK BRIMSTONE

あ	愛国心	3C7
11E	あいこくしん	*

Pictograph of a heart 心

心	シン、こころ	heart, feelings	11E
沁	シン、し.みる	penetrate; soak in	沁
蕊	ズイ、しべ	pistil; stamen	蕊
蘂	ズイ、しべ	pistil; stamen	蘂
応	オウ	respond, react	11E
應	OLD FORM OF 応 (JINMEI)	respond, react	11E
贋	ガン、にせ	counterfeit; forgery	贋

雛	やがて	soon after; presently; almost; all but; no more than; after all	雛
軈	やがて	soon after; presently; almost; all but; no more than; after all; (kokuji)	軈
膺	ヨウ、オウ、むね	breast; strike	膺

11F 行 BLACK BRIMSTONE

⿰	運行	2–9
11F	うんこう	*

Pictograph of crossroads 行

行	コウ、ギョウ、アン、い-く、ゆ-く、おこな-う	go, conduct, column	11F
衍	エン、あまり、しく、はびこ.る	overflowing	衍
衙	ガ、ギョ、ゴ	government office	衙
圻	ガケ、いけ	cliff; used in proper names	圻
銜	カン、くつわ、くわ.える	horse's bit	銜
愆	ケン、あや.まる	mistake; fault; offence	愆
絎	コウ、く.れる、く.ける	blind stitch	絎
哢	さそ.う	(kokuji); invite; entice	哢
衜	ちどり	plover	衜
裄	ゆき	sleeve length; (kokuji)	裄

11G 羽 BLACK BRIMSTONE

ぁ 11G	羽毛 うもう	5A12 *

Pictograph of bird's wings 羽

羽	ウ、は、はね	wing, feather, bird counter	11G
栩	ウ、とち	horse-chestnut tree	栩
蓊	オウ、とう	flower stalk; vigorous growth	蓊
翕	キュウ、あ.う	gather	翕
歙	キュウ、キョウ、ショウ、す.う	come together; meet; put away; store	歙
橚	ク、くぬぎ	type of oak	橚
慴	シュウ、ショウ、おそ.れる	fear; threaten	慴
褶	ショウ、シュウ、チョウ、かさね.る	pleats	褶
煽	セン、あお.る、おだ.てる、おこ.る	fan; flap; instigate	煽
搨	トウ、う.つ、す.る	trace; rub a copy of a stone inscription	搨
榻	トウ、こしかけ、しじ	chair	榻
鶲	ひたき	crested flycatcher; peewee	鶲
翊	ヨク	flying; assist; help; respect	翊

12A 外 BLOOD STONE

⊂	占い者	11F14
12A	うらないしゃ	1|1

BLOOD STONE: Synonym for gold

Crescent moon and divination (crack in turtle shell) 外
Originally showing something emerging from the mouth; exhaling and vocalising 呼

外	ガイ、ゲ、そと、ほか、はず-す、はず-れる	outside, other, undo	12A
磧	せき、ひろ	great; see	磧
筅	セン、チョウ	whip; cane; wooden writing slate	筅
沾	セン、チョウ、テン、うるお.う、うるお.す	moisten; wet; soak; touch	沾
苫	セン、とま	rush matting	苫
站	タン	stop; halt	站
遉	テイ、うかが.う、さすが	as might be expected	遉
幀	テイ、チョウ、トウ	making books or scrolls	幀
霑	テン、うるお.う、うるお.い	moisten; water; soak	霑
點	テン、つ.ける、つ.く、た.てる、さ.す、とぼ.す、とも.す、ぼち	point; mark; speck; decimal point	點
覘	テン、のぞ.く、うかが.う	peep; peek	覘
逎	トウ、に.げる、に.がす、のが.す、のが.れる	escape; flee; abscond; dodge	逎

拈	ネン、セン、デン、ひね.る	twirl; twist; twiddle; wring	拈
黏	ネン、ねば.り、ねば.る	stick to; glutinous; sticky; glue	黏
仆	フ、たお.れる	fall; lie down; bend	仆
呼	コ、よ-ぶ	call, breathe	12A
罅	カ、ケ、ひび、すき	fissure; crack; hole	罅

12B 楽 BLOOD STONE

⊂		楽観的	2B7
12B		らっかんてき	*

Originally a type of oak whose leaves were eaten by silk worms 楽

楽	ガク、ラク、たの-しい、たの-しむ	pleasure, music	12B
爍	シャク、とか.す、ひか.る	shine; melt	爍
鑠	シャク、とろ.かす、と.かす	melt; be charmed; captivated	鑠
擽	リャク、ラク、レキ、フキ、くすぐ.る、う.つ	tickle; funny	擽
礫	レキ、つぶて、こいし	small stones	礫
轢	レキ、ひ.く、きし.る	run over	轢
橡	レキ、ヤク、ロウ、くぬぎ	oak used for charcoal	橡
櫟	レキ、ヤク、ロウ、くぬぎ	oak used for charcoal	櫟

12C 舌 BLOOD STONE

⊂	二枚舌	6A9
12C	にまいじた	*

Originally mouth + dry/forked thrusting weapon, phonetic emerge 舌

舌	ゼツ、した	tongue	12C
蛞	カツ	kind of slug	蛞
聒	カツ、かまびす.しい	noisy	聒
刮	カツ、こそ.げる、けず.る	scrape off	刮
闊	カツ、ひろ.い	wide	闊
濶	カツ、ひろ.い	wide	濶
辭	ジ、や.める	word, decline, leave	辭
銛	セン、テン、もり、すき	harpoon; gaff	銛
恬	テン、やすら.く、やす.い	composure	恬
亂	ラン、ロン、みだ.れる、みだ.る、みだ.す、みだ.れ、おさ.める、わた.る	war; disorder; riot; disturb	亂

12D 周 BLOOD STONE

⊂	六百周	4A7
12D	ろっぴゃくしゅう	0|9

Originally field completely full of crops, complete, cycle 周
One and white in its original meaning of thumbnail = hundred 百

周	シュウ、まわ-り	circumference, around	12D
箒	ささら	bamboo whisk; (kokuji)	箒
惆	チュウ、うら.む	grieve over; be	惆

		disappointed	
稠	チュウ、チョウ、おお.い、し.げる	density	稠
綢	チュウ、トウ、まとう	be clothed in; tie; detailed; fine	綢
雕	チョウ、きざ.む、わし、ほ.る	carving	雕
凋	チョウ、しぼ.む	wither; droop; lame	凋
蜩	チョウ、ひぐらし、せみ	clear-toned cicada	蜩
百	ヒャク	hundred	12D
戛	カツ、ほこ	halberd	戛
戞	カツ、ほこ	lance; tap or strike lightly	戞
栢	ハク、ヒャク、かしわ	oak	栢
陌	ハク、まち、みち	east-west path between paddies; road	陌
貊	ハク、ミャク、えびす	barbarians	貊
佰	ヒャク、ハク、おさ	100; hundred; leader of 100 men; east-west path between paddies	佰
瓸	ヘクトグラム	hectogram; 100 grams; (kokuji)	瓸
粨	ヘクトメートル	hectometre; (kokuji)	粨
竡	ヘクトリットル	hectolitre; (kokuji)	竡

12E 毎 BLOOD STONE

⊂	毎日	9I8
12E	まいにち	*

Plant and mother, fertility, richly growing plant 毎
Woman with nipples, suckling 母

毎	マイ	each, every	12E
海	あま	title of a Noh play; (kokuji)	海
誨	カイ、おし.える	instruct	誨
栂	つが、とが	hemlock; (kokuji)	栂
苺	バイ、マイ、いちご	wild strawberry	苺
母	ブ、ム、はは、ぼ、ない、なか.れ、なかれ、かんのはは	do not; must not; be not; mother radical	母
拇	ボ、おやゆび	thumb	拇
姆	ボ、モ、うば	wet nurse	姆
幮	ほろ	hood; top; awning; cover	幮

12F 筆 BLOOD STONE

⊂	筆者	4–5
12F	ひっしゃ	3|6

Hand holding brush 筆
Plant growth on a tree and/or wooden tablets bound together 葉

津	シン、つ	harbour, crossing	12F
聿	イチ、イツ、ふで、ここに、ふでづくり	brush; finally; self; relate; follow; here; fast; writing brush radical	聿
畫	ガ、カク、エ、カイ、えが.く、	picture; sketch; drawing; stroke;	畫

	かく.する、かぎ.る、はかり、ごと、はか.る	mark; divide	
劃	カク、わ.かつ、かぎ.る	divide	劃
肆	シ、つら.ねる、ほしいまま、みせ	four	肆
葎	リツ、むぐら	creepers; trailing plants; vines	葎
葉	ヨウ、は	leaf	12F
縶	セツ、セチ、きずな、つな.ぐ	leash	縶
渫	セツ、チョウ、さら.う	dredging; cleaning out	渫
卅	ソウ、さんじゅう	thirty	卅
楪	チャ	lacquered dish	楪
諜	チョウ、ちょう.ずる、うかが.う、しめ.す	spy out; reconnoitre	諜
鰈	チョウ、トウ、かれい	sole; flatfish; flounder	鰈

12G 須 BLOOD STONE

⊂	必須	3F7
12G	ひっす	*

Head and attractive forehead, face 須

顔	ガン、かお	face	12G
睿	エイ、あき.らか	intelligence; imperial	睿
壑	ガク、カク、たに	valley	壑
贋	ゲン、ガン	fake; counterfeit	贋
鬚	シュ、ス、ひげ	beard; moustache	鬚
濬	シュン、さら.う	deep; dredge	濬

| 頽 | タイ、くず.れる | decline; slide | 頽 |
| 藐 | ビョウ、バク、かろ.んじる、とお.い | make light of; far away; beautiful | 藐 |

13A 孝 BORAX

⚝	孝行	3–1
13A	こうこう	*

Old man + child 孝

| 孝 | コウ | filial piety | 13A |
| 哮 | コウ、た.ける、ほ.える | roar; howl; growl; bellow | 哮 |

13B 氏 BORAX

⚝	氏名	7C14
13B	しめい	2|6

Originally ladle, now hill, prominent hilltop living 氏
Originally rice stored deep inside a building 奥

氏	シ、うじ	clan, family, Mr	13B
棔	コン、ねむのき	silk tree	棔
帋	シ、かみ	paper; stationary; document	帋
祗	シ、つつし.む、まさに	respectful	祗
鳲	シ、とび	kite	鳲
岻	ジ、ニ	name of a mountain	岻
舐	シ、ねぶ.る、な.める	lick; lap up; burn up;	舐

		taste; undergo; underrate; despise	
胝	チ、あかぎれ	chap; crack; callus	胝
詆	テイ、タイ、そし.る、しか.る	vilify; denounce	詆
柢	テイ、ね	root; founded on	柢
牴	テイ、ふ.れる	touch	牴
觝	テイ、ふ.れる	touch; feel; collide with; conflict with	觝
緡	ビン、コン、ミン、さし、つりいと、なわ、ぜにさし	paper string	緡
愍	ビン、ミン、あわ.れむ	pity; mercy; compassion	愍
罠	ビン、ミン、わな、あみ	trap; snare	罠
奥	オウ、おく	heart; interior	13B
礇	イク	jewel	礇
燠	ウ、イク、オウ、おき、あたたか.い	embers	燠
粤	エツ、ここに	alas	粤
澳	オウ、イク、オク、おき、くま	curving shoreline; bend in river	澳
墺	オウ、イク、きし	land; shore; Austria	墺
懊	オウ、じれった.い、なや.む	in distress; provoking; irritating; impatient; vexed	懊

13C 刀 BORAX

⚜	竹刀	4C17
13C	しない*	*

Curved sword, cut 刀

刀	トウ、かたな	sword	13C
釼	ケン、つるぎ	sword; dagger; sabre	釼
衂	ジク、はなぢ	nosebleed	衂
靭	ジン、ニン、サ、サイ、サツ、うつぼ、うつお、しな.やか、ゆぎ	soft; pliable; quiver	靭
靱	ジン、ニン、サ、サイ、サツ、うつぼ、うつお、しな.やか、ゆぎ	soft; pliable; quiver	靱
靮	ジン、ニン、サ、サイ、サツ、うつぼ、うつお、しな.やか、ゆぎ	soft; pliable; quiver	靮
刃	ジン、ニン、は、やいば、き.る	blade; sword; edge	刃
忍	ジン、はか.る	fathom	忍
仞	ジン、はか.る	fathom	仞
枛	トウ	type of tree	枛
釖	トウ、かたな、そり	knife; sword	釖
叨	トウ、みだりに	truly; graciously; gratuitously; ravenously	叨
屶	なた、たな	used in proper names	屶
邉	ヘン、あた.り、ほと.り、-べ	edge; margin; side; border	邉
邊	ヘン、あた.り、ほと.り、-べ	edge; margin; side; border	邊
粱	リョウ、あわ	high quality rice	粱
簗	リョウ、やな	weir; fish trap	簗
茘	レイ、リ、レン、おおにら	scallion; small onion	茘

13D 黒 BORAX

꩜	黒人	3D
13D	こくじん	*

Originally flame with window and marks of soot, black 黒

13E 通 BORAX

꩜	通勤	4B7
13E	つうきん	*

Chinese only raised, originally sun rising above a brushwood fence 通

通	ツウ、ツ、とお-る、とお-す、かよ-う	pass, way, commute	13E
鯒	こち	flathead (fish); (kokuji)	鯒
誦	ショウ、ジュ、ズ、とな.える、よ.む	recite; chant	誦
涌	ユウ、ヨウ、ユ、わ.く	boil; ferment; seethe; uproar; breed	涌
甬	ヨウ	road with walls on both sides	甬
蛹	ヨウ、さなぎ	chrysalis; pupa	蛹
慂	ヨウ、すす.む、すす.める	direct; advise	慂
俑	ヨウ、トウ、ユウ	effigy	俑

13F 沿 BORAX

꩜	鉛筆	3

| 13F | えんぴつ | * |

Hollowed out boat 沿

13G 夜 BORAX

| ⛢ | 夜明け | 2–4 |
| 13G | よあけ | * |

Clear moon 夜

夜	ヤ、よ、よる	night	13G
腋	エキ、セキ、わき	armpit; side	腋
掖	エキ、たす.ける、わきばさ.む	side (of body); carry under arm	掖
鵺	コウ、ヤ、ぬえ	fabulous night bird; chimera	鵺
亠	トウ、なべぶた	kettle lid radical	亠

14A 辛 BRICK

| ▦ | 辛苦 | 5A11 |
| 14A | しんく | 0\|6 |

Tattooist's needle, piercing, slaves, hardship, bitterness 辛
Originally gourd split into two equal halves 両

辛	シン、から-い	sharp, bitter	14A
綷	サイ、こと	breath; life	綷
妛	シ、あなど.る、おろか、みにく.い、みだる	despise; contempt; ugly; same as	妛
滓	シ、サイ、おり、か.す	dregs; grounds	滓

Kanji Alchemy III

妾	ショウ、めかけ、そばめ、わらわ	concubine	妾
襯	シン、はだぎ	underwear	襯
椄	セツ、ショウ、つ.ぐ	graft	椄
辮	ベン、ヘン、あ.む	braid	辮
辯	ベン、ヘン、わきま.える、わ.ける、はなびら、あらそ.う	speech; dialect	辯
辦	ベン、ヘン、わきま.える、わ.ける、はなびら、あらそ.う	manage; do; handle; deal with	辦
辨	ベン、ヘン、わきま.える、わ.ける、はなびら、あらそ.う	discrimination; dispose of; distinguish	辨
瓣	ベン、ヘン、わきま.える、わ.ける、はなびら、あらそ.う	petal; valve	瓣
両	リョウ	both, pair, coin	14A
輌	リョウ	numerary adjunct for vehicles	輌
輛	リョウ	counter for large vehicles	輛
裲	リョウ、うちかけ	ancient robe	裲
魉	リョウ、こだま	spirits of trees and rocks	魉
俩	リョウ、たくみ	skill	俩
兩	リョウ、ふたつ	old Japanese coin; both; counter for vehicles; two	兩

14B 前 BRICK

ⅢⅢ	朝飯前	2A5
14B	あさめしまえ	*

Originally putting on one's clogs (hollowed out wood) and go 前

前	ゼン、まえ	before, front	14B
翦	セン	scissors; cut; clip; annihilate	翦
剪	セン、き.る、つ.む	clip; snip; cut	剪
揃	セン、ただす	straighten (an arrow)	揃
箭	セン、や	arrow	箭
愈	ユ、いよいよ、まさ.る	be superior; heal; more and more; increasingly; finally; beyond doubt	愈

14C 台 BRICK

IIIII	台風	6B9
14C	たいふう	*

Originally mound of earth on the top of which one is stationed 台

台	ダイ、タイ	platform, stand	14C
貽	イ、おく.る	leave behind; gift	貽
飴	イ、シ、あめ、やしな.う	rice jelly; candy	飴
詒	イ、タイ、あざむ.く	deceive; cheat; give; leave behind	詒
怡	イ、よろこ.ぶ	rejoice; enjoy	怡
駘	タイ	stupid	駘
颱	タイ	typhoon	颱
紿	タイ、あざむ.く	deceive	紿
抬	タイ、もた.げる	lift; raise	抬
笞	チ、むち、しもと	whip; rod; scourge; crime punishable by flogging	笞

14D 弟 BRICK

	弟子	4C4
14D 並	でし	*

Previously showing two and large, double large, supersize; fat 太
Set order in binding a stake (used as a weapon), sequence 弟

弟	テイ、ダイ、デ、おとうと	younger brother	14D
俤	おもかげ、てい	face; looks; vestiges; trace; (kokuji)	俤
睇	テイ、ダイ	looking askance at	睇
涕	テイ、なみだ、な.く	tears; sympathy	涕
剃	テイ、まい、そ.る、す.る	shave	剃

14E 妻 BRICK

	夫妻	8E14
14E	ふさい	*

Hand holding broom, house wife 妻

妻	サイ、つま	wife	14E
帰	キ、かえ.る、かえ.す、おく.る、とつ.ぐ	home coming; arrive at; lead to; result in	帰
皈	キ、かえ.る、かえ.す、おく.る、とつ.ぐ	home coming; arrive at; lead to; result in	皈
帚	シュウ、ソウ、ほうき	broom	帚

筍	ジュン、シュン、イン、たけのこ、たかんな	bamboo shoot	筍
睫	ショウ、まつげ	eyelashes	睫
駸	シン	speed; horses running	駸
悽	セイ、いたむ	be sad; be sorrowful	悽
萋	セイ、サイ	luxuriant growth; beautiful	萋
凄	セイ、サイ、すご.む、さむ.い、すご.い、すさ.まじい	bitter cold; miserable; dreary	凄
帚	ソウ、シュウ、ほうき	broom	帚
箒	ソウ、シュウ、ほうき	broom	箒
筝	ソウ、ショウ、こと	koto	筝
箏	ソウ、ショウ、こと	koto	箏
褄	つま	skirt; (kokuji)	褄

14F 西 BRICK

▦	泰西	2E4
14F	たいせい	*

Originally basket, wine press 西

西	セイ、サイ、にし	west	14F
襾	ア、け、にし	cover; place on top of; west radical variant	襾
洒	シャ、ソン、サイ、セン、セイ、すす.ぐ、あら.う	wash; sprinkle	洒

哂	シン、わら.う	derisive laugh; sneer	哂
篥	リキ、リツ、リチ	horn; flageolet	篥

14G 少 BRICK

ⅢⅢ	即**妙**	8B8
14G	そくみょう	*

Original meaning is "smaller than small", tiny size 少

少	ショウ、すく-ない、すこ-し	a little, few	14G
鯊	サ、シャ、さめ、はぜ	goby (fish)	鯊
莎	サ、シャ、はますげ	sedge	莎
娑	シャ、サ	old woman	娑
鈔	ショウ	selection; summary; 1/10 shaku	鈔
杪	ビョウ、ショウ、こずえ	twig; treetop	杪
渺	ビョウ、びょう.たる	tiny; boundless	渺
緲	ビョウ、ミョウ	faint; far off	緲
眇	ビョウ、ミョウ、びょう.たる、すがめ	minuteness; squint	眇

Chapter 3 Gemini

15A 古 CALCINATION

ℝ	考古学	9D17
15A	こうこがく	*

Skull-like mask, ancestors, old 古

古	コ、ふる-い、ふる-す	old	15A
楜	コ	pepper	楜
葫	コ	garlic	葫
蝴	コ	butterfly	蝴
鈷	コ	cobalt	鈷
蛄	コ	mole cricket; cicada	蛄
鴣	コ	partridge	鴣
痼	コ	chronic illness	痼
估	コ、あきな.う、あた.い	price; business; selling	估
沽	コ、あた.い、あら.い、う.る	price; buying & selling	沽
罟	コ、あみ	net	罟
涸	コ、カク、か.れる、からす、こお.る	dry up; mature	涸
涸	コ、カク、か.れる、からす、こお.る	wither; droop; lame	涸
餬	コ、かゆ	rice broth	餬

姑	コ、しゅうとめ、しゅうと、おば、しばらく	mother-in-law	姑
怙	コ、たの.む	depend; rely on; father	怙
詁	コ、よみ	exegesis; critical analysis of classical texts	詁
做	サ、サク、ソ、な.す、つく.る	make	做

15B 番 CALCINATION

®	順番	4E12
15B	じゅんばん	*

Rice plant + field, planting follows set order, roster, turn 番

番	バン	turn, number, guard	15B
蟋	シツ	cricket; grasshopper	蟋
瀋	シン	juice; broth	瀋
潘	ハン	water in which rice has been washed	潘
鐇	ハン	hatchet; vanadium	鐇
鷭	ハン、バ、ばん	waterhen; gallinule	鷭
膰	ハン、ひもごり、ひもろぎ	offerings to gods	膰
釆	ハン、ベン、サイ、と.る、いろどり、のごめ	separate; divide; topped rice radical	釆
繙	ハン、ホン、ひもと.く	peruse	繙
燔	ハン、や.く	burn	燔
蟠	ハン、わだかま.る、わらじむし	coiled up	蟠

| 旛 | ヘン、ハン、はた | flag | 旛 |
| 旙 | ヘン、ハン、はた | a pennant; a banner | 旛 |

15C 斤 CALCINATION

ⒸⓇ	斤目	11C25
15C	きんめ	1‖4

Axe with shaped handle 斤
Original meaning is hill + growing plant, confusion with the character for commander 師
Three mouths, group of people, becoming group of things 品

斤	キン	axe, weight	15C
沂	ギ、キ、ギン	name of a Chinese river	沂
圻	キ、ギン、さか.い	region surrounding the capital	圻
釿	キン	hatchet	釿
掀	キン、ケン	raise; hoist	掀
听	キン、ポン、ド、わら.う	open-mouthed laughter; listen to; pound (sterling, lb)	听
忻	キン、よろこ.ぶ	rejoice; open one's heart	忻
鑿	サク、のみ、うが.つ	chisel	鑿
嶄	ザン、サン	steep or high mountain	嶄
鏨	サン、ザン、たがね	cold chisel	鏨
槧	ザン、セン、サン、ふだ	printed book	槧
塹	ザン、セン、ほり、あな	moat; ditch	塹
慚	ザン、はじ、はじ.る	feel ashamed	慚
慙	ザン、はじ、はじ.る	ashamed; humiliated;	慙

		shameful	
斫	シャク、き.る	cut with a sword	斫
晰	シャク、セキ、あきらか	clear	晰
晳	シャク、セキ、しろ.い	clear	晳
蜥	シャク、セキ、とかげ	a lizard	蜥
晢	セイ、セツ、あきらか	light of stars; shine	晢
淅	セキ	wash rice	淅
浙	セツ	name of a Chinese river	浙
泝	ソ、さかのぼる	go upstream	泝
拆	タク、セキ、さく、ひらく	open	拆
柝	タク、ひょうしぎ	sounding sticks	柝
躓	チ、つまず.く	stumble	躓
噺	はなし	talk; (kokuji)	噺
師	シ	teacher, model, army	15C
篩	シ、サイ、ふる.う	sieve; sift; screen	篩
鰤	シ、ソウ、ぶり、はまち、かます	yellowtail	鰤
品	ヒン、しな	goods, quality, kind	15C
癌	ガン	cancer; cancerous evil	癌
嵒	ガン、いわ、けわ.しい	rock	嵒

15D 市 CALCINATION

℞	市場	4–7
15D	しじょう	*

Originally stop + confines + waterweed, levelling out of sell/buy 市

市	シ、いち	city, market	15D
鬧	トウ、ドウ、さわが.しい	quarrel; dispute hotly	鬧
閙	ドウ、トウ、さわが.しい	noisy	閙
沛	ハイ	big rain; swamp	沛
珮	ハイ、おびだま	bauble; jewel	珮
佩	ハイ、は.く、お.びる、おびだま	wear; put on (a sword)	佩
旆	ハイ、はた	flag	旆
霈	ハイ、ひさめ	big rain; long rainy spell	霈

15E 形 CALCINATION

ⓡ	人形	4–4
15E	にんぎょう	*

Lattice window + hairs/pattern 形

形	ケイ、ギョウ、かた、かたち	shape, pattern	15E
荊	ケイ、いばら	thorn; brier; whip	荊
笄	ケイ、こうがい	hairpin; crossbar of anchor; metal rod on sheath	笄
桁	ケイ、ひじき	rafter; placename	桁
妍	ケン、うつく.しい	beauty; splendour	妍

15F 事 CALCINATION

ⓡ	一事	4–2
15F	いちじ	*

Formerly hand and flag on a pole, identifying guild? Work, worker/servant 事

事	ジ、ズ、こと	thing, matter, act	15F
事	ジ、シ、ズ、こと、つか.う、つか.える	affair; matter; business; to serve; accident; incident	事
駛	シ、は.せる、はや.い	run fast	駛

15G 谷 CALCINATION

®	幽谷	7A10
15G	ゆうこく	*

Deeply, widely split opening, valley 谷

谷	コク、たに	valley, gorge	15G
却	キャク、かえ.って、しりぞ.く、しりぞ.ける	instead; on the contrary; rather	却
郤	ゲキ、キャク、ケキ	crevice; interstice	郤
浴	サコ、セコ	ravine; valley	浴
峪	はざま	ravine; gorge; gap	峪
榕	ヨウ	no known meaning	榕
榕	ヨウ、あこう	evergreen mulberry	榕
鎔	ヨウ、と.ける、と.かす、いがた	fuse; melt	鎔
熔	ヨウ、と.ける、と.かす、いがた	fuse; melt	熔
慾	ヨク	covetousness; greed; passion; desire; craving	慾

峪	ヨク、たに		ravine	峪

16A 長 CAMPHOR

xo	長持ち	3B3
16A	ながもち	*

Originally showing an old man with flowing long hair 長

長	チョウ、なが-い	long, senior	16A
萇	チョウ	type of plant	萇
悵	チョウ、いた.む、うら.む	be sad	悵
漲	チョウ、みなぎ.る	overflow	漲

16B 京 CAMPHOR

xo	東京	8G8
16B	とうきょう	0|2

House on a hill, noble 京
Original meaning is a prominent person arriving at a prominent house on the hill 就
Originally tied sack with a pole thrust through, sun thrusting through, dawn? 東

京	キョウ、ケイ	capital	16B
鐄	キョウ	kind of percussion instrument	鐄
亰	キョウ、ケイ、キン、みやこ	capital city	亰
勍	ケイ、つよ.い	strong; fierce	勍

毫	ゴウ、コウ、ごう.も、すこし	fine hair; brush; not at all	毫
猶	ジョウ、ユウ、ヨウ、なお	condition	猶
肬	ユ、ユウ、いぼ	wart; tumour; goitre; papule	肬
疣	ユ、ユウ、いぼ	wart	疣
喨	リョウ、ロウ	clear voice	喨
東	トウ、ひがし	east	16B
杲	コウ、あきらか、たか.い	clear; high	杲
杳	ヨウ、くら.い、はるか	darkness; dimly	杳

16C 高 CAMPHOR

ⅩO	高最	2E8
16C	こうさい	*

Pictograph of a tall watchtower 高

高	コウ、たか-い、たか、たか-まる、たか-める	tall, high, sum	16C
槁	コウ、か.れる	die (vegetation)	槁
嚆	コウ、さけ.ぶ	call	嚆
鎬	コウ、しのぎ、なべ	sword-blade ridges	鎬
敲	コウ、たた.く	strike; beat; hit	敲
犒	コウ、ねぎら.う	thanks; reward	犒
蒿	コウ、よもぎ	mugwort	蒿
稾	コウ、わら、したがき	draft; manuscript; rough copy	稾
亳	ハク	an ancient Chinese capital	亳

16D 朝 CAMPHOR

XO	朝廷	4C3
16D	ちょうてい	*

Originally sun rising through plants, rise + river 朝

朝	チョウ、あさ	court, morning	16D
澣	カン、あら.う	wash	澣
翰	カン、はね、ふで、やまどり、ふみ	letter; writing brush	翰
瀚	カン、ひろ.い	wide & large	瀚

16E 可 CAMPHOR

XO	可決	12C20
16E	かけつ	1|3

Mouth + twisting waterweed/ seek an exit 可
Mouth, meaning to tell + woman phonetically expressing to comply 如

可	カ	approve, can, should	16E
婀	ア、あだ、あだ.っぽい、たおやか	charm; flirtation	婀
痾	ア、やまい	chronic illness	痾
猗	イ、ア、ああ	luxuriant growth; gentle; docile	猗
欹	イ、キ、そばだ.てる、そばだ.つ	prick up (one's ears)	欹
倚	イ、キ、よ.る、たの.む	lean on; rest	倚

		against	
渦	カ	name of Chinese river	渦
軻	カ	difficult progress	軻
謌	カ、うた、うた.う	sing; recite; carol; poem; tanka; slander; defame	謌
柯	カ、え、ふる	handle	柯
呵	カ、か.す、しか.る、わら.う	scold; blow on; reprove	呵
哥	カ、コ、あに、うた	big brother	哥
訶	カ、しか.る、せ.める	scold	訶
彁	カ、セイ	no known meaning	彁
舸	カ、ふね	large boat	舸
畸	キ	difference; strange; cripple	畸
剞	キ、きざ.む	carve	剞
奇	キ、く.しき、あや.しい、くし.くも、めずら.しい	strange; strangeness; curiosity	奇
碕	キ、さき、さい、みさき	cape; spit; promontory	碕
崎	キ、さき、さい、みさき	steep; promontory	崎
掎	キ、ひ.く	pull; hold back	掎
如	ジョ、ニョ	similar, equal	16E
洳	ジュ	wet	洳
絮	ジョ、ショ、わた	cotton	絮
茹	ジョ、ニョ、ゆ.でる、う.でる	boil; seethe	茹

16F 説 CAMPHOR

ⱮO	説得	10B8
16F	せっとく	0‖4

Non General Use character exchange, barter, person dispersing words 説
Old form shows hand and shell/valuable item, something to gain 得
Formerly showing nuggets in the ground + covering, phonetic to shine 金

説	セツ、ゼイ、と-く	preach, explain	16F
枳	キ、シ、からたち	trifoliate orange tree; thorny tree used for hedges	枳
兇	キョウ、おそ.れる、わる.い	wickedness	兇
況	キョウ、まし.て、いわ.んや、おもむき	still more; stillness	況
咒	ジュ、シュ、シュウ、まじな.う、のろ.い、まじない、のろ.う	spell; curse; malediction	咒
棕	シュ、ソウ	hemp palm	棕
蛻	ゼイ、セイ、タイ、もぬ.ける、ぬけがら	insect moulting	蛻
兌	ダ、エイ、エツ、タイ、よろこ.ぶ	exchange	兌
鐇	バン	name	鐇
得	トク、え-る、う-る	gain, potential	16F

碍	ガイ、ゲ、さまた.げる	obstacle	碍
金	キン、コン、かね、かな	gold, money, metal	16F
淦	カン、コン、あか	bilge water	淦
崟	ギン、みね	peak; mountaintop; steep; lofty	崟
釛	コク、かね	gold	釛

16G 直 CAMPHOR

XO	直立	8C3
16G	ちょくりつ	1|2

Eye + needle and corner, fix with direct piercing stare 直
Formerly dog and four mouths, mouths/receptacles have become the dominant meaning 器

直	チョク、ジキ、ただ-ちに、なお-す、なお-る	direct, upright, fix	16G
稙	ショク、チョク	early-maturing rice	稙
矗	チョク、シュク、チク、なお.い	luxuriance	矗
悳	トク	ethics; morality; virtue	悳
器	キ、うつわ	vessel, utensil, skill	16G
噐	キ、うつわ	vessel; receptacle; implement; instrument; ability	噐
嚻	ゴウ、キョウ、かしま.しい、	noisy; boisterous	嚻

	かまびす.しい	

17A 門 CAPUT MORTUUM

Tm	表門	9B19
17A	おもてもん	*

Pictograph of a gate with a double door 門

門	モン、かど	gate, door	17A
繝	カン、ケン	a method of dyeing	繝
澗	カン、ケン、たに、たにみず	valley river	澗
關	カン、せき、かか.わる、からくり、かんぬき	connection; barrier; gateway; involve; concerning	關
嫻	カン、なら.う、みやびやか	elegant; refined; skilful	嫻
嫺	カン、なら.う、みやびやか	refined; elegant; skilled	嫺
癇	カン、ひきつけ	bitter; hot temper; irritable; nervous	癇
椚	くにぎ、くぬぎ	oak used for charcoal; (kokuji)	椚
閏	ケイ、ギョク、ジュン、うるう	intercalation; illegitimate throne	閏
閂	サン、セン、かんぬき	gate bar	閂
閊	つか.える	be blocked; (kokuji)	閊
鬥	とうがまえ、たたかいがまえ	broken gate radical	鬥
壛	まま	steep slope	壛
們	モン、ともがら	plural suffix	們

捫	モン、な.でる	to stroke	捫
悶	モン、もだ.える、もだえ.る	be in agony; worry	悶
閖	ゆり、ゆ.る、ゆ.れる	shake while rinsing; pan for gold; (kokuji)	閖
燗	ラン、カン、かん.する	warming sake	燗
聯	レン、つら.なる、つら.ねる	party; gang; clique	聯
聯	レン、つら.なる、つら.ねる	party; gang; clique	聯

17B 父 CAPUT MORTUUM

Tm	雷親父	2A1
17B	かみなりおやじ	*

Originally showing hand holding stick, rod of correction 父

父	フ、ちち	father	17B
釜	フ、かま	kettle; cauldron; iron pot	釜

17C 感 CAPUT MORTUUM

Tm	感情	3–10
17C	かんじょう	*

Chinese only unison, sharp weapon, trimming + mouth, all together 感

感	カン	feeling	17C
馘	カク、キョク、くびき.る、みみき.る	behead; dismiss	馘
撼	カン、うごか.す	move	撼

鰔	カン、かれい、たら	flatfish; turbot; cod	鰔
緘	カン、かん.する、と.じる	shut; seal	緘
咸	カン、ゲン	all; same	咸
轗	カン、コン	difficulty; misfortune	轗
鹹	カン、ダイ、から.い、しおからい、しおけ、せいしゅ	salty	鹹
喊	カン、ヤク、さけ.ぶ	cry; call	喊
箴	シン、いまし.める、はり	warning; counsel; precept; needle	箴
鍼	シン、はり、さ.す	needle	鍼

17D 風 CAPUT MORTUUM

Tm	一風	2B3
17D	いっぷう	*

Originally showing phoenix believed to ride the wind 風

風	フウ、フ、かぜ、かざ	wind, style	17D
嵐	おろし	wind from mountains; (kokuji)	嵐
瘋	フウ	insanity; headache	瘋
諷	フウ、そら.んじる	hint; satirize	諷

17E 泉 CAPUT MORTUUM

Tm	温泉	3–3
17E	おんせん	0|3

Pictograph of water emerging from a hole in a rock/hillside 泉

Kanji Alchemy III

泉	セン、いずみ	spring	17E
湶	セン、いずみ、ぜに	spring; fountain-head; source	湶
楾	はんぞう	container for pouring water	楾
穆	ボク、モク、やわ.らぐ	respectful; mild; beautiful	穆
曲	キョク、ま-がる、ま-げる	bend, melody	17E
髷	キョク、まげ、わげ	topknot	髷
梍	しで	type of deciduous birch tree; (kokuji)	梍
腆	テン、あつ.い	much; abundant; kind; considerate	腆

17F 矢 CAPUT MORTUUM

Tm	知合い	4A5
17F	しりあい	*

Pictograph of an arrow 矢

知	チ、しる	know	17F
矢	シ	arrow	矢
聟	セイ、むこ	son-in-law	聟
踟	チ	hesitate	踟
蜘	チ、くも	spider	蜘
椥	なぎ	type of evergreen tree	椥

17G 自 CAPUT MORTUUM

Tm	自然	3A
17G	しぜん	0|4

Nose, self 自
Formerly hands and intertwine, emulate manually + look, learn by looking, remember 覚

覚	カク、おぼ-える、さ-ます、さ-める	remember, learn, experience	17G
覚	カク、おぼ.える、さ.ます、さ.める、さと.る	memorize	覺
撹	カク、コウ、みだ.す	disturb; throw into confusion	攪
撹	カク、コウ、みだ.す	disturb; throw into confusion	搅
黌	コウ、オウ	school	黌

18A 且 CINNABAR

舌 18A	且つ又 かつまた	11C20 *

Pictograph of cairn, piled up stones on top of others 且

且	か-つ	furthermore, besides	18A
萱	ギ	day lily	萱
勗	キョク、ボウ、つと.める	be diligent	勗
渣	サ	dregs	渣
柤	サ、そ	railing	柤
雎	ショ	osprey	雎
萴	ジョ、あさがら	Chinese matrimony vine; tilling public fields; corvee; surname	萴

鋤	ジョ、ショ、ソ、す.く、すき、くわ	spade up; plough	鋤
耡	ジョ、す.く、すき	plough; spade	耡
苴	ソ、サ、シャ、ショ、つと、あさ	husk; bract; straw wrapper; souvenir gift; bribe	苴
齟	ソ、サ、ショ、かむ	uneven; bite; disagree	齟
姐	ソ、シャ、あね、ねえさん	elder sister; maidservant	姐
砠	ソ、ショ	stony hill; stony mountain	砠
岨	ソ、ショ、いしやま、そば	a rocky mountain	岨
蛆	ソ、ショ、うじ	worm; grub; maggot	蛆
咀	ソ、ショ、か.む	bite; eat	咀
疽	ソ、ショ、かさ	carbuncle	疽
詛	ソ、ショ、のろ.う	curse	詛
沮	ソ、ショ、はば.む	stop; prevent; defeated; dejected	沮
俎	ソ、ショ、まないた	altar of sacrifice; chopping board	俎
徂	ソ、ゆ.く	go	徂

18B 元 CINNABAR

吉	元来	6A8
18B	がんらい	1|1

Person with the head exaggerated, upper part, prime part 元
Originally tree and "flame-like flowers", dazzling, shine 栄

| 元 | ゲン、ガン、もと | originally, source | 18B |

晥	カン	Venus; Morningstar; place name	晥
莞	カン	type of plant	莞
浣	カン、あら.う	wash	浣
翫	ガン、もてあそ.ぶ	take pleasure in; play instrument	翫
阮	ゲン	place name	阮
芫	ゲン、ガン	type of vetch	芫
寇	コウ、あだ.する	foe; enemy; revenge; grudge; feud	寇
寇	コウ、あだ.する	bandits; thieves; enemy; invade	寇
栄	エイ、さか-える、は-え、は-える	flourish	18B
蠑	エイ	turban shell	蠑

18C 介 CINNABAR

吉	介入		2B5
18C	かいにゅう		*

Casing, something in between, armour, shell 介

介	カイ	mediate, shell	18C
个	カ、コ	counter for articles; individual	个
价	カイ	man with shellfish kanji	价
畍	カイ、さかい	circle; world	畍
疥	カイ、はたけ	scabby eruption	疥
亅	ケツ、かぎ、はねぼう	feathered stick; barb radical	亅

18D 歩 CINNABAR

�	進歩	4C3
18D	しんぽ	*

Originally doubling of foot, putting one foot in front of other 歩

歩	ホ、ブ、フ、ある-く、あゆ-む	walk	18D
陟	チョク、トク、すす.む、のぼ.る	climb; rise	陟
蘋	ヒン、うきくさ	duckweed	蘋
顰	ヒン、ひそ.める、しか.める	scowl; raise eyebrows	顰

18E 南 CINNABAR

�	南極	2A3
18E	なんきょく	0|2

Warm side of the tent, south side? 南
Push someone between two lines (constraint) into an opening, extreme 極

南	ナン、ナ、みなみ	south	18E
遖	あっぱれ	bravo; admirable	遖
喃	ナン、の.う	chatter; rattle on	喃
献	ケン、コン	dedicate, present	18E
獻	ケン、コン、たてまつ.る	offer; present; show; display	獻
極	キョク、ゴク、きわ-める、きわ-まる、きわ-み	extreme, pole	18E
函	カン、はこ、い.れる	box	函

亟	キョク、キ、ケ、しばしば、すみやか	fast; quick; sudden	亟

18F 予 CINNABAR

占	預金	4A5
18F	よきん	*

Weaving shuttle pushed to one side, prior action 予

予	ヨ	already, prior, I	18F
抒	ジョ、ショ、く.む、の.べる	tell	抒
舒	ジョ、ショ、の.べる	stretch; loosen; open; relax; mention	舒
杼	チョ、ショ、ひ、どんぐり	shuttle	杼
蕷	ヨ、いも	potato	蕷
豫	ヨ、シャ、あらかじ.め	relaxed; comfortable; at ease	豫

18G 角 CINNABAR

占	街角	4A8
18G	まちかど	0|1

Pictograph of a horn 角
Ground and coiling, phonetic to express flat, flat ground, level 均

角	カク、かど、つの	horn, angle	18G
鵤	いかる、いかるが	grosbeak; hawk finch	鵤
邂	カイ、あ.う	meet unexpectedly	邂

蟹	カイ、かに	crab	蟹
廨	カイ、ケ、やくしょ	government office	廨
墝	カク、きそ.う	barren land	墝
桷	カク、たるき	rafter	桷
懈	ケ、カイ、たわ.い、おこた.る	laziness	懈
薊	ケイ、キ、カイ、ケ、あざみ、さく、とげ	thistle	薊
均	キン	level	18G
鈞	キン、ひと.しい	equal; important point	鈞

19A 考 COPPER

♀	考案	2–1
19A	こうあん	*

Originally bent figure + long hair, twisting waterweed, old man 考

考	コウ、かんが-える	consider	19A
栲	コウ、かえ、たえ	sumac; cloth woven from tree fibres	栲

19B 半 COPPER

♀	半島	4A3
19B	はんとう	4‖6

Half a cow 半
Bird and mountain, islands in the sea where birds alight 島
Originally referring to offer to a high authority 奏

半	ハン、なか-ば	half, middle	19B
拌	ハン	stir and mix	拌
胖	ハン	half a sacrifice; ribs; abundant; plentiful	胖
袢	ハン	summer kimono; short clothing	袢
島	トウ、しま	island	19B
橿	かし	oak; mooring pole; used in proper names	橿
嶋	トウ、しま	island	嶋
搗	トウ、つ.く、か.つ	pound; husk	搗
奏	ソウ、かな-でる	play, present, report	19B
榛	シン	dense growth; thicket	榛
臻	シン、いた.る	arrive; reach; gather	臻
輳	ソウ、あつ.まる	gather	輳

19C 発 COPPER

♀	発表	2–7
19C	はっぴょう	*

Two planted feet shooting arrow from bow, dispatch 発

発	ハツ、ホツ	discharge, start, leave	19C
癈	ハイ	chronic illness; getting crippled	癈
廃	ハイ、すた.れる、すた.る	abrogate; terminate; discard	廃
醗	ハツ、かも.す	fermentation; brewing	醗

撥	ハツ、バチ、は.ねる、おさ.める	brush up; reject; exclude; eliminate; bone plectrum	撥
癶	ハツ、はつがしら	dotted tent radical	癶
發	ハツ、ホツ、た.つ、あば.く、おこ.る、つか.わす、はな.つ	departure; publish; emit; start from; disclose	發
潑	ハツ、も.る、とびち.る、そそ.ぐ	sprinkle; lively; vigorous	潑

19D 豆 COPPER

𠮷	豆腐	10G29
19D	とうふ	*

Monopedal table-cum-food vessel with contents 豆

豆	トウ、ズ、まめ	beans, miniature	19D
饐	イ、エイ、エツ、す.える、むせ.ぶ	go bad; sour	饐
懿	イ、よい	beautiful; splendid	懿
噎	イツ、エツ、む.せる、むせ.ぶ	choke; smother	噎
殪	エイ、たお.す	die; bury	殪
磑	ガイ、う.す	mortar; hand mill	磑
刈	ガイ、カイ	scythe; suitability	刈
榿	ガイ、カイ	alder	榿
豈	カイ、ガイ、キ、あに	an interjection of surprise	豈
皚	ガイ、ギ、ゲ、カイ、しろ.い、さむ.い	white	皚

覬	キ	coveting high rank	覬
熹	キ、あぶ.る、あかるい	burn; faint light	熹
禧	キ、さいわ.い	fortunate; auspicious	禧
揆	キ、はかりごと、はか.る	category; plan; drumstick	揆
癸	キ、みずのと	10th calendar sign	癸
僖	キ、よろこぶ	enjoyment; pleasure	僖
憙	キ、よろこ.ぶ、ああ、この.む	rejoice; like; prefer; exclamation	憙
鱚	きす	sillaginoid; (kokuji)	鱚
廚	シュウ、ズ、チュ、チュウ、くりや	kitchen	廚
證	ショウ、あかし	proof; evidence; certificate; testify; verify; guarantee; witness	證
櫁	ツサ	Japanese storax; used in proper names	櫁
鐡	テツ、くろがね	iron	鐡
鐵	テツ、くろがね	iron	鐵
磴	トウ	stone steps; stone bridge	磴
鐙	トウ、あぶみ、たかつき、ひともし	stirrup (bone of the ear)	鐙
嶝	トウ、さかみち	hill; uphill path	嶝
荳	トウ、ズ、まめ	bean; nutmeg	荳
鬪	トウ、たたか.う、あらそ.う	fighting	鬪
彭	ホウ	swelling; sound of drum	彭
澎	ホウ、ヒョウ	turbulent water	澎

19E 平 COPPER

♀	平手	3A6
19E	ひらて	*

Twisting water weed, small, flat, 2 scales 平

平	ヘイ、ビョウ、たい-ら、ひら	flat, even, calm	19E
鮃	ヒョウ、ヘイ、ひらめ	flounder; flatfish	鮃
萍	ヘイ、ヒョウ、うきくさ	floating plants	萍
苹	ヘイ、ビョウ、ホウ、ほ	duckweed; mugwort	苹
泙	ホウ	surging water	泙
怦	ホウ、ヒョウ	in a hurry; excited; agitated	怦
岼	ゆり	level spot part-way up a mountain	岼

19F 言 COPPER

♀	言回し	4A3
19F	いいまわし	*

Originally mouth and sharp: articulate? 言

言	ゲン、ゴン、い-う、こと	word, say, speak	19F
罰	バツ、バチ、ハツ、はっ.する	punishment; penalty	罰
詈	リ、ののし.る	ridicule	詈
誄	ルイ、しのびごと	condolence message	誄

19G 走 COPPER

♀ 19G	奔走 ほんそう	4–3 0‖14

Frantic movement with the foot, running 走
Pictograph of a house with a window, the direction of the window is significant 向
Formerly man running and three footprints, the latter became confused with three plants 奔

歩	ホ、ブ、フ、ある-く、あゆ-む	walk	19G
徙	シ、うつ.る、うつ.す	move	徙
走	ソウ、はし.る	walk; go on foot; run; leave	走
跣	ト	barefoot	跣
向	コウ、む-く、む-ける、む-かう、む-こう	face towards, beyond	19G
餉	ショウ、け、かれい、かれい.い、べんとう	(dried) boiled rice	餉
奔	ホン	run	19G
丱	カン、ケン	saguaro-like kanji; horn-shaped locks of hair; young; tender	丱
卉	キ、ケ、くさ	grass	卉
蒭	シュウ、ス、スウ、まぐさ	to cut grass; hay; fodder	蒭
皺	シュウ、スウ、しわ、しぼ	wrinkles; creases; folds	皺
鄒	スウ、シュ、シュウ	place name	鄒
芻	スウ、シュウ、ス、まぐさ	grass cutting; hay	芻

趣	スウ、ソク、しゅ、おもむ.く、はし.る	run; go; quick; tend towards	趣
艸	ソウ、くさ、くさかんむり、そうこう	grass; plants; grass radical	艸
屮	テツ、サ、ひだりて、ふるくさ	left hand; old grass radical	屮
蟷	トウ	mantis	蟷
蟒	ボウ、モウ、うわばみ、おろち	boa constrictor; python	蟒
莽	ボウ、モウ、くさ	grass; grassy field	莽
本	ホン、もと	advance quickly; to go back and forth; origin; source	本

20A 亜 CORAL

↳	亜熱帯	2C8
20A	あねったい	0|2

Underground dwelling, crooked, hunchback 亜
Once written as eye covered by the dark night, dream might be an associated meaning 夢

亜	ア	next, sub-, Asia	20A
唖	ア、アク、おし	mute; dumb	唖
錏	ア、エ、しろこ、しころ	armour havelock; helmet neck guard	錏
堊	アク、ア、オ、いろつち、しろつち	whitewash	堊
壺	コ、つぼ	jar; pot; hinge knuckle; one's aim	壺
壷	コ、つぼ	jar; pot	壷

壼	コン	palace corridor passageway	壼
椏	また	crotch of a tree	椏
鐚	ワ、ア、びた、しころ	coin of smallest value	鐚
夢	ム、ゆめ	dream	20A
儚	ボウ、モウ、はかな.い、くら.い	fleeting; fickle	儚
梦	ム、ボウ、ゆめ、ゆめ.みる、くら.い	dream; visionary; wishful	梦

20B 主 CORAL

🔄	主催	5A
20B	しゅさい	*

Originally ornately stemmed burning oil lamp, master 主

20C 身 CORAL

🔄	身分	3–1
20C	みぶん	*

Miscopied body instead of bow and arrow 身

身	シン、み	body	20C
麝	ジャ、シャ	musk deer	麝

20D 秋 CORAL

🔄	秋分	2B7

20D	しゅうぶん	*

Rice plant + fire, dry autumn crop-fires caused by Foehn 秋

秋	シュウ、あき	autumn	20D
楸	シュウ、きささげ、ひさぎ	Japanese catalpa	楸
甃	シュウ、しきがわら、いしだたみ	floor tile	甃
鰍	シュウ、シュ、かじか、いなだ、どじょう	bullhead	鰍
愀	シュウ、ショウ	respect	愀
湫	シュウ、ショウ、くて	wetlands; marsh; not	湫
啾	シュウ、な.く	cry; whimper; neigh	啾
鞦	シュウ、ふらん.に、しりがい	swing	鞦

20E 衣 CORAL

↳		衣桁	6A5
20E 並		いこう	*

Originally showing collar and sleeves, clothing 衣
Combining the early form of clothing and fur, fur clothing, outside, surface 表

衣	イ、ころも	garment	20E
裟	けさ	surplice	裟
稷	ショク、きび	millet	稷
禝	ショク、きび	proper name	禝
謖	ショク、シュク、た.つ	arise	謖
猥	ワイ、みだ.ら、みだり.に	obscene	猥

20F 米 CORAL

ᗡ	新米	3
20F	しんまい	*

Pictograph of a rice plant 米

20G 呂 CORAL

ᗡ	風呂	4–6
20G	ふろ	*

Former Jinmei character vertebrae, also joined blocks 呂

宮	キュウ、グウ、ク、みや	palace, shrine, prince	20G
營	エイ、いとな.む、いとな.み	camp; perform; build; conduct (business)	營
筥	キョ	round basket	筥
閭	リョ、ロ、さと	rural area	閭
絽	ロ、リョ	silk gauze	絽
欄	ロ、リョ	kind of quince	欄
梠	ロ、リョ、ひさし	kind of quince	梠

21A 死 CRUCIBLE

ʊ	早死に	2–5
21A	はやじに	*

Originally variant of meatless bone, death + person 死

死	シ、し-ぬ	death	21A
歹	ガツ、ガチ、タイ、がつへん、いちたへん、しにがまえ	bare bone; bad; wrong; death radical	歹
薨	コウ、こう.じる、みま.かる	die	薨
屍	シ、しかばね	corpse	屍
夙	シュク、つとに、はやい	bright and early; long ago; early in life	夙
甍	ボウ、ミョウ、いらか	roof tile; tiled roof	甍

21B 乗 CRUCIBLE

♉	乗り降り	4E2
21B 並	のりおり	0|1

Originally person on top of a tree, climb a tree, mount 乗
Building + woman, referring to a woman resting quietly during menses 安

安	アン、やす-い	restful, ease, cheap	21B
鮟	アン	angler-fish	鮟
宀	ベン、メン、うかんむり	shaped crown; katakana u radical	宀
降	コウ、お-りる、お-ろす、ふ-る	fall, alight, descend	21B
絳	コウ、あか	red	絳

21C 軍 CORAL

♉	空軍	4A8
21C	くうぐん	*

Originally circle of carts, carts drawn into a circle, army 軍

軍	グン	military, army	21C
鶤	ウン、コン、とうまる、しゃも	type of black songbird	鶤
暈	ウン、ぼか.す、ぼか.る、かさ、くま、ぼかし、めまい	halo; corona; fade	暈
皸	クン、キン、ひび、あかぎれ	skin cracks or roughness	皸
皹	クン、キン、ひび、あかぎれ	skin cracks or roughness	皹
諢	コン	joke; jest; colloquial	諢
琿	コン	jewel	琿
渾	コン、すべ.て、にご.る	all; turbidity	渾
褌	コン、ふんどし	loincloth	褌

21D 与 CORAL

♉	与え主	2A4
21D	あたえぬし	*

Originally four hands, many interlocking hands, joint effort 与

与	ヨ、あた-える	give, convey, impart, involvement	21D
寫	シャ、うつ.す、うつ.る	write; draw; sketch; compose	寫

寫	シャ、うつ.す、うつ.る	be photographed; copy; describe	寫
嶼	ショ、しま	island	嶼
襷	たすき	cord to hold up sleeves; (kokuji)	襷

21E 受 CRUCIBLE

㋓ 21E	受付 うけつけ	3–3 *

Hand reaching down 受

受	ジュ、う-ける、う-かる	receive	21E
綬	ジュ、ひも	ribbon	綬
笊	ソウ、ざる、す	bamboo basket	笊
抓	ソウ、つ.ねる、つ.める、つね.る、つま.む	pick; pinch; summarize	抓

21F 反 CRUCIBLE

㋓ 21F	反応 はんのう*	8–3 *

Cliff, phonetic turn over + hand 反

反	ハン、ホン、タン、そ-る、そ-らす	oppose, anti, reverse, bend, cloth, measure	21F
鈑	バン、ハン	sheet metal	鈑
叛	ハン、ホン、そむ.く	disobey; defy; go back on; rebel; rebellion	叛
汳	ヘン、ベン	proper name	汳

109

21G 相 CORAL

♉	相談	4A7
21G	そうだん	1|5

Eye watching from behind the tree, careful observation 相
Heart/feelings and brain, thoughts in the brain 思

相	ソウ、ショウ、あい	mutual, minister, aspect	21G
囗	イ、コク、くにがまえ	box or enclosure radical	囗
凵	カン、うけばこ、かんにょう	open box enclosure; open box radical	凵
冂	キョウ、ケイ、まきがまえ、えながまえ、どうがまえ、けいがまえ	upside-down box radical	冂
廂	ショウ、ソウ、ひさし	eaves; canopy; visor; hallways	廂
笥	ス、シ、け、はこ	lunch box; clothes chest	笥
孀	ソウ、やもめ	widow	孀
匚	ホウ、はこがまえ	box-on-side enclosure radical	匚
思	シ、おも-う	think	21G
腮	サイ、あご、えら	jaw	腮
顋	サイ、あご、えら	lower part of face; jaw; gills of a fish	顋
鰓	サイ、シ、えら	gills; gill slits	鰓
濾	ロ、リョ、こ.す	filter	濾
鑢	ロ、リョ、やすり	file; rasp	鑢

Chapter 4 Cancer

22A 真 DAY

⊕	真昼	4F7
22A	まひる	1|0

Originally person upside-down, (dead?), spirit, essence, truth 真
Originally indicating the bright section of the day 昼

真	シン、ま	true, quintessence	22A
瞋	シン、い.かる、いか.らす	be angry	瞋
嗔	シン、いか.る	be angry	嗔
癲	テン	insanity	癲
顛	テン、いただき	overturn; summit; origin	顛
巓	テン、いただき	summit	巓
鷆	テン、シン、かすい	yellow-white mottled songbird	鷆
鷏	テン、シン、かすい	yellow-white mottled songbird	鷏

22B 度 DAY

⊕	程度	2–1
22B	ていど	*

Measure various things with the hand, measurement 度

| 度 | ド、ト、タク、たび | degree, times | 22B |

| 鍍 | ト、めっき | plating; gilding | 鍍 |

22C 列 DAY

✢		列席	4A4
22C		れっせき	0|1

Cut to the bone, set sequence for dismembering a carcass 列
Convoluted development, formerly pictograph of a rush mat 席

列	レツ	row, line	22C
粲	サン、いい	bright	粲
餐	サン、ソン、の.む、くら.う	eat; drink; swallow	餐
冽	レツ、レイ、きよ.い	cold	冽
洌	レツ、レイ、きよ.い	pure	洌
席	セキ	seat, place	22C
蓆	セキ、むしろ	straw mat; matting	蓆

22D 眼 DAY

✢		千里眼	9–9
22D		せんりがん	0|5

Stop and stare, scrutinise (eye on legs) 眼
Person and one, the body once signified one thousand (two thousand = two horizontal strokes) 千

眼	ガン、ゲン、まなこ	eye	22D
狠	ガン、ゲン、コン、もと.る	vicious; cruel; severely; extreme	狠

艱	カン、ケン、なや.む、かた.い、なや.み	difficult; trying; be distressed; parent's funeral ceremony; mourning; perilous	艱
垠	ギン、ゴン、きし、さか.い	limit; boundary	垠
齦	ギン、コン、はぐき	gums	齦
踉	コン、くび.す	heel	踉
很	コン、コウ、ギン、もと.る	disobey; dispute; very; go against; be contrary to	很
艮	コン、ゴン、うしとら	north east (Oriental zodiac); stopping; good radical	艮
褪	タイ、トン、あ.せる、ぬ.ぐ	fade; discolour	褪
腿	タイ、もも	thigh; femur	腿
千	セン、ち	thousand	22D
瓩	キログラム	kilogram; 1000 grams; (kokuji)	瓩
粁	キロメートル	kilometre; (kokuji)	粁
竏	キロリットル	kilolitre; (kokuji)	竏
阡	セン	thousand	阡
仟	セン、ち、かしら	thousand	仟

22E 旨 DAY

✧	趣旨	5–4
22E	しゅし	*

Something sweet that is spooned into the mouth, lingering 旨

| 旨 | シ、むね | tasty, good, gist | 22E |

皀	キュウ、ヒョク、キョウ、コウ	fragrant; grain	皀
鮨	シ、キ、すし	sushi; seasoned rice	鮨
鬯	チョウ、かおりぐさ	fragrant herbs	鬯
梠	ユウ	sickle handle; type of tree	梠

22F 皿 DAY

| ⊕ | 灰皿 | 6C13 |
| 22F | はいざら | * |

Pictograph of a vessel 皿

皿	さら	dish, bowl, plate	22F
隘	アイ、ヤク、せま.い	narrow; obstruct	隘
縊	イ、エイ、くび.る、くび.れる	strangle	縊
鎰	イツ、かぎ	unit of weight	鎰
謚	エキ、シ、おくりな	laughing	謚
諡	エキ、シ、おくりな	posthumous name	諡
鹽	エン、しお	salt	鹽
鰮	オン、いわし	sardine	鰮
醢	カイ、ひしお、ししびしお、しおから	salted meat	醢
洫	キョク、みぞ	ditch	洫
鷁	ゲキ	waterfowl which flies high but not against the wind	鷁
恤	ジュツ、シュツ、めぐ.む、あわ.れむ、うれ.える	relieve; have mercy	恤

| 滷 | ロ | brine | 滷 |
| 鹵 | ロ、しお、しおち、たて | salt | 鹵 |

22G 進 DAY

✧	進呈	12F22
22G	しんてい	1|1

Move with bird 進
Bamboo abacus 算

進	シン、すす-む、すす-める	advance	22G
帷	イ、とばり	curtain; screen	帷
崖	ガイ、サイ、スイ、がけ	cliff; bluff; precipice	崖
癨	カク	heatstroke; sunstroke	癨
霍	カク、にわか	quick; sudden	霍
匯	キ、エ、カイ、ワイ、がい、めぐ.る	whirl; swirl	匯
虧	キ、か.ける	wane (moon)	虧
舊	キュウ、ふる.い、もと	old things; old friend; old times; former; ex-	舊
摧	サイ、サ、くだ.く	break; smash; crush; familiar; popular	摧
隹	サイ、スイ、とり、ふるとり	bird; old bird radical	隹
囃	サツ、ソウ、はや.す	play (music); accompany; beat time; banter; jeer; applaud	囃
讎	シュウ、あだ、むく.いる	enemy; revenge	讎
讐	シュウ、あだ、むく.いる、あ.たる	enemy; revenge	讐

售	シュウ、う.る	sell; be popular	售
騅	スイ、あしげ	grey horse	騅
雖	スイ、いえど.も、これ	although; however	雖
暹	セン	sunrise	暹
寉	つる	crane (bird)	寉
罹	リ、ラ、かか.る	catch; get	罹
藺	リン、い	rush, used for tatami covers; surname	藺
躙	リン、にじ.る、ふ.む	edge forward; trample	躙
躪	リン、にじ.る、ふ.む	edge forward; trample	躪
淮	ワイ、エ、カイ	name of a Chinese river	淮
算	サン	calculate	22G
簒	サン、セン、うば.う	rob	簒

23A 丙 DECOCTION

+B	丙種	3–3
23A	へいしゅ	0|1

Large altar with sturdy legs 丙
Formerly plank of wood, bed, building/house could be a miscopying of sickness, sickbed 床

丙	ヘイ	C ,3rd	23A
鞆	とも	archer's arm protector; (kokuji)	鞆
炳	ヘイ、あきらか	clear & bright	炳
陋	ロウ、いや.しい、せま.い	narrowness; meanness; humbleness	陋

床	ショウ、とこ、ゆか	bed, floor, alcove	23A
广	ゲン、まだれ	dotted cliff radical	广

23B 式 DECOCTION

←B	開会式	3–2
23B	かいかいしき	*

Carpenter's square and stake, measured intervals, order 式

式	シキ	ceremony, form	23B
弑	シ、シイ、しい.する	murder one's lord or father	弑
軾	ショク、シキ、しきみ	front railing on a carriage	軾

23C 干 DECOCTION

←B	干潟	6B13
23C	ひがた	*

Forked thrusting weapon 干

干	カン、ほ-す、ひ-る	dry, defence	23C
駻	カン	rage; run wild	駻
奸	カン、おか.す	wickedness; mischief; rudeness	奸
悍	カン、たけし、あらし	rough; clumsy; violent	悍
杆	カン、てこ	shield; pole	杆
桿	カン、てこ	shield; pole	桿
骭	カン、はぎ	leg; shin	骭
旱	カン、ひでり	drought; dry weather	旱
扞	カン、ふせ.ぐ	restrain	扞

捍	カン、ふせ.ぐ	defend; protect	捍
罕	カン、まれ	bird-catching net; rare	罕
稈	カン、わら	straw; hollow stem	稈
訐	ケツ、あば.く	divulge; reveal	訐
幵	ヘイ	put together	幵

23D 者 DECOCTION

ᛐB	作者	10O15
23D	さくしゃ	2|3

Originally box for storing kindling, odds and ends, plebs 者
Originally showing two hands, two fires and rising smoke, brushwood on fire 蒸

者	シャ、もの	person	23D
赭	シャ、あかつち	red	赭
奢	シャ、おご.る、おご.り	extravagance; luxury	奢
偖	シャ、さて	well; now	偖
薯	ショ、いも	potato	薯
藷	ショ、ジョ、いも	potato	藷
墸	チョ	hesitate	墸
猪	チョ、い、いのしし	pig; hog	猪
楮	チョ、こうぞ	paper mulberry	楮
躇	チョ、チャク、ためら.う	hesitate	躇
瀦	チョ、みずたまり	pool; puddle	瀦
潴	チョ、みずたまり	pond; a pool	潴
闍	ト、ジャ	watch tower; used phonetically	闍

屠	ト、チョ、ほふ.る	slaughter; butcher; slay	屠
睹	ト、み.る	look at; see	睹
覩	ト、み.る	look at; see	覩
蒸	ジョウ、む-す、む-れる、む-らす	humid	23D
涵	カン、ひた.す	immerse	涵
拯	ショウ、ジョウ、すく.う	help	拯
烝	ジョウ、ショウ、む.す、もろもろ	many; offer; dedicate; to steam	烝

23E 充 DECOCTION

+B	充分	6C6
23E	じゅうぶん	1‖1

New born baby with amniotic fluid 充
Old form indicates a spinning weight, rotating amongst people, convey 伝
Stylised representation of three points 小

充	ジュウ、あ-てる	full, fill, provide	23E
毓	イク、そだ.つ、そだ.てる、はぐく.む	bring up; grow up; raise; rear	毓
醯	ケイ、カイ	vinegar	醯
吮	セン、シュン、す.う	suck	吮
蔬	ソ、ショ、あおもの	greens; vegetables	蔬
梳	ソ、と.く、と.かす、す.く、けず.る、くしけず.る	comb (hair)	梳

旒	リュウ、はたあし	counter for flags	旒
小	ショウ、ちい-さい、こ、お	small	23E
瑣	サ、ちいさ.い、くさり	small; chain	瑣

23F 求 DECOCTION

+B	球広い	3A2
23F	たまひろい	*

Originally fur coat, desirable object 求

求	キュウ、もと-める	request, seek	求
裘	キュウ、グ、かわごろも、けごろも	leather clothing	裘
逑	キュウ、つれあ.い	pair; gather; meet	逑

23G 出 DECOCTION

+B	出演者	4B3
23G 並	しゅつえんしゃ	*

Descend, stop and start 出
Once written with foot and a line of containment, emerging foot 出

出	シュツ、スイ、で-る、だ-す	emerge, put out	23G
黜	チュツ、しりぞ.ける	draw back	黜
柮	トツ	to cut; a stump	柮
咄	トツ、はなし、しか.る	pshaw; god forbid	咄

24A 副 DIGEST

	副業	4B6
24A	ふくぎょう	*

Chinese only full wine jar and altar, blessed by the gods, fortunate 副

福	フク	good fortune	24A
蝠	フク	bat	蝠
逼	フク、ヒツ、ヒョク、ヒキ、せま.る、むかばき	urge; force; imminent; spur on	逼
蔔	フク、ホク	giant radish; daikon	蔔
輻	フク、や	spoke (wheel)	輻
冖	ベキ、わかんむり、べきかんむり	wa-shaped crown radical	冖
匐	ホク、フク	crawl	匐

24B 送 DIGEST

	放送	6–4
24B	ほうそう	*

Royal we (Pluralis Majestatis) 送

送	ソウ、おく-る	send	24B
籐	トウ	climbing plants; vines; cane	籐
藤	トウ	rattan; cane	藤
縢	トウ、かが.る、かな、から.げる、	cross-stitch; darn	縢

䠋	むかばき トウ、わ.く	rising water	䠋

24C 橋 DIGEST

ユ		陸橋	5C12
24C 並		りっきょう	*

Originally two horizontal lines indicating area below 下
Mountain combined with up and down, pass 峠
Non General Use character tall, variant watchtower + person with bent neck, arched 橋

橋	キョウ、はし	bridge	24C
僑	キョウ	temporary home	僑
驕	キョウ、おご.る	pride; haughtiness	驕
轎	キョウ、かご	palanquin; litter	轎
嬌	キョウ、なまめか.しい	attractive	嬌
峠	とうげ	mountain pass	24C
鎹	かすがい	clamp; (kokuji)	鎹
裃	かみしも	old ceremonial garb; samurai garb; (kokuji)	裃
鞐	こはぜ	clamp; fastener	鞐
垰	たわ、とうげ、たお、あくつ	mountain pass; ancient kuni; low ground	垰
下	カ、ゲ、した、しも、もと、さ-げる、さ-がる、くだ-る、くだ-す、くだ-さる、お-ろす、お-りる	base, under, lower	24C
圷	あくつ	low-lying land;	圷

閇			(kokuji)	閇
閉	ヘイ、と.じる、と.ざす、し.める、し.まる、た.てる		shut; close; obstruct; block up	閉
抃	ベン、う.つ		strike with hand	抃
卞	ベン、ヘン、ハン		law; rule; rash; hasty	卞

24D 炎 DIGEST

上	気炎	3–4
24D	きえん	*

Double flame, excessive fire/heat 炎

炎	エン、ほのお	inflammation, flame, blaze	24D
痰	タン	sputum; phlegm	痰
餤	タン	proceed; offer	餤
毯	タン	wool rug	毯
啖	タン、く.う、くらわ.す	eat	啖

24E 決 DIGEST

上	快楽	2A7
24E	かいらく	*

Pulled apart by water 決

決	ケツ、き-める、き-まる	decide, settle, collapse	24E
夬	カイ、ケツ、ケチ、わ.ける	decide; determine; archery glove	夬
鴂	ケイ、ケキ、ケツ、もず	shrike	鴂

決	ケチ、ケツ、き.める、き.まる、さ.く	decide; determine; judge	決
刔	ケツ、えぐ.る	scoop out; gouge	刔
抉	ケツ、えぐ.る、こじ.る、くじ.る	gouge; hollow out; bore; pry	抉
缺	ケツ、ケン、か.ける、か.く	lack; gap; fail	缺
袂	ベイ、ケツ、たまと、たもと	sleeve; foot (of hill); edge	袂

24F 緑 DIGEST

ᇈ	記録	3D1
24F	きろく	*

Liquid oozing from basket (from a crude wine press) 緑

緑	リョク、ロク、みどり	green	24F
碌	ロク、ろく.な	satisfactory	碌

24G 童 DIGEST

ᇈ	児童	4A5
24G	じどう	*

Slave standing on the ground carrying heavy sack 童

童	ドウ、わらべ	child	24G
橦	シュ、ショウ、トウ	pole	橦
艟	ドウ、ショウ、トウ、いくさぶね	fighting ship	艟
潼	ドウ、トウ	high	潼

僮	トウ、ドウ、しもべ、わらべ	child; servant; foolishness	僮
幢	トウ、はた	flag; banner	幢

25A 重 DISSOLUTION

🖥	重さ	6A3
25A	おもさ	*

Person standing on the ground carrying heavy sack 重

重	ジュウ、チョウ、え、おも-い、かさ-ねる、かさ-なる	heavy, pile, -fold	25A
踵	ショウ、かかと、くび.す、きび.す、つ.ぐ	heel	踵
鍾	ショウ、シュ、あつ.める、さかずき、かね	spindle; gather; collect	鍾
慟	ドウ、トウ、なげ.く	be sad; grieve	慟

25B 員 DISSOLUTION

🖥	吏員	5–2
25B	りいん	*

Originally round kettle, persons gathered around 員

員	イン	member, official	25B
殞	イン、ウン、おち.る、し.ぬ	fall; die	殞
隕	イン、エン、ウン、おち.る	fall	隕

Kanji Alchemy III

25C 役 DISSOLUTION

🖌	兵役	11C14
25C	へいえき	0|3

Strike with axe, phonetic throw 役
Plant radical + plant with prominent head growing in shady delineated area, fungi 菌

役	ヤク、エキ	role, service, duty	25C
慇	イン	courtesy	慇
殷	イン、アン、さかん	flourishing	殷
繋	ケイ、か-かる、つな-ぐ	tie	繋
轂	コク、こしき	hub (of wheel)	轂
殳	シュ、また、ほこ、ほこつくり、るまた	pike; windy - again radical	殳
芟	セン、サン、か.る	cut; clip; trim; harvest; mow	芟
椴	タン、ダン、トド、むくげ	fir	椴
蕁	ダン、タン、むくげ	rose of Sharon; althea	蕁
澱	デン、テン、おり、ど.ろ、よど.み、よど.む	sediment; grounds; dregs; stagnant	澱
癜	デン、テン、なまず	leukoderma; piebald skin	癜
臀	デン、トン、しり	buttocks; hips; butt; rear	臀
醱	トウ	rebrew; ferment again	醱
骰	トウ、さい	dice; bones	骰
緞	ドン、タン	damask	緞

菌	キン	fungus, bacteria	25C
箘	キン	a type of bamboo; bamboo shoots; dice	箘
筠	キン	a type of bamboo; bamboo shoots; dice	筠
麕	キン、クン、のろ	roe deer	麕

25D 睪 DISSOLUTION

⌂	射睪	2A11
25D	しゃこう	*

Originally reversal of calamity, happiness 幸

幸	コウ、さいわ-い、さち、しあわ-せ	happiness, luck	25D
驛	エキ	station	驛
繹	エキ、ヤク、たずね.る、ぬ.く	pull out	繹
懌	エキ、よろこ.ぶ	rejoice	懌
圉	ギョ、ゴ、うまか.い、ひとや	prison; horse tender; ostler	圉
辜	コ、つみ	sin; crime	辜
睾	コウ	testicles	睾
釋	シャク、セキ、とく、す.てる、ゆる.す	explain	釋
鐸	タク	large hand bell	鐸
擇	タク、えら.ぶ	select; choose; pick out	擇
澤	タク、さわ、うるお.い、うるお.す、	swamp	澤

	つや		
譯	ヤク、わけ	translate; decode; encode	譯

25E 共 DISSOLUTION

🖵 25E	洪水 こうすい	6A7 *

Originally two hands offering a jewel, both, jointly together 共

共	キョウ、とも	together	25E
拱	キョウ、コウ、こまぬ.く、こまね.く	arch; fold arms	拱
蛬	キョウ、ころぎ、きりぎりす	cricket	蛬
哄	コウ	resound; reverberate	哄
鬨	コウ、グ、とき	fight; war cry	鬨
鬨	コウ、とき	war cry	鬨
饌	セン、サン、そな.える	food; offering	饌
哢	ロウ、さえず.る	chirp; twitter; warble	哢

25F 練 DISSOLUTION

🖵 25F	錬金術 れんきんじゅつ	3E6 *

Sack, bundle, disperse, threads soften by boiling 練

| 練 | レン、ね-る | refine, knead, train | 25F |

鶇	トウ、ツ、つぐみ	thrush	鶇
鶫	トウ、ツ、つぐみ	thrush	鶫
闌	ラン、た.ける、たけなわ、てすり	rise high; be well along	闌
爛	ラン、ただ.れる	be sore; inflamed; bleary; fester	爛
瀾	ラン、なみ	large waves	瀾
襴	ラン、リン	a kind of cloth	襴

25G 肖 DISSOLUTION

▽	宵月	5D9
25G	よいずき	0|1

Flesh of the body + variant of little, phonetic resemble, kids 肖
Pictograph of a crescent moon 月

肖	ショウ	be like, be lucky	25G
逍	ショウ	saunter; loaf	逍
悄	ショウ、うれ.える	anxiety	悄
峭	ショウ、きび.しい、けわ.しい	high & steep	峭
誚	ショウ、せ.める	censure; blame	誚
銷	ショウ、ソウ、け.す、と.ける、かわ.す、とろ.かす	erase; shut (door)	銷
鮹	ショウ、ソウ、たこ	octopus	鮹
蛸	ソウ、ショウ、たこ	octopus	蛸
稍	ソウ、ショウ、やや、ようやく	slightly	稍
趙	チョウ、ジョウ、キョウ	nimble; late-going	趙

月	ゲツ、ガツ、つき		moon	25G
朏	ヒ、ハイ		new moon; crescent moon	朏

26A 探 DISTILLATION

		探究者	2
26A		たんきゅうしゃ	*

Originally chimney-like hole, deep part of the river 探

26B 章 DISTILLATION

		憲章	3A4
26B		けんしょう	*

Tattooist's needle, identify slaves, mark, sign, badge 章

章	ショウ	badge, chapter	26B
瘴	ショウ	miasma	瘴
璋	ショウ	ceremonial jewelled implement	璋
鱆	ショウ、たこ	octopus	鱆
嶂	ショウ、みね	steep; lofty	嶂

26C 族 DISTILLATION

		家族	5–7
26C		かぞく	*

Arrow under a streaming banner tied to a pole, mustering 族

族	ゾク	clan, family	26C
簇	ゾク、ソウ、ソク、むら.がる	group; crowd; swarm	簇
蔟	ゾク、ソウ、まぶし	gather together	蔟
嗾	ゾク、ソク、ソウ、けしか.ける、そそのか.す	egg on; instigate	嗾
鏃	ソク、ゾク、やじり	arrow head; barb	鏃
旄	ボウ、モウ	tassel on a flag; long haired cow; old man	旄
蜉	ユウ	mayfly	蜉
游	ユウ、リュウ、あそ.び、あそ.ぶ、およ.ぐ	float; swim	游

26D 羊 DISTILLATION

| ✡ | 羊飼い | 9B17 |
| 26D | ひつじかい | * |

Pictograph of a sheep 羊

羊	ヨウ、ひつじ	sheep	26D
解	カイ、ゲ、と.く、と.かす、と.ける、ほど.く、ほど.ける、わか.る、さと.る	notes; key; explanation; understanding	解
羌	キョウ、ああ、えびす	barbarian	羌
姜	キョウ、ガ、こう	Chinese surname; ginger	姜
羹	コウ、カン、あつもの	hot soup	羹

羹	コウ、カン、あつもの	hot soup	羹
羔	コウ、こひつじ	lamb	羔
躾	しつ.ける、しつけ	training; (kokuji)	躾
庠	ショウ、まなびや	school	庠
鱶	ショウ、ヨウ、ふか、ひもの	shark	鱶
蘚	セン、こけ	moss	蘚
癬	セン、たむし	ringworm	癬
瀁	ヨウ	drift; flow; overflowing; vast	瀁
佯	ヨウ、いつわ.る	pretend; feign; false; deceitful	佯
癢	ヨウ、かゆ.い	itchy	癢
痒	ヨウ、かゆ.がる、かさ、かゆ.い	itchy	痒
恙	ヨウ、つつが.ない	illness	恙
羝	ラン、テイ、おひつじ	male sheep; ram	羝

26E 食 DISTILLATION

⌇	直 情 径 行	6–1
26E	ちょくじょうけいこう	1|2

Warp threads of the loom, incomplete, bare, light 径
Originally food in a long-stemmed dish, covered food in a dish 食

径	ケイ	path, direct	26E
頚	ケイ、くび	neck; head	頚

食	ショク、ジキ、く-う、く-らう、た-べる	food, eat	26E
蝕	ショク、むしば.む	eclipse; occultation; be defective	蝕
飭	チョク、チキ、いまし.める、ただ.す	correct; rectify	飭

26F 星 DISTILLATION

| ❧ | 出来星 | 2A4 |
| 26F | できぼし | * |

Originally a trebling of sun and phonetic birth/life 星

星	セイ、ショウ、ほし	star	26F
猩	ショウ、セイ、ソウ、しょうじょう	orangutan	猩
腥	セイ、ショウ、なまぐさ.い	bloody; smelling of fish; raw smelling	腥
涅	ネツ、デツ、そ.める	black soil	涅
捏	ネツ、テツ、ネチ、こ.ねる、ね.る、つく.ねる	knead; mix	捏

26G 委 DISTILLATION

| ❧ | 国際捕鯨委員会 | 2A3 |
| 26G | こくさいほげいいいんかい | 2\|5 |

Rice plant and woman, pliable 委
Old form shows marked area and enclosed 国

委	イ	committee; entrust to; leave to; devote; discard	26G
逶	イ	long; winding; oblique	逶
痿	イ、な.える	atrophy; go numb; be paralysed	痿
矮	ワイ、アイ、ひく.い	low; short	矮
国	コク、くに	country, region	26G
梱	カイ、そこ、はこ、くぬぎ	bottom; box; type of oak tree	梱
幗	カク	woman's head covering; veil	幗
膕	カク、コク、キョク、ひかがみ	hollow of knee	膕
摑	カク、つか-む	catch; seize; grasp; hold; arrest; capture	摑
圀	コク、くに	country	圀

27A 穴 DRAGON'S BLOOD

穴	穴埋め	4A2
27A	あなうめ	*

Space opened up in the ground and covered, dwelling, hole 穴

穴	ケツ、あな	hole	27A
鴥	イツ	flying fast; swooping	鴥
竊	セツ、ぬす.む、ひそ.かに	steal; secret; private; hushed	竊

27B 択 DRAGON'S BLOOD

⅏	選択	3A3
27B	せんたく	3|4

Originally take in hand and watch over file of prisoners, arrange 択
Originally expressing to follow someone along a road, movement + threads + together 選

沢	タク、さわ	marsh, moisten, much, many, benefit	27B
槹	コウ	well sweep	槹
皐	コウ、さつき	the high land along a river	皐
鐸	タク	bell; surname	鐸
選	セン、えら-ぶ	elect	27B
啜	セツ、テツ、すす.る	suck; sip	啜
錣	テツ、テイ、しころ	armour neckplates	錣
畷	テツ、テイ、セイ、なわて	rice field ridge path	畷
輟	テツ、や.める	stop; mend	輟

27C 灰 DRAGON'S BLOOD

⅏	灰塗れ	2B3
27C	はいまみれ	*

Formerly hand and fire: fire that one can hold in the hand? 灰

灰	カイ、はい	ashes	27C
詼	カイ、たわむれ	jest	詼
狄	テキ、えびす	barbarian	狄

| 逖 | テキ、とお.い | far | 逖 |

27D 面 DRAGON'S BLOOD

🐉	暗黒面	2–3
27D	あんこくめん	*

Formerly face and covering, that which covers the face, mask 面

面	メン、おも、おもて、つら	face, aspect, mask	27D
靦	テン	unashamed	靦
緬	メン、ベン	fine thread; Burma	緬
湎	メン、ベン、おぼ.れる、しず.む	drown; be immersed	湎

27E 息 DRAGON'S BLOOD

🐉	休息	2–2
27E	きゅうそく	0|5

Nose + heart = essence of life, breathing air 息
Person and tree, shady place for rest 休

息	ソク、いき	breath, rest, child	27E
憩	ケイ、いこ.い、いこ.う	rest; take rest	憩
熄	ソク、き.える、や.む	cessation	熄
休	キュウ、やす-む、やす-まる、やす-める	rest	27E
咻	キュウ	be contrary to	咻
貅	キュウ	brave heraldic beast	貅
烋	コウ、キュウ、キョウ	boasting; fortunate; beautiful	烋

鮇	ゴリ、めばる、まて、こち	bullhead; rockfish; razor clam; flathead	鮇
豸	タイ、チ、むじなへん	snake; legless insect; badger or clawed dog radical	豸

27F 波 DRAGON'S BLOOD

ⓢ	波乗り	8A7
27F	なみのり	1‖4

Hand pulling the hide of an animal with the head still attached 波
Formerly covered in flame and strength/effort, do physical work under torchlight 労
Attractive woman (plus sun) and house; bawdy house, revelry 宴

皮	ヒ、かわ	skin, leather	27F
玻	ハ	glass	玻
碆	ハ	arrowhead; weight attached to an arrow by a cord	碆
坡	ハ、ヒ、つつ.み	dike; dam; slope; bank	坡
跛	ハ、ヒ、びっこ、ちんば	lame; lameness; odd shoe	跛
菠	ハ、ホ、ほうれんそう	spinach	菠
鞁	ヒ	reins; saddle cover	鞁
陂	ヒ、ハ、つつみ	levee; embankment; hill; slope	陂
労	ロウ	labour, toil	27F
癆	ロウ	rash; pain; debilitation	癆
撈	ロウ、リョウ	catch fish	撈

勞	ロウ、ろう.する、いたわ.る、いた.ずき、ねぎら.う、つか.れる、ねぎら.い	thank for; reward for	勞
宴	エン	banquet	27F
堰	エン、ふ.せる	dam; weir	堰

27G 非 DRAGON'S BLOOD

ᔑ	非行	7B18
27G	ひこう	*

Wings of a bird spreading apart as it is flies off 非

非	ヒ	not, un-, fault	27G
薤	カイ、らっきょう、にら	scallion; shallot	薤
韭	キュウ、ク、にら	leek radical	韭
韮	キュウ、ク、にら	leek	韮
懺	ザン、サン、くい.る	remorse	懺
懴	ザン、サン、くい.る	regret; repent; confess sins	懴
徘	ハイ、さまよ.う	wander	徘
琲	ハイ、つらぬく	string of many pearls	琲
裴	ハイ、ヒ、ベ、たちもとお.る	long robes	裴
朏	ヒ	be separated	朏
翡	ヒ	kingfisher	翡
蜚	ヒ、あぶらむし	beetle; cockroach	蜚
匪	ヒ、あら.ず、かたみ	negation; wicked person	匪
菲	ヒ、うす.い	thin; inferior	菲

榧	ヒ、かや	Japanese nutmeg; plum-yew	榧
鯡	ヒ、にしん、はららご	herring	鯡
誹	ヒ、ハイ、そし.る	ridicule; slander	誹
腓	ヒ、ふくらはぎ、こむら、こぶら	calf (of leg)	腓
霏	ヒ、もや	falling rain or snow	霏

28A 去 DRAM

| ⚠ | 過去 | 4A6 |
| 28A | かこ | * |

Originally double lid on a rice container, consumption, gone? 去

去	キョ、コ、さ-る	go, leave, past	28A
怯	キョウ、コウ、ひる.む、おびえ.る、おじる、おび.える、おそ.れる	cowardice; wince; flinch; hesitate; waver	怯
溘	コウ	sudden; unexpected	溘
盍	コウ、おお.う、なんぞ	come together; congregate; meet; cover	盍
刧	コウ、ゴウ、キョウ、おびや.かす	threat; long ages	刧
闔	コウ、とびら	doors	闔
琺	ホウ	enamel	琺

28B 令 DRAM

| ⚠ | 司令官 | 7F7 |

Kanji Alchemy III

28B	しれいかん	*

Originally people summoned to hear the orders of their lord 令

令	レイ	order, rule	28B
埒	ハバ	alluvial terraced land	埒
囹	レイ	prison	囹
蛉	レイ	dragonfly; moon moth	蛉
鴒	レイ	wagtail	鴒
齢	レイ、よわ.い、とし	age	齢
聆	レイ、リョウ、きく	listening; realizing	聆
苓	レイ、リョウ、みみなぐさ	plant; herb; mushroom	苓

28C 医 DRAM

▲	産婦人科医	2B9
28C	さんふじんかい	*

Formerly expressing to attack with alcohol (arrow + quiver + strike + wine jar) 医

医	イ	doctor; medicine	28C
欸	アイ、カイ	exclamation	欸
埃	アイ、ほこり、ちり	dust	埃
矣	イ	sentence particle	矣
醫	イ、い.やす、い.する、くすし	medicine	醫
肄	イ、なら.う	learn; striving; effort	肄
翳	エイ、かげ、かげ.る、かざ.す、きぬがさ、くも.る、くもり	hold aloft	翳

雉	ジ、チ、きじ	pheasant	雉
俟	シ、ま.つ	wait; depend on	俟
竢	シ、ま.つ	wait for; wait until; as soon as	竢

28D 各 DRAM

| ∧ | 各駅 | 10A15 |
| 28D | かくえき | 2‖8 |

Descend, stop and start 各
Originally displaying shells/valuable items 賓
Previously rain and three fields, repetition/reverberate 雷

各	カク、おのおの	each	28D
茖	カク	mountain leek; garlic	茖
骼	カク	bleached bones	骼
挌	カク、う.つ	strike; hit; fight	挌
擱	カク、お.く	lay down; put down	擱
恪	カク、つつし.む	carefulness	恪
咯	カク、は.く	quarrel	咯
喀	カク、は.く	vomit	喀
狢	カク、ハク、バク、むじな	badger	狢
貉	カク、ハク、むじな	badger	貉
咎	キュウ、コウ、とが.める、とが	blame; censure; reprimand	咎
珞	ラク	necklace	珞
烙	ラク、カク、や.く	burn	烙

駱	ラク、かわらげ	white horse	駱
略	リャク、ほぼ、おか.す、おさ.める、はかりごと、はか.る、はぶ.く	abbreviation; omission; outline; shorten; capture; plunder	畧
輅	ロ、くるま	carriage	輅
賓	ヒン	guest, visitor	28D
繽	ヒン、おおし	disorder; scattering	繽
殯	ヒン、かりもがり	lying in state; unburied coffin	殯
擯	ヒン、しりぞ.ける	push (people) back; reject	擯
濱	ヒン、はま	beach; sea coast; river bank	濱
嬪	ヒン、ひめ	bride; marriage	嬪
檳	ビン、ヒン	betel-nut palm	檳
鬢	ビン、ヒン	sideburns	鬢
雷	ライ、かみなり	thunder	28D
擂	ライ、す.る	grind; mash; grate	擂

28E 追 DRAM

⚛ 28E	追放 ついほう	2A5 *

Pair of buttocks, phonetic chase 追

| 追 | ツイ、お-う | chase, pursue | 28E |
| 譴 | ケン、せめ.る | reproach | 譴 |

薛	セツ		type of mugwort	薛
縋	ツイ、すが.る		cling; hang on; depend	縋
鎚	ツイ、タイ、つち		hammer; mallet	鎚
鑓	やり		spear; javelin; (kokuji)	鑓

28F 代 DRAM

⚿		部屋代	3–1
28F		へやだい	*

Person + stake, phonetic replace, stand-in, exchange 代

代	ダイ、タイ、か-わる、か-える、よ、しろ	replace, world, generation, fee	28F
玳	タイ、たいまい	tortoise shell	玳

28G 振 DRAM

⚿		妊娠	7C10
28G		にんしん	0|1

Originally clam (now ngu character dragon) cutting grass, plants on field 振

Originally tall cliff, possible connotations of descending a tall cliff 厚

振	シン、ふ-る、ふ-るう	wave, swing, air, manner, after	28G
縟	ジョク、しげし	decoration	縟
褥	ジョク、しとね	cushion; mattress; bedding	褥

蓐	ジョク、ニク、しとね	bed	蓐
蜃	シン	clam	蜃
脣	シン、くちびる	lip	脣
宸	シン、のき	eaves; palace; imperial courtesy	宸
耨	ドウ、ジョク、ヌ、ジュク、くさぎ.る、くわ、すき	hoe	耨
儂	ドウ、ノウ、わし、かれ	I; my; he; his; me (used by old people)	儂
膿	ノウ、ドウ、う.む、うみ	pus; fester; discharge	膿
溽	ヒョク、ジョク、むしあつ.い	humid	溽
厚	コウ、あつ-い	thick, kind	28G
仄	ショク、ソク、かたむ.く	decline; go down; sunset	仄

Chapter 5 Leo

29A 祭 EARTH

▽	夏祭	4–1
29A	なつまつり	1|3

Hand placing meat on altar, worship 祭
Originally showing a person dancing with a mask 夏

祭	サイ、まつ-る、まつ-り	festival, worship	29A
蔡	サイ	type of tortoise used for divination	蔡
夏	カ、ゲ、なつ	summer	29A
厦	カ、サ、いえ	house	厦
廈	カ、サ、いえ	house	廈
嗄	サ、か.らす、か.れる、しゃが.れる	hoarse	嗄

29B 倍 EARTH

▽	倍加	6A4
29B	ばいか	*

Person and Chinese only spit 倍

倍	バイ	double, -fold	29B
碚	ハイ	mound; bud	碚
㕺	フ、ね.る	grow mouldy	㕺
蔀	ホウ、ダ、ダン、ブ、しとみ	latticed shutters	蔀

| 焙 | ホウ、ハイ、ほう.じる、あぶ.る | fire; roast | 焙 |

29C 然 EARTH

| ▽ | 燃焼 | 3–6 |
| 29C | ねんしょう | * |

Roast dog meat 然

然	ゼン、ネン	duly, thus, so, but	29C
壓	アツ、エン、オウ、お.す、へ.す、おさ.える	pressure	壓
黶	アン、エン、ほくろ	mole; scar; blemish	黶
厭	エン、オン、アン、オウ、ユウ、ヨウ、いや、あ.きる、いと.う、おさ.える	get tired of; satiate; bore	厭
魘	エン、ヨウ、うな.される	have a nightmare	魘
捻	ネン、よ.る、よ.れる、より、ひね.る	twist; twine; kinky	捻
靨	ヨウ、えくぼ	dimple	靨

29D 欠 EARTH

| ▽ | 炊事 | 14B5 |
| 29D | すいじ | 0‖4 |

Person yawning, wide open, vacant, lacking 欠
Formerly movement and mythical beast, phonetic expressing change, relay, sequence 遞
Present meaning is a borrowing from 貶 involving shell + lacking money/destitute 乏

欠	ケツ、か-ける、か-く	lack	29D
飲	イン、オン、の.む	drink	飲
坎	カン、あな	pitfall	坎
咨	シ、ああ、はか.る	investigate	咨
瓷	シ、かめ	high quality porcelain	瓷
粢	シ、しとぎ	millet; rice cakes	粢
遞	テイ	relay, in sequence	29D
虎	コ、とら	tiger; brave; fierce; surname	虎
遞	テイ、かわ.る、たがいに	hand over; deliver; substitute	遞
乏	ボウ、とぼ-しい	meagre, scanty, scarce	29D
泛	ハン、ホウ、うか.ぶ	to drift; float; careless; reckless	泛
貶	ヘン、おとし.める、おと.す	degrade	貶

29E 比 EARTH

▽	比肩	9D21
29E	ひけん	1|1

People sitting next to each other 比
Originally tree, tributary, and sheep. Convoluted etymology 様

比	ヒ、くら-べる	compare, ratio	29E

揩	カイ、カツ、ぬぐ.う	wipe	揩
偕	カイ、ともに	together	偕
箘	キン	a type of bamboo; bamboo shoots; dice	箘
菎	コン	a kind of fragrant herb	菎
崑	コン	place name	崑
鯤	コン	large mythical fish; roe	鯤
焜	コン、かが.やく	shine	焜
棍	コン、つえ	a cane	棍
紕	ヒ	braiding; decoration; error	紕
豼	ヒ	brave heraldic beast	豼
貔	ヒ	brave heraldic beast	貔
匕	ヒ、さじ、さじのひ	spoon; spoon or katakana hi	匕
秕	ヒ、しいな	empty grain or rice husk; chaff	秕
粃	ヒ、しな、しいな	empty grain husk	粃
妣	ヒ、なきはは	mother	妣
屁	ヒ、へ、おなら	fart; passing gas	屁
砒	ヒ、ヘイ	arsenic	砒
萆	ヒ、ヘイ	castor-oil plant	萆
牝	ヒン、めす、め-、めん	female	牝
箆	ヘイ、ハイ、へら、の、くし	spatula; arrow shaft	箆
篦	ヘイ、ハイ、へら、の、くし	spatula; arrow shaft	篦
様	ヨウ、さま	Esq.; way; manner; situation; polite suffix	29E
漾	ヨウ、ただよ.う	drift; flow	漾

29F 号 EARTH

ⵖ	番号	4B13
29F	ばんごう	*

Originally tiger's call 号
Big and emerge + words; boastful words 誇

号	ゴウ	number, call, sign	29F
兮	ケイ	auxiliary word for euphony or emphasis	兮
盻	ケイ、にら.む	glare at; toil	盻
栲	コ	type of tree; empty	栲
夸	コ、カ、ほこ.る	boast	夸
刳	コ、く.る、えぐ.る	clear; serene; cold	刳
胯	コウ、カ、コ、また	crotch	胯
攷	コウ、かんが.える	examine; test; investigate	攷
號	コウ、さけ.ぶ、よびな	mark; sign; symbol; number	號
楝	チョ、おおち、おうち	Japanese bead tree	楝
騁	テイ、はせ.る	run fast; gallop; as one pleases	騁
饕	トウ、むさぼ.る	be greedy; be ravenous	饕
聘	ヘイ、へい.する、と.う、め.す	invite	聘
娉	ヘイ、ホウ、ほ	ask after a woman's name; marry a woman; good-looking	娉

29G 有 EARTH

▽	所有者	6D9
29G	しょゆうしゃ	*

Originally right hand holding a piece of meat 有

有	ユウ、ウ、ある	have, exist	29G
鮪	キ、ユウ、イ、まぐろ、しび	tuna	鮪
膸	ズイ	marrow; pith	膸
髄	ズイ	marrow; pith	髄
隋	ズイ、スイ、タ、ダ	name of a Chinese dynasty; remains of sacrifice; bury; fall; sag	隋
随	ズイ、まにまに、したが.う	at the mercy of (the waves)	随
楕	ダ	ellipse	楕
堕	ダ、おち.る、くず.す、くず.れる	descend to; lapse into; degenerate	堕
陏	ダ、ずい	melon; wrap	陏
囿	ユウ、その	game preserve; pasture; garden	囿

30A 基 EBULLITION

⛩	基礎	6D12
30A	きそ	*

Non general use character "that", winnowing device, harvest, cycle of time 基

基	キ、もと、もとい	base	30A
淇	キ	name of a Chinese river	淇
稘	キ	straw; one year	稘
騏	キ	fast horse	騏
朞	キ、ゴ	one period	朞
棊	キ、ご	Japanese chess	棊
祺	キ、さいわ.い、やす.い	fortunate; blessed; peace of mind; security	祺
簱	キ、はた	flag; banner	簱
厮	シ、こもの	cut; divide; companion; follower	厮
廝	シ、こもの	servant	廝
嘶	セイ、いなな.く	neigh; whinny	嘶
撕	セイ、シ	warn against; break; rend; tear	撕
簸	ハ、ひ.る	winnow; fan	簸

30B 廷 EBULLITION

![]	法廷	3A1
30B	ほうてい	*

Chinese only artful, great, courtiers move to standing position on the ground 廷

廷	テイ	court, government office	30B
梃	チョウ、テイ、てこ、つえ	lever	梃

152

30C 成 EBULLITION

	促成	4A1
30C	そくせい	*

Exact and trimming halberd 成

成	セイ、ジョウ、な-る、な-す	become, make, consist	30C
筬	セイ、おさ	reed; guide for yarn on a loom	筬

30D 官 EBULLITION

	警官	4A3
30D	けいかん	0|2

Roof + buttocks, phonetic work, sedentary activity 官
Formerly hand, brush and rice field, partitioning fields on a map, diagram/picture 画

官	カン	government, official	30D
舘	カン、やかた、たて	mansion; large building; palace	舘
埠	フ、ホ、つか、はとば	wharf	埠
綰	ワン、わが.ねる、たが.ねる、たか.ねる	bend around	綰
画	ガ、カク	picture, stroke	30D
圖	ズ、ト、え、はか.る	drawing; plan	圖
鄙	ヒ、ひな、ひな.びる、いや.しい	lowly; the country; the countryside; be countrified	鄙

30E 永 EBULLITION

🅐	永遠	3–4
30E	えいえん	0|2

Picture of the confluence of tributary and main river, originally long distance 永

Two men verbally (?) competing 競

永	エイ、なが-い	long, lasting	30E
詠	エイ、よ.む、うた.う	recitation; poem; song; composing	詠
怺	こら.える	endure; (kokuji)	怺
昶	チョウ	long day; clear	昶
脈	ミャク、すじ	vein (blood, ore); pulse; hope	脈
競	キョウ、ケイ、きそ-う、せ-る	compete, vie for	30E
兢	キョウ、おそ.れる、つつ.しむ	discreet; careful	兢
竸	キョウ、ケイ、きそ.う、せ.る、くら.べる	contest; race	竸

30F 由 EBULLITION

🅐	由縁	8D5
30F	ゆえん	*

Basket/ wine press, drops falling from basket, cause 由

由	ユ、ユウ、ユイ、よし	reason, means, way	30F
届	カイ、とど.ける、とど.く	reach; arrive; report; notify; forward	届
岬	コウ、シュウ、ユウ、みさき、	gorge; ravine; in	岬

	くき、みね	the mountains; cape; promontory	
舳	ジク、チク、チュウ、ヘ、へさき、とも	bow; prow	舳
廸	テキ、みち、みち.びく、すす.む、いた.る	path; way; guide; lead; proceed; advance; reach; arrive	廸
蚰	ユウ	millipede	蚰

30G 是 EBULLITION

	是正	4A5
30G	ぜせい	0|1

Originally spoon kept on (proper) hook 是
Formerly hand + plump-thighed bird, phonetic to carry, carry in the hand 携

是	ゼ	proper, this	30G
嫣	エン	beauty	嫣
焉	エン、いずく.んぞ、ここに、これ	how; why; then	焉
篶	エン、くろだけ、すず	black bamboo; slender bamboo	篶
匙	シ、さじ	spoon	匙
寔	ショク、これ、じき、まことに	real; genuine; actual	寔
携	ケイ、たずさ-える、たずさ-わる	carry, participate	30G
攜	ケイ、たずさ-える、たずさ-わる	carry (in hand); armed with; bring along	攜

31A 県 EFFERVESCENCE

EF	県庁	2A1
31A	けんちょう	*

Originally joined threads/attach, severed head upside down in tree 県

県	ケン		prefecture	31A
纛	トウ、トク、はたぼこ、おにがしら		flag; banner	纛

31B 具 EFFERVESCENCE

EF	台所道具	2A5
31B	だいどころどうぐ	*

Originally showing hands holding up a kettle, offer a utensil 具

具	グ	equip, means	31B
懼	ク、おそ.れる	fear; overawed	懼
瞿	ク、おそ.れる、み.る	surname	瞿
颶	グ、ク	storm	颶
倶	グ、とも-に、みな	both	倶
衢	ク、みち	crossroads	衢

31C 象 EFFERVESCENCE

EF	印象	2–1
31C	いんしょう	0|1

Pictograph of an elephant 象
Originally showing a hand pressing down on a bending person, press down 印

象	ショウ、ゾウ	elephant, image	31C
橡	ショウ、ゾウ、とち、くぬぎ	horse chestnut	橡
印	イン、しるし	seal, sign, symbol	31C
卩	セツ、わりふ、ふしづくり	seal radical	卩

31D 迅 EFFERVESCENCE

EF	束の間	6–14
31D	つかのま	1‖4

Variant of east/tied sack with pole thrust through, bundle 束
Movement and element expressing fast 迅
Formerly person and quiver with arrows, prepared to fight? 備

束	ソク、たば	bundle, manage	31D
諫	カン、いさ.め、いさ.める	admonish; dissuade	諫
諌	カン、いさ.め、いさ.める	admonish; dissuade	諌
柬	カン、ケン、えら.ぶ	select; pick out	柬
揀	カン、ケン、えら.ぶ	select	揀
悚	ショウ、おそ.れる	fear	悚
竦	ショウ、すく.む、おそ.れる、つつし.む	crouch; cower	竦
疎	ソ、ショ、うと.い、うと.む、まば.ら	neglect; careless; lax	疎
敕	チョク、いまし.める、みことのり	an imperial order or decree	敕
嫩	ドン、ノン、わか.い	young; weak	嫩

溂	ラツ	opposed; biased	溂
剌	ラツ、もと.る	opposed; biased	剌
喇	ラツ、ラ	chatter; rattle on	喇
楝	レン、おおち、おうち	Japanese bead tree	楝
鰊	レン、にしん	herring	鰊
迅	ジン	fast, intense	31D
嫈	ケイ、ひとりもの	all alone; without any family; worry	嫈
備	ビ、そな-える、そな-わる	equip, prepare	31D
憊	ハイ、ヘイ、つか.れる	fatigue	憊
糒	ビ、ハイ、ほしい、ほしい.い	dried boiled rice	糒
韛	ヒ、ビ、フク、ふいご	bellows	韛

31E 免 EFFERVESCENCE

EF	逸品	4F12
31E	いっぴん	0|2

Women's genitals + crouching person, child birth, escape 免
Original meaning is a big, strong, piercing insect, horsefly 強

免	メン、まぬか-れる	escape, avoid	31E
冤	エン	false charge; hatred	冤
寃	エン	grievance; injustice; wrong	寃
巉	ザン、サン	rising precipitously; rising steeply	巉
纔	サン、ザン、サイ、わずか、ひたた	a little	纔
讒	ザン、サン、そし.る	defamation	讒

兔	ト、ツ、うさぎ	rabbit; hare	兔
菟	ト、ツ、うさぎ	dodder (plant)	菟
莵	ト、ツ、うさぎ	dodder (plant)	莵
輓	バン、おそ.い、ひ.く	pull	輓
悗	バン、マン	be perplexed	悗
俛	フ、ベン、メン、ふ.せる	look down; diligent	俛
冕	ベン、メン、かんむり	crown	冕
強	キョウ、ゴウ、つよ-い、つよ-まる、つよ-める、し-いる	strong	31E
繦	キョウ、むつき、ぜにさし	string of coins; child's obi; nappy	繦
襁	キョウ、むつき	diaper	襁

31F 区 EFFERVESCENCE

EF	区別	5B13
31F	くべつ	*

Originally enclosure with three mouths, smaller enclosures
Wards 区

区	ク	ward, section	31F
嫗	ウ、オウ、あたた.める、おうな	old woman; mother	嫗
謳	オウ、ウ、うた.う	extol; declare; express	謳
欧	オウ、うた.う、は.く	Europe	欧
鴎	オウ、かもめ	seagull	鴎
殴	オウ、ク、なぐ.る、たた.く	beat; fight with fists; hit; to strike; brawl	殴

嘔	オウ、ク、は.く、むかつ.く、うた.う	vomit; nauseated	嘔
甌	オウ、ほとぎ、はち、かめ	small jar; jug	甌
傴	ク、ウ、かが.む、せむし	bend over; stoop; bow	傴
區	ク、オウ、コウ	ward; district	區
驅	ク、か.ける、か.る	spur a horse on; expel; drive away	驅
嶇	ク、けわ.しい	steep	嶇
軀	ク、むくろ、からだ	body; corpse; tree with rotten core	軀
樞	スウ、シュ、とぼそ、からくり	pivot; door	樞

31G 及 EFFERVESCENCE

EF	及第点	4C3
31G	きゅうだいてん	*

Originally person + hand reaching out to seize 及

及	キュウ、およ-ぶ、およ-び、およ-ぼす	reach, extend, and	31G
躱	タ、かわ.す	dodge; parry; avoid	躱
朵	ダ、タ、えだ	branch	朵
ノ	ヘツ、えい、よう、ノのかんむり	katakana no radical	ノ

32A 央 ELEMENT

⊕	震央	3A7

32A	しんおう	*

Person with a yoke on the neck, restrained at the middle 央

央	オウ	centre	32A
暎	エイ、ヨウ、うつ.す、うつ.る、は.える	sun beginning decline; reflect	暎
霙	エイ、ヨウ、みぞれ	sleet	霙
泱	オウ	billowy clouds; deep and broad	泱
秧	オウ、なえ	rice; seedlings	秧
怏	オウ、ヨウ、うら.む	dissatisfaction; grudge	怏
鞅	オウ、ヨウ、むながい	martingale; breast harness; saddle girth; fetter; shackle; carry on back	鞅
殃	オウ、ヨウ、わざわい	misfortune; disaster; calamity	殃

32B 君 ELEMENT

⑨	君主	3A5
32B	くんしゅ	*

Hand holding stick to govern and mouth 君

君	クン、きみ	lord, you, Mr	32B
尹	イン、おさ、ただ.す	an official rank	尹
窘	キン、たしな.める、くるし.む	rebuke	窘
梱	クン	type of fruit tree	梱
羣	グン、む.れる、むれ、むら、	group; crowd;	羣

161

	むら.がる	multitude; mob	
裙	クン、もすそ	hem; underwear	裙

32C 更 ELEMENT

❀	今更	4A4
32C	いまさら	*

Originally, enforce + third rate, enforced change of guard 更

更	コウ、さら、ふ-ける、ふ-かす	anew, change, again, grow late	32C
哽	コ	obstruct	哽
粳	コウ、うるち、ぬか	ordinary rice	粳
哽	コウ、むせ.ぶ	sob; get choked up	哽
甦	ソ、コウ、よみがえ.る	be resuscitated; revived	甦

32D 昔 ELEMENT

❀	今昔	6–3
32D	こんじゃく	*

Originally sun/day and piling up, accumulating, the past 昔

昔	セキ、シャク、むかし	olden times, past	32D
醋	サク、す	vinegar	醋
藉	シャ、セキ、ジャク、かり.る、ふ.む	carpet; lend; borrow; make excuses; spread out	藉
鵲	シャク、ジャク、かささぎ	magpie	鵲

32E 宿 ELEMENT

⌘	宿題	2–2
32E	しゅくだい	*

Originally rush mat + building + person, resting 宿

宿	シュク、やど、やど-る、やど-す	lodge, shelter, house	32E
蓿	シュク	clover; medic	蓿
鏥	シュウ、さび	rust; corrosion	鏥

32F 全 ELEMENT

⌘	安全	3–3
32F	あんぜん	0|2

Jewel under cover, precious, perfect, whole, complete 全
Originally pictograph of a fire and flames 火

全	ゼン、まった-く	whole, completely	32F
痊	セン	heal	痊
筌	セン、うけ、うえ	fish trap; weir	筌
銓	セン、はか.る	measure; scales; weigh	銓
火	カ、ひ、ほ	fire	32F
炙	シャ、セキ、あぶ.る	roast; broil; toast; cauterize	炙
炒	ソウ、ショウ、い.る、いた.める	broil; parch; roast; fry	炒

32G 不 ELEMENT

⌘	玉杯	3A6

32G	ぎょくはい	*

Pictograph of a calyx 不

不	フ、ブ	not, un-, dis-	32G
坏	ハイ、つき、おか	bowl	坏
胚	ハイ、はらみ、はら.む	embryo	胚
丕	ヒ、おお.きい	large; great; grand; glorious; distinguished	丕
痞	ヒ、つかえ	constipation; costiveness in chest or intestines	痞
罘	フ、うさぎあみ	rabbit catching net	罘
抔	ホウ、ハイ、など、すく.う	and so forth	抔

33A 冬 EQUAL PARTS

dP	寒村	4A13
33A 並	かんそん	*

Old form phonetically expresses "become compact" and ice, winter 冬
Originally expressing binding of rushes to the wall of a house to insulate against cold 寒

寒	カン、さむ-い	cold, midwinter	33A
騫	ケン	lift up; err; hopping	騫
蹇	ケン、いざ.る、あしなえ、なや.む	cripple	蹇
搴	ケン、と.る、ぬ.く	take; hoist; pull out; shrink	搴
謇	ケン、ども.る	stutter; speak frankly	謇

賽	サイ	dice; temple visit	賽
寨	サイ、とりで	fort	寨
冬	トウ、ふゆ	winter	33A
鮗	このしろ	gizzard shad; (kokuji)	鮗
螽	シュウ、いなご	grasshopper	螽
夊	スイ、ゆき、すいにょう	winter variant radical	夊
夂	チ、しゅう、ふゆがしら	winter radical	夂
鼕	トウ	beating of drums	鼕
疼	トウ、うず.く、いた.む	ache; pain; tingle; fester	疼
苳	トウ、ふき	butterbur; bog rhubarb	苳

33B 建 EQUAL PARTS

dP	建物	3–1
33B	たてもの	*

Movement of an erect brush 建

| 建 | ケン、コン、た-てる、た-つ | build, erect | 33B |
| 腱 | ケン、キン | tendon | 腱 |

33C 単 EQUAL PARTS

dP	簡単	5H12
33C	かんたん	*

Forked thrusting weapon 単

| 単 | タン | simple, single, unit | 33C |

嬋	セン	beautiful	嬋
蝉	セン、せみ	cicada	蝉
闡	セン、みち.る	clarify	闡
鄲	タン	place name	鄲
禅	タン、ゼン、ひとえ	thin kimono; undergarment	禅
襌	タン、ゼン、ひとえ	thin kimono; undergarment	襌
憚	タン、タ、はばか.る	hesitate; shrink; awe	憚
驒	タン、ダン、タ、ダ、テン	dappled grey horse	驒
殫	タン、つき.る	become exhausted; all	殫
箪	タン、はこ	bamboo rice basket	箪
篳	ヒチ、ヒツ、まがき	fence	篳
蹕	ヒツ、さきばらい	one who precedes king in procession	蹕

33D 帯 EQUAL PARTS

dP	熱**帯**魚	2B
33D	ねったいぎょ	0|1

Cloth and belt with items attached to it 帯
Original meaning is earthen barrier, be firmly in place, be located 在

在	ザイ、あ-る	exist, outskirts, suburbs	33D
恠	カイ、ケ、あや.しい、あや.しむ	suspicious; mystery; apparition	33D

Kanji Alchemy III

33E 壮 EQUAL PARTS

dP	強壮	6D6
33E	きょうそう	*

Originally bed + samurai/male/ erect male organ 壮

壮	ソウ	manly, strong, grand, fertile	33E
奘	ジョウ、ソウ、さかん	large; great	奘
牂	ジョウ、ソウ、さかん	large; powerful; stout; thick	牂
爿	ショウ、ソウ、しょうへん	left-side kata radical	爿
牀	ショウ、ソウ、ゆか	bed; couch; bench; chassis	牀
賍	ソウ	bribery	賍
寐	ビ、ね.る	sleep	寐

33F 召 EQUAL PARTS

dP	大詔	8–7
33F	たいしょう	0|1

Mouth + person bending as they answer their master's summons 召
Rice plant and mouth, softness, pliant in speech 和

召	ショウ、め-す	summon, partake, wear	33F
邵	ショウ	place name	邵
韶	ショウ	music; spring	韶
劭	ショウ、つと.める	recommend; work hard; beautiful	劭
迢	チョ、チョウ	far off; distant	迢
齠	チョウ	baby teeth; young child	齠

髟	チョウ、うな.る、うな.い	long hair; groan	髟
貂	チョウ、てん	marten; sable	貂
和	ワ、オ、やわ-らぐ、やわ-らげる、なご-む、なご-やか	Japan, peace, soft	33F
呝	ワ	follow; childless	呝

33G 井 EQUAL PARTS

⅊	井戸	3–2
33G	いど	*

Pictograph of a well 井

井	セイ、ショウ、い	well	33G
畊	キョウ、コウ、たが.やす	plough; cultivate	畊
穽	セイ、おとしあな	sunken trap	穽

34A 害 ESSENCE

⿱	殺害	3–2
34A	さつがい	*

Originally old (skull), inverted basket, cover head to smother? 害

害	ガイ	harm, damage	34A
豁	カツ、ひら.ける、ひろ.い	empty	豁
瞎	カツ、めくら、かため	blind eye; one eye	瞎

34B 末 ESSENCE

芓	週末	2B2
34B	しゅうまつ	*

Tree with additional branches at the top, tip of tree 末

末	マツ、バツ、すえ	end, tip	34B
秣	マツ、バツ	proper name	秣
秣	マツ、バツ、まぐさ、まぐさかう	fodder	秣

34C 幾 ESSENCE

芓	幾つ	3A2
34C	いくつ	1‖5

Short thread + variant of broad bladed halberd, loom 幾
Jinmei character originally expressing (emerging) plant 芝
Originally pair of shears + cut 刈

幾	キ、いく	how many, how much	34C
饑	キ、う.える	hunger; thirst	饑
譏	キ、そし.る	slander; disparage; censure; criticize	譏
刈	か-る	reap, cut, shear	34C
苅	ガイ、カイ、か.る	cutting (grass)	苅
乂	ガイ、カイ、ゲ、おさ.める、か.る	mow; cut grass; subdue	乂

艾	カイ、ゲイ、もぐさ、よもぎ、おさ.める、か.る	moxa; sagebrush; wormwood; mugwort	艾
刋	カン、セン、き.る、けず.る	cut; whittle	刋
駁	ハク、バク、ぶち、まじ.る、まだら	refutation; contradiction	駁

34D 付 ESSENCE

宀	仕付	5–9
34D	しつけ	*

Originally person + hand, reach out and give something to someone 付

付	フ、つ-ける、つ-く	attach, apply	34D
枌	たぶ、たふ	type of evergreen camphor tree	枌
苻	フ	kudzu-like plant	苻
坿	フ	slope; hill	坿
柎	フ、うてな	raft; calyx	柎
拊	フ、は.る、うつ、な.でる	slap; strike	拊
腑	フ、はらわた	viscera; bowels	腑
俯	フ、ふ.す、うつむ.く、ふ.せる	bend down; lie prostrate	俯
吋	フ、ホ	blow; command	吋
鮒	ホ、フ、ブ、ふな	carp	鮒

34E 康 ESSENCE

半	健康体	2A1
34E	けんこうたい	*

Hands holding pestle pounding cereals 康

康	コウ	peace, health	34E
慵	ヨウ、ショウ、ものうい	languid	慵

34F 漢 ESSENCE

半	漢字	6H7
34F	かんじ	*

Originally Han river gleaming like a flaming arrow 漢

漢	カン	Han China, man	34F
瑾	キン	jewel	瑾
饉	キン、う.える	hunger	饉
懃	キン、ゴン、ねんごろ	courtesy	懃
覲	キン、まみ.える	see; have an audience with	覲
槿	キン、むくげ	rose of Sharon	槿
攤	タン、ひら.く	open; broaden; apportion	攤
儺	ナ、ダ、おにやらい	exorcism	儺

34G 要 ESSENCE

半	重要	3–2

34G	じゅうよう	*

Originally two hands holding a waist, middle part, pivot, essential 要

要	ヨウ、い-る	need; main point; essence; pivot	34G
僊	セン	hermit	僊
韆	セン	swing; trapeze	韆

35A 民 EXTRACTION

⇌	移民	3–4
35A	いみん	*

Needle in the eye, blind, slave, lowly people, commoners 民

民	ミン、たみ	people, populace	35A
聚	シュウ、シュ、あつ.まる	assemble	聚
驟	シュウ、にわか、はせ.る	run; suddenly	驟
泯	ビン、ベン、ミン、メン、ほろ.びる	die out; dim	泯
岷	ビン、ミン	name of a Chinese river; name of a Chinese mountain	岷

35B 勢 EXTRACTION

⇌	勢力	4A4
35B	せいりょく	*

Kneeling to plant a tree 勢

勢	セイ、いきお-い	power, force	35B

盖	ガイ、カイ、コウ、ふた、けだ.し、おお.う、かさ、かこう	cover; lid; flap	盖
蓋	ガイ、カイ、コウ、ふた、けだ.し、おお.う、かさ、かこう	cover; lid; flap	蓋
囈	ゲイ	foolish talk	囈
褻	セツ、けが.れる、な.れる	filthy	褻

35C 銭 EXTRACTION

⇆	金銭	6–13
35C	きんせん	*

Halberd cutting bone 浅

銭	セン、ぜに	sen, coin, money	35C
桟	サン、セン、かけはし	crosspiece	棧
盞	サン、セン、さかずき	sake cup	盞
残	ザン、のこ.る、のこ.す、そこな.う、のこ.り	left over; remain; balance	殘
牋	セン	paper; label; letter; composition	牋
浅	セン、あさ.い	shallow; not deep; superficial	淺
戔	セン、サン	damage; remain; slight	戔
綫	セン、すじ	thread; line	綫
錢	セン、ぜに、すき	100th of yen	錢
賎	セン、ゼン、いや.しい、いや.しむ、いや.しめる、しず、やす.い	despise; low-life; poverty	賤

賤	セン、ゼン、いや.しい、いや.しむ、いや.しめる、しず、やす.い	despise; low-life; poverty	賤
濺	セン、そそ.ぐ	sprinkle; splash	濺
餞	セン、はなむけ	farewell gift	餞
踐	セン、ふ.む	step on; trample; practice; carry through	踐

35D 即 EXTRACTION

⇔	即刻	2C
35D	そっこく	*

Originally taking one's place at the table, food + person 即

35E 暁 EXTRACTION

⇔	暁星	2E13
35E	ぎょうせい	1|5

Chinese only high, trebling of earth 暁
Old form expresses dry and empty bowl, exhaust extended meaning 尽

暁	ギョウ、あかつき	dawn, light, event	35E
翹	ギョウ、あ.げる、つまだ.てる	excellence	翹
僥	ギョウ、キョウ	luck; seek; desire	僥
嶢	ギョウ、けわ.しい	high; towering	嶢
蟯	ギョウ、ジョウ	intestinal worm	蟯

澆	ギョウ、そそ.ぐ	sprinkle; thing; shallow; frivolous	澆
磽	コウ、キョウ	rocky; barren	磽
蕘	ジョウ、たきぎ、きこり	firewood	蕘
繞	ジョウ、ニョウ、めぐ.る、まわ.る、もとう.る、まとう	surround; return	繞
饒	ジョウ、ニョウ、ゆたか	abundant	饒
撓	トウ、キョウ、コウ、ジョウ、たわ.む、しな.う、しお.る、たわ.める、みだ.す、みだ.れる	bend; train; lithe	撓
橈	ドウ、ジョウ、ニョウ、かい、かじ、たわ.む、たわ.める	oar; scull; paddle	橈
鐃	ドウ、ニョウ、どら	gong	鐃
遶	ニョウ、ジョウ、めぐ.る	surround	遶
尽	ジン、つ-くす、つ-きる、つ-かす	use up, exhaust	35E
贐	シン、はなむけ	going away present; parting gift	贐
侭	ジン、まま、ことごとく	as it is; because	侭
儘	ジン、まま、ことごとく	as it is; because	儘
燼	ジン、もえのこり	embers	燼
壔	まま	steep slope	壔

35F 川 EXTRACTION

⇌		川床	8C2

| 35F | かわどこ | 3\|0 |

Originally showing water flowing between two banks 川
Originally sandbank in a river, separate area, province 州
Right hand and mouth. Right hand indicates strength 右

川	セン、かわ	river	35F
巛	セン、かわ、まがりがわ	curving river radical	巛
州	シュウ、す	state, province	35F
馴	シュウ、シュン	horse's buttocks; horse's tail	馴

35G 的 EXTRACTION

| ⇆ | 的外れ | 4C4 |
| 35G | まとはずれ | * |

White, conspicuous and pictograph of a ladle/scoop, setting apart, target 的

的	テキ、まと	target, like, adjectival suffix	35G
芍	シャク	peony	芍
杓	シャク、チョウ、テキ、ヒョウ、ひしゃく	ladle, scoop	杓
妁	シャク、なこうど	go-between	妁
葯	ヤク	pollen pod at tip of stamen; type of tall grass	葯

Chapter 6 Virgo

36A 兆 FERMENTATION

☫ 36A	前兆 ぜんちょう	6-6 *

Cracks appearing on a heated turtle shell, divination 兆

兆	チョウ、きざ-す、きざ-し	sign, omen, trillion	36A
晁	チョウ、あさ	proper name	晁
誂	チョウ、あつら.える、いど.む	order	誂
佻	チョウ、ジョウ、ヨウ、かる.い	frivolity	佻
窕	チョウ、ヨウ、うつく.しい	quiet	窕
銚	チョウ、ヨウ、なべ	sake bottle	銚
姚	ヨウ、チョウ、うつく.しい	beautiful	姚

36B 陸 FERMENTATION

☫ 36B	陸海 空 りくかいくう	2–2 *

Hill and mound (Chinese only), land 陸

陸	リク	land	24C
逵	キ、おおじ	broad road	逵
淕	リク、ロク	sleet; slush; name of a wetland	淕

36C 戒 FERMENTATION

☫	戒行	2–1
36C	かいぎょう	*

Two hands holding a halberd, threat, commanding, punishing 戒

戒	カイ、いまし-める	command, admonish	36C
誡	カイ、いまし.める	admonish; warn; prohibit	誡

36D 鏡 FERMENTATION

☫	望遠鏡	2–1
36D	ぼうえんきょう	*

Non general use character finish, sound + bent figure 境

境	キョウ、ケイ、さかい	boundary, border	36D
竟	キョウ、ケイ、おわ.る、ついに、わた.る	end; finally	竟

36E 包 FERMENTATION

☫	小包み	6A18
36E	こづつみ	0|4

Originally embryo in womb 包
Formerly hand/arm, bird, village and river, phonetic envelop, embrace 擁

包	ホウ、つつ-む	wrap, envelop	36E
雹	ハク、ヒョク、ボク、ひょう	hail	雹

枹	フ、ホウ、ほ、ばち	gong stick; drum stick; type of tree	枹
鮑	ホ、ホウ、あわび	abalone	鮑
匏	ホ、ホウ、ひさご	gourd	匏
圮	ホウ	collapse; break	圮
炮	ホウ、あぶ.る	burn; roast	炮
蚫	ホウ、あわび	abalone; dried fish; surname	蚫
庖	ホウ、くりや	kitchen	庖
麭	ホウ、こなもち	sticky rice ball	麭
髱	ホウ、たぼ	top knot; bun; coiled hair knot	髱
皰	ホウ、にきび	pimple	皰
苞	ホウ、ヒョウ、つと	husk; bract; straw wrapper; souvenir gift; bribe	苞
鉋	ホウ、ビョウ、かんな	carpenter's plane	鉋
皰	ホウ、ビョウ、にきび	pimple	皰
咆	ホウ、ほ.える	bark; roar; get angry	咆
疱	ホウ、もがさ	smallpox; blister	疱
袍	ホウ、わたいれ	coat	袍
萢	ヤチ、ヤラ	bog; wetlands; used in proper names	萢
擁	ヨウ	embrace, protect	36E
癰	ヨウ、はれもの	boil; carbuncle	癰
壅	ヨウ、ふさ.ぐ	plug up; shut up	壅
雍	ヨウ、やわらぐ	mild; congenial; block; obstruct	雍
雝	ヨウ、ユ、ふさ.ぐ、やわら.ぐ	softening; mitigation	雝

36F 利 FERMENTATION

	利益	3C7
36F	りえき	*

Reaping the harvest, pouring forth 利

利	リ、き-く	profit, gain, effect	36F
鯏	あさり、うぐい	short necked clam; dace; chub; (kokuji)	鯏
黍	ショ、きび	millet	黍
悧	リ	clever	悧
蜊	リ、あさり	a kind of bivalve	蜊
犂	リ、レイ、リュウ、すき	plough	犂
犁	リ、レイ、リュウ、すき	plough	犁
藜	レイ、あかざ	goosefoot; wild spinach	藜

36G 観 FERMENTATION

	観光	4–14
36G	かんこう	5‖5

Chinese only heron 観
Formerly depicting a variant of fire + bending person, fire carried overhead, torch? 光
Formerly showing child and hands, disposing of a child, abandon 棄

観	カン	watch, observe	36G
鑵	カン、かま	steam boiler	鑵
罐	カン、かま	steam boiler (left side only)	罐

諠	カン、ケン、かまびす.しい	noisy; disputatious	諠
勸	カン、ケン、すす.める	persuade; recommend; advise; encourage; offer	勸
鸛	カン、こうのとり	Japanese stork	鸛
潅	カン、そそ.ぐ	pour into; irrigate; shed (tears; flow into; concentrate on)	潅
灌	カン、そそ.ぐ	pour	灌
觀	カン、み.る、しめ.す	outlook; look; appearance; condition; view	觀
懽	カン、よろこ.ぶ	rejoice	懽
驩	カン、よろこ.ぶ	greetings; be happy; celebrate	驩
歡	カン、よろこ.ぶ	delight; joy	歡
顴	ケン、カン	cheek bone	顴
權	ケン、ゴン、おもり、かり、はか.る	authority; power; rights	權
欅	つき	keyaki; zelkova tree	欅
棄	キ	abandon, renounce	36G
弃	キ、すて.る	reject; abandon; discard	弃
岾	くら	shrine in the mountains	岾
光	コウ、ひか-る、ひかり	light, shine	36G
胱	コウ	bladder	胱
恍	コウ、とぼ.ける、ほ.れる	unclear; senile; stupid; joke	恍
絖	コウ、ぬめ、わた	white rice	絖

37A 量 FILTRATION

33	重量	2
37A	じゅうりょう	*

Originally heavy sack left on the ground 量

37B 侖 FILTRATION

33	絶倫	6B11
37B	ぜつりんの	*

Chinese only arrange, align neatly (bamboo tablets bound together) 侖

倫	リン	principles, ethics	37B
册	サツ、サク、ふみ	counter for books; volume	册
跚	サン	stagger; reel; stumble	跚
刪	サン、けず.る	cut down	刪
鑰	ヤク、かぎ	lock	鑰
龠	ヤク、ふえ	flute	龠
籥	ヤク、ふえ	three-holed flute	籥
棆	リン	camphor tree	棆
侖	リン、ロン、おも.う	think; be methodical	侖
淪	リン、ロン、しず.む	sink; ripple	淪
崙	ロン	place name	崙
崘	ロン	Kunlun Mountains in Jiangsu	崘

37C 義 FILTRATION

33	意義	4–7
37C	いぎ	*

Sheep (praiseworthy) + I, consider oneself praiseworthy 義

義	ギ	righteousness	37C
嶬	ギ	high; steep	嶬
羲	ギ、キ	used in proper names	羲
曦	ギ、キ	the sun	曦
蟻	ギ、あり	ant	蟻
礒	ギ、ガ、いそ、いわお	rock; beach; shore	礒
犠	ギ、キ、いけにえ	sacrifice	犠
艤	ギ、ふなよそおい	landing a boat	艤

37D 布 FILTRATION

33	絹布	6A2
37D	けんぷ	*

Hand beating cloth 布

布	フ、ぬの	cloth, spread	37D
匝	キョウ、ソウ、めぐ.る	go around	匝
箍	コ、たが	barrel hoop	箍

37E 告 FERMENTATION

33	広告	3B7
37E	こうこく	*

Variant growing plant, phonetic proffer, proffer from the mouth 告

告	コク、つ-げる	proclaim, inform	37E
皓	コウ	bright; pure	皓
窖	コウ、キョウ、あなぐら	cellar	窖
誥	コウ、つ.ぐ	state; give instructions	誥
靠	コウ、もた.れる、たが.う、よ.る	lean on	靠
梏	コク、カク、てかせ	manacles	梏
鵠	コク、コウ、くぐい、まと	swan	鵠
慥	ゾウ、たし.かに	certainly; doubtless	慥

37F 失 FILTRATION

33	失業	5–4
37F	しつぎょう	*

Originally lose by slipping from the hand 失

失	シツ、うしな-う	lose	37F
軼	イツ、テツ、すぎ.る	pass along	軼
佚	イツ、テツ、たのし.む、のが.れる	lost; hide; peace; mistake; beautiful; in turn	佚
帙	チツ、ふまき	Japanese book cover	帙
跌	テツ、あやまつ、つまず.く	stumble	跌

Kanji Alchemy III

37G 変 FILTRATION

33	変遷	5A17
37G	へんせん	0|1

Originally Chinese only tied together, phonetic reverse 変
Originally thread and cut threads, meaning join threads, patching 継

変	ヘン、か-わる、か-える	change, strange	37G
奕	エキ、ヤク	large	奕
絲	シ、いと	thread	絲
燮	ショウ、やわ.らげる	moderate; alleviate; boil over low heat	燮
迹	セキ、シャク、あと	mark; print; impression	迹
蠻	バン、えびす	barbarian	蠻
轡	ヒ、くつわ、たづな	bit (horse)	轡
變	ヘン、か.わる、か.える	change; strange	變
鸞	ラン	fabulous mythical bird; imperial	鸞
欒	ラン、おうち、ひじき、まどか、まるい	chinaberry tree; round; harmonious	欒
鑾	ラン、すず	bells on emperor's carriage	鑾
巒	ラン、みね	small peak	巒
戀	レン、こ.う、こい、こい.しい	in love; yearn for; miss; darling	戀
攣	レン、つ.る、ひ.く	crooked; bent	攣
臠	レン、みそな.わす、きりみ	witness	臠

灣	ワン、いりえ	gulf; bay; inlet	灣
弯	ワン、ひ.く	curve; stretching a bow	弯
彎	ワン、ひ.く	curve; stretching a bow	彎
継	ケイ、つ-ぐ	inherit, follow, patch, join	37G
繼	ケイ、つ.ぐ、まま	succeed; inherit; patch; graft (tree)	繼

38A 争 FIRE

△	戦争	4C5
38A 並	せんそう	*

Hand reaching down to take hold of someone and restrain 争
Originally cooked rice and vapours, spirit extended meaning 気

戦	セン、いく-さ、たたか-う	fight, war	38A
錚	ソウ	gong	錚
崢	ソウ	high; steep	崢
諍	ソウ、ショウ、いさか.う、あらそ.う、いさ.める、うった.える	quarrel	諍
気	キ、ケ	spirit	38A
愾	ガイ、キ、ケ、キツ、ためいき	anger; breathlessness	愾
气	キ、ケ、いき、きがまえ	spirit; steam radical	气

38B 以 FIRE

△	以内	2–1
38B	いない	*

Originally person behind a plough 以

以	イ	starting point, means, use, through, because	38B
苡	イ、シ、ワ、くさ	adlay; plantain	苡

38C 砕 FIRE

△	砕氷船	5D12
38C	さいひょうせん	0|2

Marked clothing indicating slave or soldier 砕
Formerly water and an element that represents cracks in ice 氷

砕	サイ、くだ-く、くだ-ける	break, smash	砕
倅	サイ、ソツ、ソチ、せがれ	son; my son	倅
伜	サイ、ソツ、ソチ、せがれ	son; my son	伜
淬	サイ、にらぐ	anneal; quench; temper	淬
膵	スイ	pancreas	膵
翠	スイ、かわせみ、みどり	colour green; kingfisher	翠
萃	スイ、サイ、あつ.まる	collect; gather; assemble	萃
悴	スイ、せがれ、やつ.れる	becoming emaciated; son	悴
忰	スイ、せがれ、やつ.れる	suffer; become emaciated; haggard	忰

瘁	スイ、つか.れる	take sick; fatigue	瘁
埣	ソツ	barren land	埣
卒	ソツ、シュツ、そつ.する、お.える、お.わる、ついに、にわか	soldier; private; die	卒
猝	ソツ、にわか	sudden	猝
氷	ヒョウ、こおり、ひ	ice, hail, freeze	38C
冫	ヒョウ、こおり、にすい	two-stroke water radical or ice radical	冫
冰	ヒョウ、こおり、ひ、こお.る	ice; hail	冰

38D 博 FIRE

△	博物館	5–10
38D	はくぶつかん	*

Spread, big, extensive 博

博	ハク、バク	extensive, spread, gain, gamble	38D
愽	タン	grieving	愽
慱	タン	grieving	慱
槫	タン、セン	hearse	槫
摶	タン、セン、まる.い	roll into a ball; slap	摶
搏	ハク、う.つ、と.る	seize; spring upon; strike	搏
膊	ハク、ほじし	arm	膊
賻	フ	condolence gift	賻
傅	フ、かしず.く、つく、もり	tutor	傅
榑	フ、くれ	unbarked lumber	榑
溥	フ、ハク、あまねし	far and wide	溥

38E 奴 FIRE

△	奴隷	3–6
38E	どれい	*

Woman, compliance, work 奴

奴	ド	slave, servant, guy	38E
拏	ダ、ナ、つか.む、ひ.く	catch; arrest	拏
弩	ド、おおゆみ、いしゆみ	bow (arrow)	弩
呶	ド、ド、ウ、かまびす.しい	noisy	呶
駑	ド、にぶ.い	slow horse; foolish fellow	駑
孥	ド、ヌ、つまこ	child; wife and children; servant; slave	孥
帑	トウ、ド、かねぐら	money repository	帑

38F 良 FIRE

△	良心	6D8
38F	りょうしん	2|7

Originally sieve selecting the good 良
Phonetically expressing partner for a woman, husband 婿

良	リョウ、よ-い	good	38F
糧	リョウ、ロウ、かて	food; provisions	糧
琅	ロウ	a precious stone	琅
瑯	ロウ	a precious stone	瑯
螂	ロウ	mantis	螂
榔	ロウ	betel palm tree	榔
莨	ロウ、たばこ	tobacco	莨

朗	ロウ、ほが.らか、あき.らか	clear; bright; distinct	朗
踉	ロウ、リョウ	stagger; falter	踉
婿	セイ、むこ	son-in-law	38F
丐	カイ、こ.う	beggar; beg; give	丐
胥	ショ、ソ、あい、み.る、みな	together; mutual; subordinate official	胥
壻	セイ、むこ	son-in-law	壻
蛋	タン	barbarian; egg	蛋
蜑	タン、あま	egg	蜑
眄	ベン、メン、かえり.みる	looking askance	眄
麺	メン、ベン、むぎこ	noodles; wheatflour	麺

38G 亢 FIRE

△	航空	3A4
38G	こうくう	*

Non general use character high, originally lashing boats together in a straight line 亢

航	コウ	sail, voyage	38G
亢	コウ、たかぶる	high spirits	亢
伉	コウ、たぐ.い、なら.ぶ	same kind; compare with	伉
吭	コウ、のど	throat; neck; pivot	吭
頏	コウ、のど	alight; land; throat; neck	頏

39A 夫 FIRST MATTER

▽	夫君	5B6
39A 並	ふくん	*

Originally big male with an ornamental hairpin (sign of adulthood) 夫
Formerly mouth and standing person: person giving a verbal statement, presenting a report 呈

夫	フ、フウ、おっと	husband, man	39A
趺	シ、フ、あし	foot; calyx; sitting in the lotus position	趺
畉	フ、たがや.す	till; cultivate	畉
麸	フ、ふすま	light wheat-gluten bread	麸
麩	フ、ふすま	light wheat-gluten bread	麩
呈	テイ	present, offer	39A
酲	テイ	hangover	酲
蟶	テイ、まて	razor clam	蟶

39B 則 FIRST MATTER

▽	原則	3–3
39B	げんそく	*

Originally notches in a kettle, scale 則

則	ソク	rule, model, standard	39B
厠	シ、ショク、かわや	privy; toilet	厠
廁	シ、ショク、かわや	toilet; lavatory; mingle with	廁
惻	ソク、ショク、いた.む	be sad	惻

39C 兵 FIRST MATTER

▽	兵器	2–2
39C	へいき	*

Axe being held with both hands 兵

兵	ヘイ、ヒョウ	soldier	39C
鋲	びょう	rivet; tack; thumb tack; (kokuji)	鋲
梹	ヒン	areca nut; betel nut	梹

39D 票 FIRST MATTER

▽	投票	3A8
39D	とうひょう	*

Originally leaping tongues of flame 票

票	ヒョウ	vote, label, sign	39D
慓	ヒョウ	fast; quick	慓
驃	ヒョウ	white horse	驃
剽	ヒョウ、おびや.かす、さす	threat	剽
嫖	ヒョウ、かる.い	wanton; hedonistic	嫖
縹	ヒョウ、はなだ、はなだ.いろ	light blue	縹
飄	ヒョウ、ひるが.える、つむじかぜ	turn over; wave	飄
飆	ヒョウ、ひるが.える、つむじかぜ	whirlwind; cyclone; floating	飆
鰾	ヒョウ、ふえ、うきぶくろ	fish bladder	鰾

39E 愛 FIRST MATTER

▽	渇愛	2–2
39E	かつあい	*

Previously enveloped heart, completely covered. (convoluted etymology) 愛

愛	アイ	love	39E
曖	アイ	hidden; unclear	曖
靉	アイ、イ	clouds	靉

39F 旧 FIRST MATTER

▽	旧式	7D21
39F	きゅうしき	*

Originally crested bird with cry of 'kyuu', simplification 旧

旧	キュウ	old, past	39F
餡	アン、カン	bean jam	餡
閻	エン	town	閻
焔	エン、ほのお	flame; blaze	焔
鷽	カク、アク、うそ	long-tailed bird; dove; bullfinch	鷽
盥	カン、たらい、そそ.ぐ	tub; washbasin	盥
燬	キ、や.く	blaze	燬
猊	ゲイ	lion; the seat of a famous priest	猊
貎	ゲイ	lion; wild beast; wild horse	貎
倪	ゲイ、ガイ、きわ	stare	倪
鯢	ゲイ、さんしょううお	salamander; female whale;	鯢

		small fish; old person's teeth	
霓	ゲイ、にじ	rainbow	霓
睨	ゲイ、にら.む、にら.み	glaring at; authority; power; scowl at	睨
麑	ゲイ、ベイ、こじか、かのこ	fawn	麑
鬩	ケキ、カク、ゲキ、せめ.ぐ	quarrel	鬩
瀉	シャ、くだ.す、は.く	evacuation	瀉
舂	ショウ、うすつ.く、うすづ.く、つ.く	pound (mortar); sink; set (sun)	舂
啗	タン、く.らわす、く.う、く.らう	allure; entice	啗
諂	テン、へつら.う	flatter	諂
滔	トウ、はびこ.る	overflowing	滔
蹈	トウ、ふ.む	step on; trample; carry through; appraise; evade payment	蹈
韜	トウ、ゆぶくろ、ゆみぶくろ、つつ.む	bag; wrapping	韜

39G 采 FIRST MATTER

⬇	喝采	4–1
39G	かっさい	*

Take/gather/pluck, hand + tree/shrub 采

采	サイ、と-る	dice; form; appearance; take; colouring; general's baton	39G
綵	サイ、あや、あやぎぬ	colourful	綵

40A 別 FIXATION

🌱 40A	誘**拐** ゆうかい	2–2 *

Variant of bone 別

別	ベツ、わか-れる	split, differ, special	40A
枴	カイ、つえ	cane; walking stick	枴
捌	ハツ、ハチ、ベツ、さば.く、さば.ける、は.け	handle; deal with; dispose of; sell	捌

40B 林 FIXATION

🌱 40B 並	林間 りんかん	5F15 *

Ideograph of trees 林
Trail of rice plants in an ordered regularly spaced row 歷

林	リン、はやし	woods, forest	40B
爨	サン、かし.ぐ、かまど	cook; boil	爨
礬	バン、ハン	alum	礬
樊	ハン、まがき	cage; fence; pen; enclosure	樊
攀	ハン、よ.じる	climb; scale	攀
梺	ふむと、ふもと	base of a mountain	梺
醂	ラン、リン、あわ.す、さわ.す	remove astringency; bleach in water	醂
菻	リン	kind of thistle	菻
痳	リン	gonorrhoea	痳
罧	リン	luring fish with a bonfire	罧

霖	リン、ながあめ、ながめ	long rainy spell	霖
歷	レキ	history	40B
轣	レキ	creaking sound	轣
靂	レキ	violent; thunder; lightening	靂
癧	レキ	swollen neck glands	癧
櫪	レキ、かいばおけ、くぬぎ	manger; fodder trough; horse barn	櫪
瀝	レキ、したた.る	dropping	瀝

40C 又 FIXATION

♇	最大	4A4
40C 並	さいだい	*

Originally warrior's helmet, attack + take 最
Originally pictograph of the right hand, again is borrowed meaning 又

最	サイ、もっと-も	most, -est	40C
榱	サイ、ふし	knot in wood	榱
又	また	or again	40C
扠	サ、さて、さ.す	well; now	扠
扨	サ、さて、さ.す	well; now	扨
釵	サイ、サ、かざし、かんざし	ornamental hairpin	釵

40D 吉 FIXATION

♇	妥結	3A8

| 40D | だけつ | 0\|2 |

Originally double-lidded container, plenty, good fortune 吉
Woman and hand reaching down, phonetic possibly expressing soft and delicate, pliant? 妥

吉	キチ、キツ	good luck, joy	40D
劼	カツ、ケチ	be careful; hard; strive	劼
拮	カツ、ケツ、キツ、はた.らく	be imminent	拮
黠	カツ、さと.い、わるがしこ.い	crafty	黠
佶	キツ、キチ	healthy; correct	佶
髻	ケイ、キツ、たぶさ、みずら、もとどり	samurai topknot	髻
頡	ケツ、キツ、カツ、ケチ	take wing; fly up	頡
纈	ケツ、ケチ、しぼり	tie-dyeing; purblind	纈
襭	ケツ、つまばさ.む、はさ.む	tuck into one's obi	襭
妥	ダ	peaceful, tranquil	40D
綏	スイ、タ、やす.い	peaceful; cheap; grab strap	綏
餒	ダイ、イ、う.える	hunger; spoil	餒

40E 参 FIXATION

| ♀ | 参加 | 2–19 |
| 40E | さんか | * |

Originally attractive woman, kneeling with three ornamental hairpins 参

| 参 | サン、まい-る | attend, go, be in | 40E |

		love, be at a loss	
樛	キュウ、つが、まと.う	bend; droop; undulate; to entwine; to be clad in	樛
摎	ク、キュウ	tie into a bundle; coil around	摎
膠	コウ、キョウ、にかわ、にべ	glue; isinglass	膠
参	サン、シン、まい.る、まじわる、みつ	three; going; coming; visiting	参
驂	サン、そえうま	extra driver or horse	驂
惨	サン、みじ.め、いた.む、むご.い	sad; pitiful; wretched; cruel	惨
蔘	シン、サン	luxurious growth of grass	蔘
滲	シン、し.みる、にじ.む	imbued with	滲
蓼	シン、リク、リョウ、たで	luxurious grass; a smart weed	蓼
鯵	ソウ、あじ	horse mackerel	鯵
鰺	ソウ、あじ	horse mackerel	鰺
繆	ビュウ、キュウ、ボク、リョウ、あやま.る、まと.う	error; wrap around	繆
謬	ビュウ、ビョウ、ミュウ、あやま.る	mistake	謬
勠	リク、あわ.せる	combine; join forces	勠
戮	リク、リュウ、ロク、キョウ、ク、ころ.す、けず.る	kill	戮
鏐	リュウ	gold	鏐
廖	リョウ	empty; name	廖
寥	リョウ、さび.しい	lonely	寥

醪	ロウ、もろみ、にごりざけ	unrefined sake or shoyu	醪

40F 弓 FIXATION

⻗	弓道	5B11
40F 並	きゅうどう	*

Pictograph of a bow 弓
Chinese only not and water binding being undone, disperse 沸

引	イン、ひ-く、ひ-ける	pull, draw	40F
矧	シン、は.ぐ、いわ.んや、はぐき、はぎ	feather (arrow)	矧
蚓	ズ、イン、みみず	earthworm	蚓
弓	キュウ、ゆみ	bow	40F
痍	イ、きず	injury	痍
洟	イ、テイ、はな.しる、はな.じる	tear; nasal discharge	洟
儁	シュン、すぐ.れる	excellence; talented person	儁
雋	シュン、セン、すぐ.れる	excel	雋
鐫	セン、ほ.る、え.る、き.る、のみ	carve; engrave; chisel	鐫
弓	テ	phoneme only	弓
姨	テイ、イ、いもと、いもうと、おば	younger sister	姨
銕	テツ、くろがね	iron; strong; solid; firm	銕
弭	ビ、ミ、や.める、や.む、ゆはず	stop; cease; notches where drawstring is attached to the bow	弭

40G 豕 FIXATION

𠂇	豚肉	7D17
40G	ぶたにく	0|1

Flesh and pig 豚
Pictograph showing the graining of the flesh 肉

豚	トン、ぶた	pig, pork	40G
彝	イ、つね	moral principle	彝
彝	イ、つね	moral principle	彝
櫞	エン	kind of lemon tree	櫞
掾	エン、テン、じょう	help; subordinate official; obsolete government service rank	掾
喙	カイ、がい、くちばし	beak	喙
溷	コン、かわや、けが.れる、にご.る、みだ.れる	get muddy	溷
豕	シ、いのこ	pig; hog; pig radical	豕
邃	スイ、おくぶか.い	deep; profound	邃
隧	スイ、ツイ、みち	fall; go around	隧
燧	スイ、ひうち、ひきり、のろし	signal fire	燧
燹	セン、のび	prairie fire	燹
彖	タン	divination	彖
冢	チョウ、つか、おお.う	mound; hillock	冢
篆	テン	seal-style characters	篆
椽	テン、えん、たるき	rafter; porch	椽
遁	トン、のが.れる	deceive; hide; conceal; flee	遁
蠡	レイ、ライ、リ、ラ、	worm-eaten; conch	蠡

	にな、ひさご		
肉	ニク	meat, flesh	40G
俎	ソ、ショ、いた、まないた	altar of sacrifice; chopping board	俎

41A 牙 FLOWERS OF SATURN

巧		象牙の塔	4B4
41A		ぞうげのとう	*

Former NGU character picturing interlocking fangs 牙

牙	ガ、ゲ、きば	tusk; fang	41A
鴉	ア、からす	crow; raven	鴉
呀	ガ、カ、あ	open one's mouth; bare one's teeth; empty	呀
訝	ガ、ゲ、いぶか.る	doubt	訝
谺	コ、カ、こだま	tree spirit	谺

41B 折 FLOWERS OF SATURN

巧		折衷	5–1
41B		せっちゅう	*

Originally chop down trees, longstanding miscopy 折

折	セツ、お-る、おり、お-れる	bend, break, occasion	41B
断	ダン、た.つ、ことわ.る、さだ.める	sever; cut off; interrupt	断

41C 侯 FLOWERS OF SATURN

ｵﾝ	侯爵	3–2
41C	こうしゃく	0‖2

Originally meet, greet, target range or archery 侯
Rice plant and child, young rice plant, young 季
Convoluted, originally a vessel that is lifted with two hands to drink the contents 爵

侯	コウ	marquis, lord	41C
篌	ゴ、コウ	type of harp	篌
猴	コウ、さる	monkey	猴
季	キ	season	41C
悸	キ	pulsate; shudder	悸
爵	シャク	baron	41C
嚼	シャク、か.む	bite	嚼

41D 述 FLOWERS OF SATURN

ｵﾝ	述語	4–5
41D 並	じゅつご	*

Originally entrance of a primitive dwelling 入
Originally hand with bits (of glutinous rice) sticking to it 述

述	ジュツ、の-べる	state, relate	41D
朮	ジュツ、シュツ、チュツ、もちあわ、おけら	a type of millet; a type of herb	朮
入	ニュウ、い-る、い-れる、はい-る	to get in ,to go in, to come in, to flow	41D

		into, to set, to set in	
杁	イリ	sluice; spout; floodgate; penstock	杁
圦	イリ	sluice; spout; floodgate; penstock	圦
叺	かます	straw bag; (kokuji)	叺
鳰	にお	grebe	鳰

41E 司 FLOWERS OF SATURN

ㄅ		司会者	6–8
41E		しかいしゃ	*

Originally mirror image of anus, sedentary work? 司

司	シ	administer, official	41E
逅	コウ、あ.う、まみ.える	meet	逅
垢	コウ、ク、あか、はじ	dirt; grime; earwax	垢
詬	コウ、ク、ののし.る、はじ、はずかし.める	ridicule	詬
梔	シ、くちなし	gardenia	梔
卮	シ、さかずき	large goblet; apt; fitting	卮
巵	シ、さかずき	large winecup; apt; fitting	巵
覗	シ、のぞ.く、うかが.う	peep; peek; come in sight	覗
祠	シ、ほこら、まつる	small shrine	祠

41F 倹 FLOWERS OF SATURN

ㄅ		倹約	5E14

41F	けんやく	*

Originally two talking persons examining horses, discuss 僉

倹	ケン	thrifty, frugal	41F
鹼	ケン、カン、セン、あ.く	saltiness	鹼
嶮	ケン、けわ.しい	inaccessible place; impregnable position; steep place; sharp eyes	嶮
臉	ケン、セン、レン	area between eye and cheek; face	臉
劍	ケン、つるぎ	sword	劍
剱	ケン、つるぎ	sword	剱
劎	ケン、つるぎ	sword	劎
瞼	ケン、まぶた	eyelids	瞼
簽	セン、かご	label; signature	簽
僉	セン、みな	all	僉
歛	レン	tighten; also	歛
斂	レン、おさ.める	tighten; stiffen	斂
匲	レン、くしげ、はこ	cosmetics box	匲
奩	レン、くしげ、はこ	lady's vanity case; trousseau	奩
瀲	レン、なぎさ	brimming; rippling	瀲

41G 倉 FLOWERS OF SATURN

倉	創造	2B7
41G	そうぞう	*

Cover, preserving + door, that which is covered behind a door 倉

倉	ソウ、くら	warehouse, sudden	41G
滄	ソウ	ocean	滄
艙	ソウ	hold (ship)	艙
愴	ソウ、いたま.しい、いた.む	sad; pathetic	愴
蹌	ソウ、ショウ、うご.く、よろ.めく	move; stagger	蹌
瘡	ソウ、ショウ、かさ	wound; boil; syphilis	瘡
搶	ソウ、ショウ、つ.く	thrust; poke; come together; assemble	搶
鎗	ソウ、ショウ、やり	spear; lance; javelin	鎗

42A 復 FURNACE

⊟	復習	5–5
42A	ふくしゅう	*

Chinese only go back, food Chinese only container of reversible shape + inversed foot 復

復	フク	again, repeat	42A
馥	クク、ヒョク、フク、か、かお.る	perfume	馥
鰒	フク、あわび、ふぐ	abalone	鰒
輹	フク、とこしばり	connection between axle and carriage	輹
愎	フク、ヒョク、もと.る	go against; disobey	愎
蝮	フク、まむし	viper; adder; asp	蝮

42B 果 FURNACE

⊟	果汁	6A7
42B	かじゅう	*

Originally fruit on a tree, replaced by rice field, abundant crop, outcome 果

果	カ、は-たす、は-てる、は-て	fruit, result, carry out	42B
踝	カ、くるぶし	ankle	踝
顆	カ、つぶ	grain (e.g. rice)	顆
夥	カ、ワ、おびただ.しい	immense; tremendous	夥
剿	ソウ、ショウ	destroy	剿
勦	ソウ、ショウ	destroy; steal	勦
槊	ソウ、す、すく.う、た.える	nest; dip up; scoop up; come to an end	槊
裹	ホウ、カ、つつ.む	wrap; pack up; cover; conceal	裹

42C 必 FURNACE

⊟	必然	5A4
42C	ひつぜん の	*

Originally halberd/lance between two poles (to prevent break) 必

必	ヒツ、かなら-ず	necessarily	42C
瑟	シツ、おおごと	large koto	瑟
謐	ヒツ、しずか	quiet	謐
樒	ミツ、しきみ、じんこう	tree whose branches are placed on Buddhist graves	樒

| 樒 | ミツ、しきみ、じんこう | Japanese star anise | 樒 |

42D 志 FURNACE

⊟	意志	4-4
42D 並	いし	*

Pictograph of an extended finger 一
Emerging plant, movement of the heart, intent 志

志	シ、こころざ-す、こころざし	will, intent	42D
痣	シ、あざ、ほくろ	birthmark; mole	痣
一	イチ、イツ、ひと、ひと-つ	one	42D
弌	イチ、イツ、ひと-、ひと.つ	one	弌
壹	イチ、イツ、ひとつ	one	壹
辷	すべ.る、すべ.らす	glide; skate; slip; fail in exams; (kokuji)	辷

42E 佳 FURNACE

⊟	絶佳	7E18
42E	ぜっか	*

Non general use character edge/angle/jewel, raised earthen paths 佳

佳	カ	beautiful, good	42E
哇	ア、アイ、エ、ワ、かい、けい	fawning child's voice; laughing child's voice	哇
蛙	ア、ワ、かえる、かわず	frog	蛙

鞋	アイ、カイ、わらじ、くつ	straw sandals	鞋
恚	イ、いか.る	anger	恚
卦	カ、カイ、ケ、うらかた	a divination sign	卦
啀	ガイ、いがむ	wrangle; growl at	啀
崖	ガイ、がけ	cliff; bluff; precipice	崖
鮭	カイ、ケイ、さけ、しゃけ、ふぐ	salmon	鮭
眦	ガイ、まなじり	glare; angry look	眦
硅	カク、キャク、ケイ、やぶ.る	silicon	硅
畦	ケイ、あぜ、うね	rice paddy ridge; furrow; rib	畦
桂	ケイ、うちき、うちかけ、うちぎ	ancient ordinary kimono	桂
罫	ケイ、カイ、ケ	ruled line	罫
褂	ケイ、カイ、ケ、うちき、うちかけ	ancient ordinary kimono	褂
挂	ケイ、カイ、ケ、か.ける	hang	挂
閨	ケイ、ケ、ねや	bedroom	閨
珪	ケイ、たま	jade sceptre or tablet (authority symbol)	珪
幇	ホウ、たす.ける	help	幇

42F 加 FURNACE

⊟	添加	3G4
42F	てんか	*

Add strength to an argument by adding one's own words 加

加	カ、くわ-える、くわ-わる	add, join	42F
跏	カ	sitting in the lotus position	跏
笳	カ、あしぶえ	reed flute	笳
枷	カ、かせ、からざお	shackles; irons; handcuffs; bonds	枷
痂	カ、ケ、かさ、かさ.ぶた	scab; dry up; slough	痂

42G 胃 FURNACE

▭		胃酸	3A12
42G		いさん	*

Pictograph of the stomach and (underneath) flesh of the body 胃

胃	イ	stomach	42G
渭	イ	name of Chinese river	渭
蝟	イ、はりねずみ	hedgehog	蝟
悁	エン、ケン	anger; worry; impatience	悁
娟	エン、ケン	beauty of face	娟
捐	エン、す.てる	throw away	捐
喟	キ、カイ、なげ.く	moan	喟
涓	ケン	drop; pure	涓
狷	ケン	short-tempered	狷
鵑	ケン	cuckoo	鵑
蹐	セキ	stealthy footsteps	蹐
鶺	セキ	wagtail	鶺
瘠	セキ、ジャク、やせ.る	get thin; lose weight; become sterile	瘠

Chapter 7 Libra

43A 居 GLASS

古	住居	3A2
43A	じゅうきょ	*

Slumped figure and old, so staying immobile, in one place 居

居	キョ、い-る	be, reside	43A
倨	キョ、コ、おご.る	pride; squatting with legs outstretched	倨
踞	キョ、コ、うずく.まる	crouch; cower	踞

43B 臣 GLASS

古	大臣	4D7
43B	だいじん	*

Eye, wide eyed alertness, guard, servant, subject 臣

臣	シン、ジン	retainer, subject	43B
頤	イ、おとがい、あご	chin; jaw	頤
宦	カン、つかさ	official	宦
熙	キ、たのし.む、ひか.る、ひろ.い、よろこ.ぶ、かわ.く、あきらか、ひろ.める、ひろ.まる	shine	熙

熙	キ、たのし.む、ひか.る、ひろ.い、よろこ.ぶ、かわ.く、あきらか、ひろ.める、ひろ.まる	shine	熙
豎	ジュ、たて、た.てる、こども	vertical; child	豎
贓	ソウ	bribery	贓
臧	ゾウ、ソウ、よい	good; bribe; servant	臧

43C 勇 GLASS

古	蛮勇	2–1
43C	ばんゆう	*

Originally expressing break through and strength 勇

勇	ユウ、いさ-む	courage; cheer up; be in high spirits; bravery; heroism	43C
踊	ヨウ、おど.る	jump; dance; leap; skip	踊

43D 易 GLASS

古	貿易	2A5
43D	ぼうえき	*

Originally big-eyed lizard + rays of the sun, iridescent, change 易

易	エキ、イ、やさ-しい	easy, change, divination	43D
蜴	エキ	lizard	蜴
蜴	エキ	lizard	蜴

鯣	エキ、するめ	cuttlefish	鯣
裼	セキ、テイ、はだぬ.ぐ	to bare the shoulder	裼
剔	テキ、テイ、えぐ.る、そ.る	cutting	剔

43E 妖 GLASS

古	妖精	5–4
43E	ようせい	*

Originally referred to a type of thistle (bamboo + person with bowed head) 夭

妖	ヨウ、あや-しい、なまめ-く	attractive	43E
忝	テン、かたじけな.い	grateful; indebted	忝
飫	ヨウ、オ、ヨ、あき.る	satiety	飫
夭	ヨウ、オウ、カ、わか.い、わかじに、わざわい	early death; calamity	夭
殀	ヨウ、わかじに	dying young	殀

43F 尚 GLASS

古	高尚	8B19
43F	こうしょう	1|7

Originally smoke rising out of the window of a house, height 尚
Originally expressing to offer someone a valuable object, reward/praise in return 賛

尚	ショウ	furthermore, esteem	43F
嫦	コウ、ジョウ	proper name	嫦

厰	ショウ	workshop	厰
廠	ショウ	workshop	廠
嘗	ショウ、ジョウ、かつ.て、な.める	lick; lap up; burn up; taste; undergo; underrate; despise	嘗
敞	ショウ、たか.い、ほが.らか、ひろ.い	high and flat; broad; spacious	敞
蟾	ジョウ、もむ	toad; mantis	蟾
吊	チョウ、つ.る、つる.す	suspend; hang; wear (sword)	吊
鐺	ト、ソウ、トウ、くさり、こじり、こて、なべ	chain; tip of a scabbard; flatiron	鐺
档	トウ	bookshelf; archives	档
蟷	トウ	mantis	蟷
螳	トウ	mantis	螳
洮	トウ	flow	洮
當	トウ、あ.たる、あ.てる、まさ.に	bear; accept; undertake; just	當
儻	トウ、あるいは、すぐ.れる、もし	excel; surpass; if; perhaps	儻
瞠	ドウ、トウ、みは.る	stare intently	瞠
黨	トウ、なかま、むら	party; faction; clique	黨
磴	トウ、はた、はたと	bottom; base; slap; bang; all of a sudden	磴
襠	トウ、ふんどし、まち	gusset; gore	襠
棠	トウ、やまなし	wild pear tree; crab apple tree	棠
賛	サン	praise	43F
攅	サン、あつ.まる	gather; come together	攅

鑽	サン、き.る	make fire by rubbing sticks	鑽
鑽	サン、き.る	make fire by rubbing sticks	鑽
纘	サン、サブ、つ.ぐ	succeed to; inherit	纘
賛	サン、たす.ける、たた.える	help; support; assist; aid	賛
蠶	サン、テン、かいこ、こ	silkworms	蠶
讚	サン、ほ.める、たた.える	praise; picture title	讚

43G 窓 GLASS

古	窓口	2A3
43G	まどぐち	*

Pictograph of a window with grille 窓

窓	ソウ、まど	window	43G
聡	ソウ、さと.い、みみざと.い	wise; fast learner	聡
窗	ソウ、ス、まど、てんまど、けむだし	window; pane	窗
總	ソウ、す.べて、すべ.て、ふさ	collect; overall; altogether	總

44A 墓 GLUE OF THE WISE

ぁ	墓地	8A11
44A	ぼち	0‖4

Non general use character not, sun among many plants is setting, covered 墓
Formerly birds gathered in a tree, assemble 集
Formerly a pictograph of a net with hauling ropes, thread + die, phonetic interwoven 網

墓	ボ、はか	grave	44A
蟇	バ、マ、ひき	toad	蟇
蟆	バ、マ、ひき	toad	蟆
驀	バク	going straight forward	驀
寞	バク、マク、さび.しい	lonely; quiet	寞
獏	バク、ミャク	tapir	獏
貘	バク、ミャク	tapir	貘
冪	ベキ	power; exponent	冪
羃	ベキ	power; exponent	羃
糢	ボ、モ、かた、のっとる	rice snacks	糢
謨	ボ、モ、はか.る	plan; deliberate	謨
摸	モ、モウ、バク、ボ、マク	search; imitate; copy	摸
網	モウ、あみ	net, network	44A
惘	ボウ、モウ、あき.れる	unclear; be astonished	惘
魍	モウ、ボウ	spirits of mountains and streams	魍
罔	モウ、ボウ、あみ、し.いる、ない	net	罔
集	シュウ、あつ-まる、あつ-める、つど-う	gather, collect	44A
襍	ザツ、ゾウ、まじ.える、まじ.る	mixed; blended; mix; mingle	襍

44B 亭 GLUE OF THE WISE

☞	料亭	2–1
44B	りょうてい	*

Simplification of tall, building + nail, phonetic stop/stay 亭

亭	テイ	pavilion, inn	44B
渟	テイ、とど.まる	stop	渟

44C 協 GLUE OF THE WISE

☞	日本放送協会	3A1
44C	にっぽんほうそうきょうかい	*

Trebling of strength and ten, expressing many; strength of many persons, cooperate 協

協	キョウ	cooperate	44C
恊	キョウ、あわ.せる、かな.う	threaten	恊

44D 属 GLUE OF THE WISE

☞	付属	3A8
44D	ふぞく	*

Variant of tail + ngu character caterpillar 属

属	ゾク	belong, genus	44D
嘱	ショク、しょく.する、たの.む	request; send a message	嘱
蜀	ショク、ゾク、いもむし	green caterpillar; Szechwan	蜀

矚	ショク、ソク、み.る	look intently	矚
觸	ショク、ふ.れる、さわ.る	touch; feel; hit; proclaim; announce; conflict; contact	觸
屬	ゾク、ショク、さかん、つく、やから	genus; subordinate official; belong; affiliated	屬
躅	チョク、タク	tap with the feet; ruins	躅
髑	ドク、トク	skull	髑
獨	ドク、トク、ひと.り	alone; spontaneously; Germany	獨

44E 保 GLUE OF THE WISE

ꝋ	保険	2–5
44E	ほけん	*

Originally mother carrying a child in a blanket 保

保	ホ、たも-つ	preserve, maintain	44E
堡	ホ、ホウ、とりで	fort	堡
褓	ホ、ホウ、むつき	diaper	褓
葆	ホウ、ホ、し.げる	dense growth; keep; adhere to; conceal	葆
襃	ホウ、ほ.める	praise; extol	襃
呆	ホウ、ほけ.る、ぼ.ける、あき.れる、おろか	be amazed; disgusted; shocked	呆

44F 責 GLUE OF THE WISE

↻	債権者	5A5
44F	さいけんしゃ	*

Taper, phonetic demand, money which can be demanded promptly 責

責	セキ、せ-める	liability, blame	44F
嘖	サク、さいな.む、さけ.ぶ	scold; torment; chastise	嘖
簀	サク、ジャク、セキ、す	rough mat (reeds)	簀
瘠	しゃく	spasms; (kokuji)	瘠
磧	セキ、かわら	expanse of sand; pebbly beach	磧
勣	セキ、シャク、いさお、つむ.ぐ	merit; achievement	勣

44G 俊 GLUE OF THE WISE

↻	俊才	3D5
44G	しゅんさい	*

Chinese only linger/dawdle, stop/start + self and legs 俊

俊	シュン	excellence, genius	44G
梭	サ、ひ	shuttle	梭
浚	シュン、さら.える、さら.う	dredge; drag; clean	浚
逡	シュン、しりぞ.く	saunter; go back	逡
悛	シュン、セン、あらた.める	amend	悛
皴	シュン、ひび、しわ	wrinkles; cracking; creases	皴

45A 犯 GOLD

🦴	犯人	3–2
45A	はんにん	*

Pictograph of a slumped figure 犯

犯	ハン、おか-す	crime, violate, commit, assault	45A
范	ハン、いがた	bee; law; casting mould	范
笵	ハン、ボン、のり	bamboo frame; law	笵

45B 片 GOLD

🦴	片手	4–7
45B 並	かたて	*

Tree cut in half, thin piece 片
Formerly depicting an intricately patterned collar, (complex) writing 文

文	ブン、モン、ふみ	writing, text	45B
紊	ビン、ブン、みだ.れる	disturb	紊
旻	ビン、ミン、あきぞら	the autumn sky	旻
閔	ビン、ミン、あわ.れむ、うれ.える	grieve; be sad; pity	閔
憫	ビン、ミン、あわれ.む、うれ.える	anxiety; mercy	憫
駁	ブン、モン	zebra with yellow eyes and red mane	駁
吝	リン、しわ.い、やぶさ.かな、おし.む	miserly; stingy; sparing	吝
悋	リン、ねた.む、やぶさか、お.しむ	stingy	悋

45C 那 GOLD

🖋	旦**那**	2C6
45C 並	だんな	*

Specially interwoven cloth, rare 希
City where furs where worn, ancient barbarian kingdom 那

那	ナ	what?	45C
娜	ダ、ナ	graceful	娜
希	キ	desire, hope for, rare	45C
鯑	かずのこ	yellow fish (herring) eggs (sushi); (kokuji)	鯑
晞	キ、かわ.く	dry out; expose to the sun	晞
唏	キ、なげ.く	lament; grieve	唏
欷	キ、なげく	cry	欷
淆	コウ、ま.じる	turbidity; mixing	淆

45D 爆 GOLD

🖋	**爆**発	2A1
45D	ばくはつ	*

Expose rice to the sun 爆

爆	バク		burst, explode	45D
瀑	バク、ハク、ホウ、ボウ、ホク、ボク、たき、にわかあめ		waterfall	瀑

45E 修 GOLD

	悠然	4C6
45E 並	ゆうぜん	*

Brushing specks of dirt off clothes, elegant 修
Formerly hand striking person with a stick and tree, something straight, line 条

修	シュウ、シュ、おさ-める、おさ-まる	practice, master	45E
蓨	シュウ	(used only in compounds)	蓨
絛	ジュウ、ジョウ、トウ、さなだ	braid	絛
倏	シュク、たちまち	quick; prompt	倏
筱	ゾウ、ショウ、しの	dwarf bamboo; diminutive in person's name	筱
攸	ユウ、ところ	relaxed; at ease; place	攸
条	ジョウ	clause, item, line	45E
滌	デキ、テキ、ジョウ、あら.う	rinse; wash	滌

45F 貫 GOLD

	貫通	2–1
45F	かんつう	*

Originally two shells/units of money threaded on a string 貫

| 貫 | カン、つらぬ-く | pierce | 45F |
| 槓 | カン | grove | 槓 |

45G 任 GOLD

⚭ 45G	妊婦 にんぷ	4A10 *

Person + spindle, burden borne by a person, duty 任

任	ニン、まか-せる、まか-す	duty, entrust	45G
霪	イン	rain lasting at least ten days	霪
恁	イン、ジン、ニン	like this; thus	恁
婬	イン、みだれ-、ひた.す、ほしいまま、みだ.ら、みだ.れる	lewdness; licentiousness	婬
郢	エイ	place name	郢
荏	ジン、ニン	bean	荏
袵	ジン、ニン、こくび、おくみ、しとね	neck of a garment; gusset; gore	袵
衽	ジン、ニン、こくび、おくみ、しとね	neck of a garment; gusset; gore	衽
霆	テイ、いかづち	lightning; thunder	霆
妊	ニン、ジン、はら.む、みご も.る	be(come) pregnant	妊
凭	ヒョウ、ヘイ、もた.れる、よ.る	lean on; recline on; lie heavy	凭

46A 示 GRADE OF FIRE

示	宗教	5F8
46A	しゅうきょう	1‖3

Altar with drops of blood/wine 示
Originally sitting on a piece of cloth as it is being spread out 展
Hand and thickly growing plant, religious offering from the forest 拝

示	ジ、シ、しめ-す	show	46A
蒜	サン、にんにく、ひる、のびる	garlic	蒜
棕	シュ、ソウ	hemp palm	棕
祟	スイ、たた.る、たた.り	curse; haunt	祟
淙	ソウ	sound of running water	淙
粽	ソウ、ちまき	rice dumplings steamed in bamboo leaves	粽
廩	リン、くら	rice storehouse	廩
稟	リン、ヒン、こめぐら	salary in rice	稟
懍	リン、ラン	fear; tremble	懍
展	テン	unfold	46A
輾	テン、ネン、きし.る、めぐ.る	squeak	輾
碾	テン、ひ.く、う.す	mortar; grind	碾
拝	ハイ、おが-む	worship, respectful	46A
湃	ハイ	sound of waves	湃

46B 築 GRADE OF FIRE

築	建築	2A3

46B	けんちく	*

Hand striking instrument 築

恐	キョウ、おそ-れる、おそ-ろしい	fear, awe	46B
跫	キョウ、あしおと	sound of footsteps	跫
鞏	キョウ、かたい	hard	鞏
蛩	キョウ、こおろぎ	cricket	蛩

46C 矛 GRADE OF FIRE

矛	矛先	4A8
46C	ほこさき	*

Barbed lance 矛

矛	ム、ほこ	halberd, lance, spear	46C
鞣	ジュウ、ニュウ、なめ.す、なめしがわ	tanned leather	鞣
蹂	ジュウ、ふ.む	step on	蹂
糅	ジュウ、ま.じる	mix	糅
揉	ジュウ、も.む、も.める	rub; massage; shampoo; debate vigorously; train; coach; worry; get in trouble	揉
懋	ボウ、し.げる、つと.める	strive; flourish	懋
楙	ボウ、しげる	name of plant; lush	楙
袤	ボウ、ながさ	length	袤
鶩	ボク、ブ、ム、あひる	domestic duck	鶩

46D 鳥 GRADE OF FIRE

隹		候鳥		4C11
46D 並		こうちょう		*

Pictograph of a bird 鳥
Chinese only hawk, phonetic level, possibly settled on a level 准

准	ジュン	quasi-, conform, permit	46D
準	ジュン、じゅん.じる、じゅん.ずる、なぞら.える、のり、ひと.しい、みずもり	correspond to; proportionate to; conform; imitate	準
鳥	チョウ、とり	bird	46D
嗚	ウ、オ、ああ	weep; ah; alas	嗚
塢	オ、ウ	fortress embankment; village	塢
鴛	オウ、	female mandarin duck	鴛
鶯	オウ、うぐいす	nightingale; bush warbler	鶯
鴬	オウ、うぐいす	nightingale	鴬
雁	ガン、かり、かりがね	wild goose	雁
鴈	ガン、かり、かりがね	wild goose	鴈
梟	キョウ、ふくろう	owl; expose	梟
鷦	ショウ	wren	鷦
鵆	ト、チョウ、つた	type of bird; vine	鵆

46E 渦 GRADE OF FIRE

ず	渦巻き	4A4
46E	うずまき	*

Bone/vertebrae, flexibility, ease of movement 渦

渦	カ、うず	whirlpool, eddy	46E
蝸	カ、かたつむり	snail	蝸
堝	カ、るつぼ	crucible; melting pot	堝
窩	カ、ワ、むろ	cave; pouch	窩
喎	カイ、ケ、クウ、カ、よこしま、くちがゆがむ、ゆが.む	crooked mouth; evil; dishonest	喎

46F 輸 GRADE OF FIRE

ず	輸出	4
46F	ゆしゅつ	*

Chinese only affirmation, originally convey, boat + cap off, phonetic transfer 輸

46G 能 GRADE OF FIRE

ず	大熊座	4–2
46G	おおぐまざ	0|1

Pictograph of a bear, ability "abearability" 能
Originally small bits of thread + two devices to twist threads, control 率

能	ノウ		ability, can, Noh	46G
擺	ハイ、ひら.く		push open	擺
羆	ヒ、ひぐま、しぐま		brown bear	羆
率	ソツ、リツ、ひき-いる		rate, command	46G
蟀	シュツ		cricket; grasshopper	蟀

47A 禁 GRANATE

舌		禁煙	2–1
47A		きんえん	*

Altar + forest phonetic. Abstain, abstain for religious reasons 禁

禁	キン	ban, forbid	47A
噤	キン、つぐ.む	shut up	噤

47B 規 GRANATE

舌		規制	2–1
47B		きせい	2|0

Originally prune a tree, order 制
Adult male and look, observe carefully, looked upon as a standard 規

制	セイ	system, control	47B
掣	セイ、セツ、ひ.く	pull back; restrain	掣

47C 二 GRANATE

舌		武者	5A8

47C 並	むしゃ	*

Two fingers 二
Advance on foot with a halberd 武

武	ブ、ム	military, warrior	47C
贇	イン	beautiful	贇
斌	ヒン、フン、うるわ.しい、あき.らか	beautiful; harmony of appearance	斌
鋖	ブ	tin plate	鋖
鵡	ブ、ム	cockatoo	鵡
二	ニ、ふた、ふた-つ	two	47C
膩	ジ、ニ、あぶら、あぶらあか	smooth; oily	膩
弍	ニ、ジ、ふた-、ふた.つ、ふたた.び	two	弍
貳	ニ、ジ、ふた.つ、そえ	two	貳
貮	ニ、ジ、ふた.つ、そえ	number two	貮

47D 余 GRANATE

余	余暇	7A4
47D	よか	2|6

Cover + wooden cross frame, roomy ample 余
False + day, phonetically expressing space, day of leisure 暇

余	ヨ、あま-る、あま-す	excess, ample, I	47D
蜍	ショ	toad	蜍
敘	ジョ、つい.ず、ついで	describe, confer	敘
餘	ヨ、あま.る、あま.り、あま.す	surplus; excess; remainder	餘

畲	ヨ、シャ	new field	畲
暇	カ、ひま	leisure, free time	47D
鍜	カ	armour neck plates	鍜
瑕	カ、あら、きず、なんぞ	flaw; blemish	瑕
鰕	カ、えび	shrimp; prawn; lobster	鰕
假	カ、ケ、かり、かり.る	temporary; interim; assumed (name); informal	假
遐	カ、とお.い、なんぞ	distant	遐
葭	カ、よし、あし	reed	葭

47E 舎 GRANATE

舎	田舎	2–1
47E	いなか*	*

Originally mouth/breathe + ample, easily, relax 舎

舍	シャ	house, quarters	47E
舍	セキ、シャ、やど.る	inn; hut; house; mansion	舍

47F 識 GRANATE

舎	常識	3–2
47F	じょうしき	*

The marker that produces words, intelligence, knowledge 識

識	シキ	knowledge	47F
熾	シ、おこ.る、おこ.す、さかん	kindling fire	熾
幟	シ、のぼり	flag; banner; streamer	幟

47G 屯 GRANATE

击	屯営	4A4
47G	とんえい	*

Originally sprouting plant + bud 屯

屯	トン	barracks, camp, post	47G
邨	ソン、むら	village; hamlet; rustic	邨
噸	トン	tonne; 1000 kilograms	噸
噸	トン	tonnage; (kokuji)	噸
飩	ドン、トン	Japanese noodles	飩

48A 因 GUM

🜊	因果 関係	4–3
48A	いんがかんけい	*

Big man + enclosure, prisoner, cause of imprisonment? 因

因	イン、よ-る	cause, be based on, depend on	48A
氤	イン	spirited	氤
茵	イン、しとね	cushion; mattress	茵
烟	エン、けむ.る、けむり、けむ.い	smoke	烟

48B 牛 GUM

🜊	耕作	5F14
48B 并	こうさく	*

Chinese only plough, or serrated wood 耕
Pictograph of a cow's head and horns 牛

耕	コウ、たがや-す	till, plough	48B
耜	シ、すき	plough	耜
牛	ギュウ、うし	cow	48B
桙	ウ、ほこ	halberd	桙
吽	コウ、ウン、イン、オン、グ、ほえ.る	bark; growl	吽
忸	ジク、ジュウ、はじ.る	shame	忸
衄	ジク、はなぢ	nose bleed	衄
狃	ジュウ、な.れる、なら.う	get used to; learn	狃
遲	チ、おく.れる、おく.らす、おそ.い	late; tardy; slow; delay	遲
稺	チ、ジ、いと.けない、おさ.ない、おく.て、お.ごる	infancy	稺
鈕	チュウ、ジュウ、ぼたん、つまみ	button	鈕
鵚	ボウ、とき	crested ibis	鵚
鉾	ボウ、ム、ほこ	halberd; arms; festival float	鉾
犇	ホン、ひし.めく、ひしひし、は.しる	clamour; crowded	犇
犖	ラク、まだらうし	brindled cow; bright; excel	犖
牢	ロウ、かた.い、ひとや	prison; jail; hardness	牢

48C 偉 GUM

𢆶	偉人	5B4

48C	いじん	*

Chinese only leather/hide, originally patrol, move all around 偉

偉	イ、えら-い	great, grand	48C
圍	イ、かこ.む、かこ.う、かこ.い	enclose; surround; encircle; preserve; store; keep	圍
幃	イ、キ、とばり	bag	幃
韋	イ、そむ.く、なめしがわ	tanned leather radical	韋
諱	キ、いみな、い.む	posthumous (real) name	諱

48D 曽 GUM

🧪	僧院	6G2
48D	そういん	*

Originally build up, steam from a rice cooker 曽

曽	ソ、ソウ、かつ-て、すなわ-ち	formerly; once; before; ever; never; ex-	48D
噌	ソ、しょう	used in place names	噌
甑	ソウ、ショウ、こしき	rice-steaming pot	甑

48E 綿 GUM

🧪	綿雪	2–3
48E	わたゆき	*

White, threads, and cloth/cotton 綿

綿	メン、わた	cotton, cotton wool	48E
帛	ハク、きぬ	cloth	帛
棉	メン、わた	cotton	棉
緜	メン、わた、つら.なる	cotton	緜

48F 句 GUM

𤤄	文句	7E18
48F	もんく	*

Mouth + cover/wrap/encircle, intertwining words, phrase 句
Plant and encircle + head of rice(plant), plant with a circular head 菊

句	ク	phrase, clause	48F
椈	キク	oak	椈
鞫	キク	investigate a crime	鞫
麹	キク、こうじ	malt; yeast	麹
恟	ク	foolish; fear	恟
煦	ク、あたた.める	warm	煦
枸	ク、コウ	quince tree	枸
狗	ク、コウ、いぬ	puppy; dog	狗
劬	ク、つか.れる	become tired; work busily	劬
苟	コウ、ク、いやしく.も	any; at all; in the least	苟
鉤	コウ、ク、かぎ	hook; barb; gaff; brackets	鉤
鈎	コウ、ク、かぎ	hook; barb; gaff; brackets	鈎

佝	コウ、ク、せむし	foolish; stopped over	佝
蒟	コン、ク	devil's tongue (plant)	蒟
荀	ジュン、シュン	type of plant; proper name	荀
徇	ジュン、シュン、あまねし、したが.う、とな.える	herald; announce; follow; obey; seek; lay down one's life	徇
筍	ジュン、シュン、イン、たけのこ、たかんな	bamboo shoot	筍
恂	ジュン、シュン、まこと	sincere; fear; sudden; blinking	恂
勹	ホウ、つつ.む、つつみがまえ	wrapping enclosure; wrapping radical	勹

48G 逆 GUM

5G	遡行	5B7
48G	そこう	*

From inverted variant of big man, opposite normal, going backwards 逆

逆	ギャク、さか、さか-らう	reverse, oppose	48G
獗	ケツ	storm around; be crazy	獗
闕	ケツ、か.ける	lack; gap; fail; imperial palace	闕
厥	ケツ、クツ、その、それ	that	厥
蹶	ケツ、ケイ、たお.れる、つまず.く	stumble	蹶

槊	サク、ほこ	halberd	槊
愬	ソ、サク、うった.える	complain of	愬
溯	ソ、サク、さかのぼ.る	go upstream; retrace the past	溯

49A 災 GYPSUM

⚎	災厄	2–19
49A	さいやく	1|13

Cliff, bending figure, danger 厄
Flood and Fire 災

厄	ヤク	misfortune, disaster	49A
檐	エン、タン、のき、ひさし	eaves	檐
簷	エン、ひさし	eaves	簷
鮠	カイ、ゲ、ガイ、はえ、はや	dace (carp); (kokuji)	鮠
厂	カン、かりがね、がんだれ	wild goose; trailing cliff radical	厂
詭	キ、いつわ.る	lie; deceive	詭
跪	キ、ひざまず.く	kneel	跪
岌	キュウ、たか.い	high; dangerous	岌
脆	ゼイ、セイ、セツ、もろ.い、よわい	brittle; fragile; easy to beat; sentimental; susceptible	脆
蟾	セン	toad	蟾
贍	セン、すく.う	have enough of; add to	贍
瞻	セン、み.る	look at	瞻
憺	タン	calm; quiet; move	憺

擔	タン、かつ.ぐ、にな.う	carry; bear; undertake	擔
膽	タン、きも	gall bladder; bravery; courage	膽
澹	タン、セン、あわ.い	calm; quiet; bland; rocking; rippling; suffice	澹
譫	トウ、セン、タン、うわごと、たわごと、うるさくしゃべ.る	delirious talk	譫
阨	ヤク、アイ、アク、せま.い、ふさが.る、せま.る	obstruct; distress; narrow	阨
扼	ヤク、アク、おさ.える	command; dominate; prevent; obstruct	扼
軛	ヤク、アク、くびき	yoke	軛
災	サイ、わざわ-い	calamity	49A
輕	ケイ、かる.い、かろ.やか、かろ.んじる	light; easy; simple; gentle	輕
莖	ケイ、キョウ、くき	stem; stalk	莖
經	ケイ、キョウ、へ.る、た.つ、たていと、はか.る、のり	classic works; pass through	經
頸	ケイ、くび	neck; head	頸
剄	ケイ、くびき.る	beheading	剄
脛	ケイ、すね、はぎ	leg; shin	脛
痙	ケイ、つ.る、ひきつ.る	have a cramp	痙
逕	ケイ、みち、こみち、さしわたし、ただちに	path	逕
徑	ケイ、みち、こみち、さしわたし、ただちに	path; diameter; method	徑
錙	シ	unit of weight; small; slight	錙

緇	シ、くろ		black clothing; priest	緇
輺	シ、こにだ、ほろぐるま、にぐるま		wagon; dray; canopied cart	輺
鯔	シ、ぼら、とど		mullet (fish)	鯔

49B 契 GYPSUM

▽		契約	3–5
49B		けいやく	0|1

Originally tally, right, proper 契
Plant and simplification of "yo", ample, phonetic expressing bitter, bitter plant 茶

契	ケイ、ちぎ-る		pledge, join	49B
禊	ケイ、カツ、みそぎ、はら.う		Shinto purification ceremony	禊
挈	ケイ、ケツ、ひっさ.げる		carry by hand	挈
齧	ゲツ、ケツ、かじ.る、か.む		gnaw; nibble; munch; have a smattering of	齧
囓	ゲツ、ケツ、かじ.る、か.む		gnaw	囓
楔	ケツ、セツ、くさび、ほうだて		wedge; arrowhead	楔
茶	チャ、サ		tea	49B
茶	タ、ズ、ト、ダ、にがな		a weed	茶

49C 券 GYPSUM

▽		拳銃	3–4
49C		けんじゅう	*

Originally expressing notched pledge 券

券	ケン	ticket, pass, bond	49C
眷	ケン、かえり.みる	look around; regard affectionately	眷
豢	ケン、カン、やしな.う	raising domestic animals	豢
劵	ケン、てがた、わりふ	become fatigued; stop	劵
棬	ケン、まげもの	wickerwork	棬

49D 雄 GYPSUM

ᰮ 49D	雄犬 めすいぬ	6D11 1|4

Bird with forearm Chinese only, phonetic fine/showy bird, male bird 雄
Hands lifting together, rise 興

雄	ユウ、お、おす	male, powerful	49D
擒	キン、とら.える、とりこ	capture; a captive	擒
羂	ケン、わな	trap; snare	羂
肱	コウ、かいな、ひじ、まるい	ability; talent; elbow; arm	肱
浤	コウ、ふか.い	rising waters; clear deep water	浤
魖	チ、すだま	mountain spirits	魖
黐	チ、リ、もち	bird-lime	黐
蘿	ラ、つた	ivy	蘿
鑼	ラ、どら	gong	鑼
邏	ラ、めぐ.る	go around; conceal	邏
漓	リ、うす.い	dropping; soak in	漓

籬	リ、まがき、かき	rough-woven fence; bamboo hedge	籬
興	コウ、キョウ、おこ-る、おこ-す	rise, raise, interest	49D
釁	キン、ちぬ.る、すき、ひま	smear with blood	釁
舁	ヨ、か.く	bear; carry	舁
譽	ヨ、ほ.まれ、ほ.める	fame; reputation; praise	譽
歟	ヨ、や、か	interrogative particle	歟

49E 豊 GYPSUM

⍦	豊胸	2–6
49E	ほうきょう	*

Originally showing food vessel and edible plant, full, plenty 豊

豊	ホウ、ゆたか	abundant, rich	49E
艶	エン、つや、なま.めかしい、あで.やか、つや.めく、なま.めく	lustre; glaze; polish; charm; colourful; captivating	艶
體	タイ、テイ、からだ、かたち	body; group; class; body; unit	體
體	タイ、テイ、からだ、かたち	the body; substance; object; reality	體
豐	ホウ、ブ、ゆた.か、とよ	bountiful; excellent; rich	豐
鱧	レイ、はも	conger; sea eel	鱧
醴	レイ、ライ、あまざけ	sweet sake	醴

49F 講 GYPSUM

ⵘ	講義	6–11
49F	こうぎ	0|3

Non general use character large amount, accumulation, two baskets piled up 講
Formerly hands joined in performing a task 挙

講	コウ	lecture	49F
構	コウ	pull; cause	構
覯	コウ、あ.う	happening to meet	覯
遘	コウ、あ.う、まみ.える	meet	遘
篝	コウ、かがりび、かがり、ふせご	campfire; fishing fire; beacon basket	篝
冓	コウ、かま.える	put together; inner palace	冓
糠	コウ、ソウ、ぬか	dregs; sediment; grounds	糠
媾	コウ、よしみ	association; intimacy	媾
稱	ショウ、たた.える、とな.える、あ.げる、かな.う、はか.る、ほめ.る	name, praise	稱
苒	ゼン	flourishing; luxuriant	苒
冉	ゼン、ネン、あや.うい	red; tan	冉
髯	ゼン、ひげ	beard; moustache	髯
挙	キョ、あ-げる、あ-がる	offer, raise, act, perform	49F

擧	キョ、あ-げる、あ-がる	offer, raise, act, perform	擧
擧	キョ、あ-げる、あ-がる	offer, raise, act, perform	擧
欅	キョ、けやき	keyaki; zelkova tree	欅

49G 並 GYPSUM

⍫	杉並木	4A3
49G	すぎなみき	0|1

Doubling of standing person, row/line, rank along side 並
Tree and hairs, tree with hair-like leaves 杉

並	ヘイ、なみ、なら-べる、なら-ぶ、なら-びに	row, line, rank with, ordinary	49G
椪	ポン	name of a place in India; Poona	椪
靈	レイ、リョウ、たま	soul; spirit	靈
櫺	レイ、リョウ、れんじ	lattice work	櫺
杉	すぎ	cryptomeria, cedar	49G
衫	サン	thin kimono	衫

Chapter 8 Scorpio

50A 玄 HOUR

⊠ 50A	玄妙 げんみょう	11A10 *

Short thread suitable for twisting, very small, hard to see 玄

玄	ゲン	occult, black	50A
拗	オウ、ヨウ、イク、ユウ、ねじ.れる、こじ.れる、す.ねる、ねじ.ける	crooked; twisted; distorted; perverted; cross	拗
眩	ゲン、カン、げん.す、くるめ.く、まぶ.しい、くら.む、まど.う、めま.い、まばゆ.い、くれ.る、ま.う	faint; dizzy	眩
痃	ゲン、ケン	cramps	痃
衒	ゲン、ケン、てら.う	show off; display; pretend	衒
鉉	ケン、つ.る	handle	鉉
呟	ゲン、つぶや.く	mutter; grumble; murmur	呟
孳	ジ、シ、う.む、しげ.る	increase; bear children	孳
茲	シ、ジ、ここ.に、し.げる	here	茲
黝	ユウ、あおぐろ	black	黝
窈	ヨウ	quiet	窈

50B 留 HOURS

⊠ 50B	留守番 るすばん	4F15 *

Horse's bit, control 留

留	リュウ、ル、と-める、と-まる	stop, fasten	50B
茆	エン、ボウ、その、かや、ぬなわ	garden; farm; yard	茆
籀	チュウ、シュウ、ジュ、よ.む	a style of calligraphy	籀
卯	ボウ、う	rabbit (zodiac sign)	卯
鉚	リュ、よいかね	gold	鉚
餾	リュウ	steaming rice	餾
霤	リュウ、あまだれ	raindrops falling from the eaves; eaves	霤
瀏	リュウ、きよ.い	clear	瀏
溜	リュウ、た.まる、たま.る、た.める、したた.る、たまり、ため	slide; glide; slip; slippery	溜
鰡	リュウ、ル	a type of fish	鰡
嚠	リュウ、ル	a clear sound	嚠
瘤	リュウ、ル、こぶ	lump; swelling	瘤
畄	リュウ、ル、と.める、と.まる、とど.める、とど.まる、るうぶる	fasten; halt; stop	畄
聊	リョウ、いささか	slightly	聊
瑠	ル、リュウ	precious stone	瑠
榴	ル、リュウ、リョウ、ざくろ	pomegranate	榴

50C 忍 HOUR

⊠	忍耐	2–2
50C	にんたい	*

Blade, phonetic bear, bear something painful in the heart? 忍

忍	ニン、しの-ぶ、しの-ばせる	endure, stealth	50C
絣	かせ、かすり	splashed dye pattern; reel; skein	絣
荵	ニン、ジン、しのぶ	hare's foot fern	荵

50D 刻 HOUR

⊠	忍耐	5A4
50D	にんたい	*

Jinmei character zodiac hog, variant of pig, phonetic carve 刻

刻	コク、きざ-む	chop, mince, engrave	50D
駭	ガイ、カイ、おどろ.く、おどろ.かす	be surprised	駭
咳	カイ、ガイ、せ.く、しわぶ.く、せき、しわぶき	cough; clear throat	咳
孩	ガイ、カイ、ちのみご	baby; infancy	孩
垓	ガイ、カイ、はて	border; boundary; staircase; hundred quintillion	垓

50E 垂 HOUR

| ⊠ | 雨垂れ | 4A2 |

| 50E | あまだれ | 0‖3 |

Originally ground + plant with leaves hanging down to ground 垂
Raindrops falling from the clouds 雨
Obscure, slumped figure, bending and phrase, used to convey interlocking parts of a building? 局

垂	スイ、た-れる、た-らす	suspend, hang down	50E
陲	スイ、ほとり	boundary	陲
捶	スイ、むちう.つ	strike; whip; slap	捶
局	キョク	office, section, end, circumstances	50E
跼	キョク、こご.む、くぐま.る、かが.む、せぐく.まる	bow; stoop; bend over; crouch	跼
雨	ウ、あめ、あま	rain	50E
霎	ショウ、ソウ	light rain; short while	霎
霄	ショウ、そら	sky	霄

50F 護 HOUR

☒	弁護士	3
50F	べんごし	*

Crested bird in hand, phonetic make dizzy, snare with words 護

50G 巻 HOUR

☒	鉢巻	2D3
50G	はちまき	*

Hands rolling rice + curled or bent body 巻

巻	カン、ま-く、ま-き	roll, reel, volume	50G
綣	ケン	attachment; affection	綣
倦	ケン、うむ	be respectful; grow tired	倦
蜷	ケン、にな	an edible river snail	蜷

51A 異 IRON

♕	異人	3–3
51A	いじん	*

Person putting on a mask, different, strange appearance 異

異	イ、こと	differ, strange	51A
驥	キ	fast horse; talent	驥
冀	キ、こいねが.う、こいねが.わくは	hope for; wish; Hebei province	冀
糞	フン、くそ	shit; faeces; excrement	糞

51B 編 IRON

♕	編集者	3A6
51B	へんしゅうしゃ	*

Originally doorplate, door + bound writing tablets 編

編	ヘン、あ-む	edit, knit, book	51B
諞	ヘン	flattering; glibness	諞

騙	ヘン、かた.る、だま.す	deceive	騙
蝙	ヘン、こうもり	bat	蝙
褊	ヘン、せま.い	narrow; small	褊
扁	ヘン、ひらたい	level; small	扁
翩	ヘン、ひるが.える	fluttering of flag	翩

51C 域 IRON

⛉	領域	7B16
51C	りょういき	*

Walk and halberd, originally walking one lap, Chinese only multiple of time 域

域	イキ	area, limits	51C
穢	アイ、エ、ワイ、けが.す、けが.れ、けが.れる	dirty	穢
鮇	イ	a type of fish	鮇
縅	おど.す	the thread/braid (of armour); (kokuji)	縅
賊	ザイ、サイ、ゾク	pirate; thief	賊
閾	シキ、イキ、キョク、ヨク、くぎり、しきい	threshold	閾
絨	ジュウ	wool cloth	絨
戉	ジュウ、エツ、えびす、まさかり	warrior; arms; savage; Ainu	戉
戎	ジュウ、えびす、つわもの	warrior; arms; barbarian; Ainu	戎
譏	シン	omen	譏
截	セツ、サイ、き.る、たつ	cut off; sever	截

繊	セン	fine; delicate; minute; graceful	纖
孅	セン、かよわ.い	delicate	孅
籤	セン、くじ、かずとり	lottery; raffle	籤
籖	セン、くじ、かずとり	lottery; raffle	籖
殱	セン、つく.す、ほろぼ.す	massacre	殱
殲	セン、つく.す、ほろぼ.す	massacre	殲

51D 宇 IRON

♔ 51D		宇頂天 うちょうてん	3A13 *

Originally roof that completely covers, firmament/heaven 宇

宇	ウ	eaves, roof, heaven	51D
于	ウ、ク、ここに、ああ、おいて に より を	going; from	于
盂	ウ、はち	bowl	盂
紆	ウ、まが.る、めぐ.る	crouch	紆
鄂	ガク	place name; frankly	鄂
萼	ガク、うてな	calyx; cup	萼
蕚	ガク、うてな	calyx; cup	蕚
愕	ガク、おどろ.く	surprised; frightened	愕
咢	ガク、おどろく	outspokenly	咢
鍔	ガク、つば	sword guard; kettle brim	鍔
鶚	ガク、みさご	osprey	鶚
鰐	ガク、わに	alligator; crocodile	鰐

| 諤 | ガク、わめ.く、あご | speaking the truth | 諤 |
| 吁 | ク、ウ、ああ | exclamation | 吁 |

51E 煩 IRON

♛	煩悩	4–1
51E	ぼんのう	*

Person with exaggerated head 煩

| 煩 | ハン、ボン、わずら-う、わずら-わす | trouble, pain, torment | 煩 |
| 鰥 | カン、コン、やもめ、やもお | widower; unmarried man | 鰥 |

51F 貴 IRON

♛	貴重	3–5
51F	きちょうな	*

Shell/money and non general use character gather, basket 貴

貴	キ、たっと-い、とうと-い、たっと-ぶ、とうと-ぶ	precious, revered	51F
瞶	キ	see everything	瞶
餽	キ、おく.る	give; provide; offer	餽
匱	キ、ひつ	chest; coffer; rice tub	匱
櫃	キ、ひつ	chest; coffer; tub	櫃
簣	キ、もっこ、あじか	earth-carrying basket	簣

51G 監 IRON

⛉	監視	6A9
51G	かんし	*

Originally person bending over to stare at water in bowl 監

監	カン	supervise, watch	51G
檻	カン、おり、おばしま、てすり	pen; corral; cell; jail	檻
鑒	カン、かんが.みる、かがみ	take warning from; learn from; pattern; example	鑒
儖	ラン	ugly	儖
欖	ラン	Chinese olive tree	欖
籃	ラン、かご	basket	籃
攬	ラン、と.る	hold (in hand)	攬
纜	ラン、ともづな	hawser	纜
繿	ラン、ぼろ	rags	繿
襤	ラン、ぼろ	rags	襤

52A 男 JUNIPER

ᓃ	憂愁	2–1
52A	ゆうしゅう	1∣3

Originally head/heart + upturned foot, walk slowly, phonetic sad 憂
Strength in the fields 男

憂	ユウ、うれ-える、うれ-い、う-い	grief, sorrow	52A

擾	ジョウ、みだ.れる、みだ.す、わずら.わしい	disturb; throw into confusion	擾
男	ダン、ナン、おとこ	man, male	52A
舅	キュウ、しゅうと	father-in-law	舅
嬲	ドウ、ジョウ、なぶ.る	sport with; ridicule; tease	嬲
娚	ナン、めおと	loud talking	娚

52B 適 JUNIPER

G	適性	5–2
52B	てきせい	*

Chinese only base/starting point, (emperor and mouth/say) 適

適	テキ	suitable, fit, go	52B
謫	タク、チャク、せ.める、とが.める	crime	謫
鏑	テキ、かぶら、かぶらや、やじり	arrow head	鏑

52C 敢 JUNIPER

G	勇敢	2C3
52C	ゆうかん	*

Originally pulling something out of a container, make-or-break effort? 敢

敢	カン	daring, tragic	52C
橄	カン	olive	橄
瞰	カン、み.る	look; see	瞰

儼	ゲン、いかめ.しい、おごそか	serious; untouched; solemnly; majestically	儼

52D 尺 JUNIPER

G	尺八	4A3
52D	しゃくはち	0|2

Span of the hand, measure 尺
Previously symbolising dividing/splitting 八

尺	シャク	measure, foot	52D
咫	シ、た	short; span	咫
呎	シャク、ふいいと	foot	呎
仗	ジョウ、チョウ、つえ、つわもの、まわり、よる	cane; stick	仗
八	ハチ、や、やっ-つ、よう	eight	52D
釟	ハチ、ハツ	forge; temper; anneal	釟
叭	ハツ	open	叭

52E 将 JUNIPER

G	将来	2D5
52E	しょうらい	*

Originally offer meat to a superior, (on a litter?) 将

将	ショウ	command, about to	52E
醤	ショウ	a kind of miso	醤
漿	ショウ、こんず	a drink	漿

奬	ショウ、ソウ、すす.める	prize; reward; give award to	奬
蒋	ショウ、ソウ、まこも、はげ.ます	reed	蒋
鏘	ソウ、ショウ	tinkling of jade or metal pendants	鏘

52F 亡 JUNIPER

&	文盲	7–9
52F	もんもう	*

Originally person no longer able to be seen, escaping 亡

亡	ボウ、モウ、な-い	die, escape, lose	52F
匸	ケイ、かくしがまえ	hiding enclosure radical	匸
肓	コウ	interior region of the body too deep to be reached by acupuncture	肓
佞	ネイ、おもね.る、よこしま	flattery; insincerity	佞
侫	ネイ、おもね.る、よこしま	flattery; insincerity	侫
虻	ボウ、あぶ	gadfly; horsefly	虻
芒	ボウ、コウ、モウ、すすき、のぎ、のげ	pampas grass; beard (grain)	芒
氓	ボウ、たみ	people	氓
茫	ボウ、とお.い	wide; extensive	茫
鋩	ボウ、ほこさき、きっさき、へさき	sword point	鋩

52G 宅 JUNIPER

G	自宅	2B2
52G	じたく	*

Roof and growing plant, 'taken root' 宅

宅	タク	house, home	52G
咤	タ、ト、しか.る	clicking (with tongue); upbraid; pity; belch	咤
侘	タ、わび.しい、ほこ.る、わ.びる	proud; lonely	侘

53A 蔵 LEAD

ｳ	蔵書	2B
53A	ぞうしょ	*

Originally concealing a wounded + incapacitated person with grass 蔵

53B 支 LEAD

ｳ	支店	7–5
53B	しじ	*

Hand holding up branch, originally break off a branch 支

支	シ、ささ-える	branch, support	53B
妓	ギ、キ、わざおぎ、うたいめ	stretch; singing girl; geisha; prostitute	妓
跂	キ、つまだ.つ、むつゆび	stand on tiptoes	跂

屐	ゲキ、ケキ、はきもの	clog	屐
皷	コ、つづみ	drum; beat; rouse	皷
翅	シ、はね、つばさ	(insect) wings; fly; merely	翅

53C 我 LEAD

| カ | 我まま | 2B8 |
| 53C | わがまま | * |

Originally broad bladed halberd with tassels, notches for kill 我

我	ガ、われ、わ	I, self, my	53C
哦	ガ	sing	哦
莪	ガ	type of thistle	莪
鵝	ガ	goose	鵝
鵞	ガ	goose	鵞
峨	ガ、けわ.しい	lofty	峨
戈	カ、ほこ、ほこづくり、かのほこ	halberd; arms; festival car; float; tasselled spear radical	戈
娥	ガ、みめよ.い	beautiful	娥
蛾	ギ、ガ、ひむし	moth	蛾

53D 犬 LEAD

| カ | 番犬 | 4A8 |
| 53D | ばんけん | * |

Originally a pictograph of a dog on its hind legs barking 犬
Pictograph originally means head, clamour and attack 顎

犬	ケン、いぬ	dog	53D
哭	コク、なげ.く、な.く	weep; moan; wail	哭
吠	ハイ、ベイ、ほえ.る、ほ.える	bark; howl; cry	吠
飆	ヒョウ、つむじかぜ	whirlwind	飆
袱	フク	cloth wrapper	袱
茯	フク、ブク、ヒ、ビ	type of mushroom	茯
厖	ボウ、おおき.い	large; mix	厖
尨	ボウ、むくいぬ	shaggy hair or dog	尨
顎	ガク、あご、あぎと	jaw; chin; gill	53D
齶	ガク、あご、はぐき	jaw	齶

53E 尊 LEAD

| ヵ | | 尊敬 | 3E11 |
| 53E | | そんけい | * |

Offer and pour wine for a superior 尊

尊	ソン、たっと-い、とうと-い、たっと-ぶ、とうと-ぶ	value, esteem, your	53E
酋	シュウ、ジュ、おさ、ふるざけ、さけのつかさ	chieftain	酋
遒	シュウ、せま.る、つよ.い	strong; unyielding; forceful	遒
逎	シュウ、せま.る、つよ.い	strong; powerful	逎
墫	シュン	cup	墫

蹲	ソン、シュン、つくば.う、うずくま.る	crouch; squat; cower	蹲
蹢	テキ、しゃが.む、たちもとお.る	squat; sit on heels; loiter	蹢
擲	テキ、チャク、ジャク、なぐ.る、なげう.つ	hit; resign	擲
迺	ナイ、ダイ、アイ、のすなわ.ちなんじ	in other words; thou; you; possessive particle	迺
廼	ナイ、ダイ、ノ、アイ、すなわ.ちなんじ	in other words; thou; you; possessive particle	廼
蕕	ユウ、ユ	foul-smelling grass	蕕
猷	ユウ、ヨウ、はかりごと、はか.る	plan; scheme; plan; plot; way	猷

53F 善 LEAD

ち	親善	3–1
53F	しんぜん	*

Originally sheep + argue, praiseworthy argument, fine debate 善

善	ゼン、よ-い	good, virtuous	53F
譱	ゼン、よ.い、い.い、よ.く、よし.とする	virtuous; good; goodness	譱

53G 延 LEAD

ち	延期	2–5

| 53G | えんき | * |

Lengthy protracted movement, foot + go and add mark 延

廴	イン、いんにょう、えんにょう	long stride or stretching radical	廴
蜒	エン、タン	meandering; serpentine	蜒
莚	エン、むしろ	straw mat	莚
筵	エン、むしろ	straw mat	筵
涎	セン、エン、よだれ	saliva; slobber	涎

54A 匿 MAGNESIA

M	匿名	3A1
54A	とくめい	*

Originally old person tending to long pliant hair, weak, young 匿

匿	トク	conceal	54A
慝	トク、わる.い	bad; evil; disaster	慝

54B 机 MAGNESIA

M	事務机	4–3
54B	じむつくえ	*

Non general use character representing small table 机

机	キ、つくえ	desk, table	54B
几	キ、きにょう、つくえ	table; table enclosure; table or windy radical	几

鳧	フ、けり、かも	wild duck; end; suffix	鳧
鳬	フ、けり、かも	wild duck; end; suffix	鳬

54C 栽 MAGNESIA

𝓜	盆栽	3A
54C	ぼんさい	*

Fancy halberd cutting/trimming 栽

54D 座 MAGNESIA

𝓜	銀行口座	2B6
54D	ぎんこうこうざ	*

Two persons sitting on the ground under a roof, gathering 座

座	ザ、すわ-る	seat, sit, gather	54D
覡	ゲキ、ケキ、かんなぎ、みこ	diviner; medium	覡
蓙	ザ、ござ	mat; matting; (kokuji)	蓙
噬	ゼイ、か.む	bite	噬
筮	ゼイ、セイ、うらな.う、めどぎ	(water) divining equipment	筮
誣	フ、しい.る、し.いる、あざむ.く	slander	誣
鵐	ブ、ム	unmottled quail	鵐

54E 従 MAGNESIA

𝓜	従業員	2B4

54E	じゅうぎょういん	*

Originally two persons moving along a road 従

従	ジュウ、ショウ、ジュ、したが-う、したが-える	follow, comply	54E
蹤	ショウ、あと	footprints; traces; tracks	蹤
慫	ショウ、すす.める	advise; persuade	慫
聳	ショウ、そび.える	rise; tower	聳
樅	ショウ、もみ	fir	樅

54F 株 MAGNESIA

ℳ	株式会社	4–6
54F	かぶしきかいしゃ	*

Originally inside of a tree trunk, often red 朱

朱	シュ	vermillion, red	54F
洙	シュ	name of a Chinese river	洙
侏	シュ	actor; supporting post	侏
茱	シュ	river ginger tree; oleaster	茱
銖	シュ	measuring unit, 1/16 of a ryou; percent; small; slight	銖
蛛	チュ、シュ	spider	蛛
誅	チュウ、チュ、ちゅう.する、ころ.す、せ.める	death penalty	誅

54G 脳 MAGNESIA

ᴍ	頭脳	2–4
54G	ずのう	*

Brain, hair, scoop, part of the head that is scooped out 脳

脳	ノウ		brain	54G
硇	ノウ		agate	硇
瑙	ノウ		agate; onyx	瑙
腦	ノウ、ドウ、のうずる		brain; memory	腦
惱	ノウ、なや.む、なや.ます、なや.ましい、なやみ		angered; filled with hate	惱

55A 斉 NIGHT

x	一斉	4A14
55A	いっせい	*

Similar heads of grain for religious offering 斉

斉	セイ	equal, similar	55A
絣	かすり	splashed pattern dyeing or weaving	絣
纃	かすり	splashed pattern dyeing or weaving	纃
剤	ザイ、スイ、セイ、かる、けず.る	medicine; drug; dose	剤
済	サイ、セイ、す.む、す.ます、すく.う、な.す、わた.す、わた.る	to help; aid; relieve; to ferry; cross	済
斎	サイ、つつし.む、とき、ものいみ	Buddhist food; room; religious purification;	斎

		worship; avoid; alike	
齏	セイ、サイ、あえもの、な.ます、あ.える	dress (salad) vegetables	齏
齎	セイ、サイ、あえもの、な.ます、あ.える	dishes seasoned with vinegar or miso	齎
擠	セイ、サイ、お.す	push aside	擠
齎	セイ、サイ、シ、もたら.す、もた.らす	bring; take; bring about	齎
儕	セイ、サイ、ともがら	companion	儕
躋	セイ、サイ、のぼ.る	climb	躋
霽	セイ、サイ、は.れる、は.らす	clear up	霽
薺	セイ、ザイ、ひと、ととの.える、なずな	water-chestnuts; caltrop	薺
臍	セイ、サイ、へそ、ほぞ	navel	臍

55B 操 NIGHT

✗	操縦 士		4–6
55B	そうじゅうし		*

Chinese only birds chirping, three mouths in tree 操

操	ソウ、みさお、あやつ-る	handle, chastity	55B
懆	ソウ	unease	懆
髞	ソウ	hurry; high	髞
澡	ソウ、あら.う	wash	澡
譟	ソウ、さわ.ぐ	shout; be noisy	譟
噪	ソウ、さわ.ぐ	be noisy	噪
躁	ソウ、さわ.ぐ	noisy	躁

55C 虚 NIGHT

✗	虚無 主義	8E25
55C	きょむしゅぎ	0|11

Originally tiger, phonetic big, + large hill with a hollow crown 虚
Enclosure with person inside, imprisoned person 囚

虚	キョ、コ	empty, hollow, dip	55C
瘧	ギャク、ガク、おこり	ague; intermittent fever	瘧
謔	ギャク、キャク、たわむ.れる	sport with	謔
醵	キョ	contribution for a feast (potluck)	醵
墟	キョ、あと	ruins	墟
遽	キョ、あわ.てる、あわただ.しい、すみやか、にわか	fear; agitation; confusion; hurry	遽
嘘	キョ、コ、うそ、ふ.く	lie; falsehood	嘘
據	キョ、コ、よ.る	to occupy; take possession of; a base	據
歔	キョ、すすりな.く	cry	歔
虔	ケン、つつし.む	respect	虔
虍	コ、とらかんむり、とらがしら	tiger spots; mottled; tiger or tiger crown radical	虍
鯱	しゃちほこ、しゃち	fabulous dolphin-like fish; killer whale; (kokuji)	鯱
褫	チ、うば.う	rob	褫
廬	ロ	hut	廬
濾	ロ	name of river in China	濾

轤	ロ	pulley	轤
蘆	ロ、あし、よし	reed; rush	蘆
鑪	ロ、いろり	hearth; fireplace; furnace	鑪
爐	ロ、いろり	fireplace; stove; oven; furnace	爐
顱	ロ、かしら、あたま	head; skull	顱
鱸	ロ、すずき	seabass	鱸
艫	ロ、とも、へさき	bow; prow; stern	艫
櫨	ロ、はぜ	wax tree; sumac	櫨
臚	ロ、リョ	skin; tell; report	臚
廬	ロ、リョ、いお、いおり、いえ	hermitage	廬
驢	ロ、リョ、うさぎうま	donkey	驢
囚	シュウ	captured, criminal, arrest	55C
饂	ウン、うどん	Japanese noodles; (kokuji)	饂
慍	ウン、オン、いか.る、いか.り、うら.む	be angry (excited)	慍
薀	ウン、オン、たくわ.える、つ.む	pile up; store; hornwort	薀
褞	ウン、オン、ぬのこ	robe	褞
蘊	ウン、つ.む	pile up	蘊
媼	オウ、おうな	mother; grandma; old woman	媼
榲	オツ	quince	榲
膃	オツ	fat; corpulent	膃
鰮	オン、いわし	sardine	鰮
瘟	オン、えやみ	contagious disease	瘟
泅	シュウ、およぐ	swim	泅

55D 専 NIGHT

✕	仁恵	3C4
55D	じんけい	*

Hand and round weighted device used in spinning 専

専	セン、もっぱ-ら	exclusive, sole	55D
蒪	シュン、ぬなわ	type of water plant	蒪
磚	セン、かわら	tile	磚
甎	セン、しきがわら、かわら	floor tiles	甎
囀	テン、さえず.る	sing; chirp; warble; chatter	囀

55E 郷 NIGHT

✕	望郷	2B1
55E	ぼうきょう	*

Originally two persons meeting over dinner, feast, community 郷

郷	キョウ、ゴウ	village, rural	55E
嚮	コウ、キョウ、さきに、むか.う	guide; direct; incline to; favour	嚮

55F 革 NIGHT

✕	革命	3–4
55F	かくめい	*

Hornless creature with flaps of skin, hairless hide, change 革

革	カク、かわ	leather, reform	55F
羈	キ、ハ、おもが.い、たづな、たび、つな.ぐ	reins; connection	羈
羈	キ、ハ、おもが.い、たづな、たび、つな.ぐ	reins; connection	羈
羈	キ、ハ、おもが.い、たづな、たび、つな.ぐ	reins	羈
霸	ハ、ハク、はたがしら	supremacy; leadership	霸

55G 没 NIGHT

✕	陷没	3A4
55G	かんぼつ	*

Originally hand holding a gong to strike large hanging bell 没

没	ボツ	sink, disappear, die, lack, not	55G
殻	カク、コク、バイ、から	husk; nutshell	殻
慤	カク、つつし.む、まこと	respectful; sincerely	慤
歾	ボツ、しぬ	die	歾
没	ボツ、モツ、おぼ.れる、しず.む、ない	not; have not; none; to drown; sink	没

56A 疑 OIL OF SATURN

𠤎	疑問	3-3
56A	ぎもん	*

Originally old man in doubt where to turn 疑

疑	ギ、うたが-う	doubt, suspect	56A
礙	ガイ、ゲ、さまた.げる	obstruct; hinder; block; deter	礙
嶷	ギョク、ギ、さと.い	wise	嶷
癡	チ、し.れる、おろか	foolish	癡

56B 垣 OIL OF SATURN

アイ	宣伝	3E4
56B	せんでん	*

Originally that which goes around a building, wall, fence 垣

宣	セン	promulgate, state	56B
桓	カン	marking post	桓
暄	ケン、あたたか.い	warm weather	暄
諠	ケン、かまびす.しい、わす.れる	forget; noisy	諠
愃	ケン、カン	abundant; generous	愃

56C 処 OIL OF SATURN

アイ	処理	2–4
56C	しょり	*

Visiting somewhere and stop sitting on a stool 処

処	ショ	deal with, place	56C
兀	コツ	high & level; lofty; bald; dangerous	兀

處	ショ、ところ、-こ、お.る	place; locale; department	處
攵	ホク、のぶん、ぼくづくり、ぼくにょう	strike; hit; folding chair radical	攵
攴	ホク、ぼくづくり、ぼくにょう、とまた	strike; hit; folding chair radical	攴

56D 旦 OIL OF SATURN

57¹	元旦	4A5
56D	がんたん	*

Simplification of carry, former ngu character dawn, sun over the horizon 旦

旦	タン	daybreak; dawn; morning	56D
妲	ダツ	female proper name	妲
怛	ダツ、タン、タツ、いた.む	be sad; be dejected; fear	怛
疸	タン	jaundice	疸
袒	タン、かたぬ.ぐ	baring the shoulder; strip to waist	袒
靼	タン、タチ、タツ、なめ.す、なめしがわ	tanned leather; smooth leather	靼

56E 滑 OIL OF SATURN

57¹	潤滑	3–5
56E	じゅんかつ	*

Skull and vertebrae, bones + flesh of the body 骨

滑	カツ、すべ-る、なめ-らか	slide, slip, smooth	56E
磆	カツ	stone implement	磆
猾	カツ、わるがしこ.い	crafty	猾
鶻	コツ、カツ、はやぶさ	falcon; eagle	鶻
榾	コツ、ほた	chip (of wood)	榾
萵	ワ	lettuce	萵

56F 叫 OIL OF SATURN

ㄢ	収入	3B
56F	しゅうにゅう	*

Originally intertwined threads, assemble, gather 叫

56G 為 OIL OF SATURN

ㄢ	行為	2B1
56G	こうい	*

Originally hand + prototype elephant, imitate form, image 為

為	イ	do, purpose	56G
譌	カ、なま.る、あやま.る	accent; dialect	譌

Chapter 9 Sagittarius

57A 哀 PHILOSOPHICAL STONE

👑	悲哀	3–4
57A	ひあい	*

Mouth + clothing phonetic to express sound of wailing 哀

哀	アイ、あわ-れ、あわ-れむ	sorrow, pity	57A
寰	カン	imperial domain; world	寰
圜	カン、エン、まる.い、めぐ.る	round; go around	圜
鐶	カン、たまき、わ	metal ring; link; drawer pull	鐶
鬟	カン、わげ、みずら	topknot; chignon; male hairstyle of looped ponytails	鬟

57B 補 PHILOSOPHICAL STONE

👑	補助	5E9
57B	ほじょ	*

Jinmei character begin, use + hand holding tool, start to use, phonetic patch 補

補	ホ、おぎな-う	make good, compensate	57B
黼	フ、ホ、あや	embroidery	黼
鯆	フ、ホ、いるか	type of herring	鯆
脯	フ、ホ、こじし、ほじし	dried meat	脯

埔	ホ	used in Chinese place names	埔
舖	ホ	shop; store	舖
匍	ホ、は.う	crawl; creep	匍
餔	ホ、フ、く.う、ゆうめし	eat; late afternoon meal	餔
鋪	ホ、フ、しく、みせ	shop; store	鋪
逋	ホ、フ、のが.れる	flee	逋

57C 享 PHILOSOPHICAL STONE

♛		享受者	4F9
57C		きょうじゅしゃ	1|8

Originally castle watchtower extending in two directions 享
Originally showing an old man leaning on a stick 老

享	キョウ	receive, have	57C
椁	カク	outer box for a coffin	椁
槨	カク	outer box for a coffin	槨
廓	カク、くるわ、とりで	enclosure; quarter; red-light district	廓
孰	ジュク、いずれ、たれ	which; how; who	孰
鶉	ジュン、シュン、うずら	quail	鶉
鐓	タイ、いしづき	ferrule; butt end	鐓
燉	トン	fiery	燉
暾	トン、あさひ	sunrise; sun's rays	暾
烹	ホウ、に.る	boil; cook	烹
老	ロウ、お-いる、ふ-ける	old, aged	57C
鰭	キ、ギ、ひれ	fin	鰭

耆	キ、シ、おい.る	senility	耆
蜆	ケン、えび	shrimp	蜆
嗜	シ、たしな.む、たしな.み、この.む、この.み	like; taste; modest	嗜
蓍	シ、めどぎ	yarrow; sericea; stalks used for divination	蓍
耋	テツ、としより	old; elderly	耋
耄	ボウ、モウ、おいぼ.れる	senility	耄
姥	ロウ	voice	姥

57D 凶 PHILOSOPHICAL STONE

| 👑 | 凶悪 | 2–3 |
| 57D | きょうあくな | * |

Container/mouth + symbol for drawing attention, empty 凶

凶	キョウ	bad luck, disaster	57D
匈	キョウ	turmoil; Hungary	匈
恟	キョウ、おそ.れる	fear	恟
洶	キョウ、わ.く	gush forth; surge	洶

57E 乳 PHILOSOPHICAL STONE

| 👑 | 乳房 | 4–9 |
| 57E | にゅうぼう | * |

Originally manually assist in removing a child from the vagina 乳

乳	ニュウ、ちち、ち	breasts, milk	57E
吼	コウ、ク、ほ.える	bark; bay; howl; bellow; roar; cry	吼
殍	ヒョウ、フ、うえじに	dying of starvation	殍
蜉	フ	kind of ant; mayfly	蜉
孵	フ、か.えす	hatch; incubate	孵
郛	フ、くるわ	earthwork enclosure around a castle	郛
孚	フ、たまご、はぐく.む	sincere; nourish; encase	孚
俘	フ、とりこ	captive	俘
艀	フ、はしけ	sampan; lighter; barge	艀
桴	フ、ばち、いかだ	drumstick; raft	桴

57F 敬 PHILOSOPHICAL STONE

♛	敬称	3–1
57F	けいしょう	*

Non general use character insignificance, person bending, speaking respectfully 敬

敬	ケイ、うやま-う	respect	57F
檠	ケイ、ゆだめ	straighten a bow; lamp stand	檠

57G 甲 PHILOSOPHICAL STONE

♛	甲虫	4A5
57G	こうちゅう	*

Hard-shelled seed with a split 甲

甲	コウ、カン	shell, armour, high, 1st,	57G

		A	
狎	オウ、コウ、な.れる、あなど.る	get used to; experienced; tamed	狎
呷	コウ、あお.る、す.う	sip; noisy; quack	呷
胛	コウ、かいがらぼね	shoulder blade	胛
匣	コウ、はこ	box	匣
閘	コウ、ひのくち	water gate; lock	閘

58A 鬼 QUICKSILVER

♘		鬼界	5B10
58A		きかい	1|8

Person crouching wearing death mask, contact spirits dead 鬼
Old forms indicate plump thighs and penetration, "trading sex" 商

鬼	キ、おに	devil, demon, ghost	58A
槐	カイ、えんじゅ	type of Japanese pagoda tree	槐
傀	カイ、おおき.い	large	傀
嵬	カイ、ギ	high and flat	嵬
隗	カイ、けわ.しい	high; steep	隗
瑰	カイ、たま、めずら.しい	strange	瑰
餽	キ、おく.る	give; provide	餽
巍	ギ、たか.い	high	巍
魏	ギ、たか.い	high; large	魏
愧	キ、はじ.る、はじ.らう、はずかし.める、とが.める	feel ashamed; shy	愧

魄	ハク、タク、たま.しい	soul; spirit	魄
商	ショウ、あきな-う	trade, deal, sell	58A
鷸	イツ、しぎ	kingfisher; snipe	鷸
裔	エイ、すそ	descendant; border	裔
烱	ケイ、キョウ、あきらか	light; clear	烱
炯	ケイ、キョウ、あきらか	light; clear	炯
冏	ケイ、キョウ、ソウ、あきらか	light; clear; bright	冏
迥	ケイ、ギョウ、はるか	far; distant	迥
絅	ケイ、ひ.く	thin silk	絅
譎	ケツ、キツ、いつわ.る、いつわ.り	deceive	譎

58B 刺 QUICKSILVER

☿	名刺	2–4
58B	めいし	*

Non general use character thorn, (tree/wood + tapering), phonetic beat 刺

刺	シ、さ-す、さ-さる	pierce, stab, thorn	58B
蕀	キョク	milwort	蕀
棘	キョク、いばら、とげ	thorn; splinter; spine; biting words; briers	棘
朿	シ、とげ	thorn	朿
棗	ソウ、なつめ	jujube	棗

58C 声 QUICKSILVER

☿	暖炉	4–3

| 58C | だんろ | 1\|3 |

Former ngu character at this point, originally draw up (hand down, up + rope) 暖
Formerly a pictograph showing the striking of a musical instrument to produce a sound 声

暖	ダン、あたた-か、あたた-かい、あたた-まる、あたた-める	warm	58C
湲	エン、カン	flowing water	湲
爰	エン、ここ.に	lead on to; therefore; then	爰
煖	ダン、カン、ケン、ナン、あたた.か、あたた.める	warm	煖
声	セイ、ショウ、こえ、こわ	voice	58C
磬	ケイ	upside-V-shaped gong	磬
謦	ケイ、しわぶき	coughing	謦
聲	セイ、ショウ、こえ、こわ	sound; voice; noise; tone; music	聲

58D 岡 QUICKSILVER

✡	静岡	4–3
58D	しずおか	*

Former ngu character hill, hill + net, draw in/up, formidable hill, phonetic strong 岡

岡	コウ、おか	hill; height; knoll; rising ground	58D
棡	コウ	mast cross beam	棡
崗	コウ、おか	hill	崗

网	モウ、ボウ、あみ、あみがしら、よんかしら、よこめ	net; net or net crown radical	网

58E 奉 QUICKSILVER

♉	棒紅	3A
58E	ぼうべに	*

Originally two hands offering thickly growing plant, offer 奉

58F 誤 QUICKSILVER

♉	誤解	4–2
58F	ごかい	*

Originally mouth/say + man with head tilted, bragging 誤

誤	ゴ、あやま-る	mistake, mis-	58F
茣	ゴ	mat; matting	茣
蜈	ゴ	centipede	蜈

58G 陵 QUICKSILVER

♉	丘陵	3–2
58G	きゅうりょう	5|2

Originally two hills 丘
Originally high hill, mound 陵

丘	キュウ、おか	hill	58G
邱	キュウ、おか	hill	邱

蚯	キュウ、みみず	earthworm	蚯
陵	リョウ、みささぎ	imperial tomb, mound	58G
菱	リョウ、ひし	water chestnut	菱
薐	ロウ、ほうれんそう	spinach	薐

59A 既 QUINTESSENCE

旡	慨嘆	3A12
59A	がいたん	*

Chinese only not without, person kneeling with head turned, unable 既

慨	ガイ	lament, deplore	59A
漑	ガイ、カイ、そそ.ぐ	pour	漑
曁	キ、およ.ぶ	and; along with; reach; extend to	曁
旡	キ、ケ、む、なし、すでのつくり	sob; choke; crooked heaven radical variant	旡
廐	キュウ、うまや	barn; stable	廐
廏	キュウ、うまや	barn; stable	廏
簪	シン、サン、かんざし	ornamental hairpin	簪
僣	シン、セン、せん.する、おご.る	boastfully usurp	僣
僭	シン、セン、せん.する、おご.る	boastfully usurp	僭
譛	シン、セン、そし.る	slander	譛
譖	シン、セン、そし.る	slander; false accusation	譖
潜	セン、ひそ.む、もぐ.る、	conceal; hide; lower	潜

	かく.れる、くぐ.る、ひそ.める	(voice); hush	
潜	セン、ひそ.む、もぐ.る、かく.れる、くぐ.る、ひそ.める	hide; conceal; secrete; hidden	潜

59B 尉 QUINTESSENCE

⟐	小尉	2–2
59B	しょい	*

Press down with something hot, ironing, put into shape 尉

尉	イ	military rank	59B
熨	イ、ウツ、のし、おさ.える、の.す、ひのし	flatiron; smooth out	熨
蔚	ウツ、イ、うち、おとこよもぎ	dense growth	蔚

59C 茂 QUINTESSENCE

⟐	繁茂	3A5
59C	はんも	*

Pictograph of halberd/battle axe 茂

茂	モ、しげ-る	grow thickly	59C
鉞	エツ、まさかり	battle axe	鉞
戍	ジュ、シュ、まもり、まも.る	protection	戍
戌	ジュツ、いぬ	sign of the dog	戌
袜	ベツ、バツ	socks	袜
韈	ベツ、モチ、バツ、マチ、くつした、たび	socks	韈

59D 隠 QUINTESSENCE

	雲**隠**れ	3–2
59D	くもがくれ	*

Chinese only compassion, care 隠

隠	イン、かく-す、かく-れる	hide	59D
隱	イン、オン、かく.す、かく.れる、よ.る	hide; conceal; cover	隱
穩	オン、おだ.やか	calm	穩

59E 激 QUINTESSENCE

	憤**激**	2–13
59E	ふんげき	*

Water, release (literally strike a person) and white, phonetic to beat, water striking 傲

激	ゲキ、はげ-しい	violent, fierce, strong, intense	59E
覈	カク、ケツ、しら.べる	investigate	覈
竅	キョウ、あな	hole; cave	竅
徼	キョウ、ヨウ、めぐ.る	seek; enquire; go around; border	徼
檄	ケキ、げき.する、ふれぶみ	written appeal; manifesto	檄
遨	ゴウ、あそ.ぶ	play; enjoyment	遨
敖	ゴウ、あそ.ぶ、おご.る	play; be proud	敖

熬	ゴウ、い.る	parch; roast	熬
鰲	ゴウ、おおがめ	huge sea turtle	鰲
嗷	ゴウ、かまびす.しい	noisy	嗷
螯	ゴウ、はさみ	claws	螯
贅	セイ、いぼ	luxury	贅
鼈	ベツ、ゴウ、すっぽん、おおがめ	snapping turtle	鼈
邀	ヨウ、むか.える、もと.める	go to meet; call	邀

59F 唐 QUINTESSENCE

🄚	唐本	2–2
59F	とうほん	*

Originally mouth + hands holding pestle, phonetic brag/boast 唐

唐	トウ、から	(T'ang) China	59F
溏	トウ	mud	溏
塘	トウ、つつみ	dike; embankment	塘

59G 甘 QUINTESSENCE

🄚	甘え	7B18
59G	あまえ	0|2

Originally something held in the mouth, savoured, sweet 甘
Phonetic substitute (original meaning = breath), for four fingers representing four 四

甘	カン、あま-い、あま-える、-あま-やかす	sweet, presume upon	59G
邯	カン	place name; tree cricket	邯

疳	カン	children's diseases	疳
蚶	カン	ark shell	蚶
箝	カン、ケン、す.げる、くびかせ、はさ.む	insert; fit into; attach (a clog thong)	箝
拑	カン、ケン、つぐ.む	shut one's mouth	拑
酣	カン、たけなわ	height of; thick of; full swing	酣
戡	カン、チン、かつ、さす	victory	戡
坩	カン、つぼ	jar; pot	坩
篏	カン、は.める、は.まる、あな	inlay; set in; fall into; rugged	篏
嵌	カン、は.める、は.まる、あな	go into; plunge; inlay	嵌
鉗	ケン、カン、つぐ.む、くびかせ	shut up	鉗
糂	ジン	mixing rice into soup	糂
斟	シン、く.む	dip water; estimate	斟
椹	ジン、チン、シン、さわら、あてぎ、くわのみ	type of cypress	椹
尠	セン、セウ、すくな.い	at least; not a little	尠
鏶	チン	unsatisfactory	鏶
碪	チン、きぬた	stone slab used for washing clothes; an anvil	碪
甜	テン、うま.い、あま.い	sweet	甜
四	シ、よ、よ-つ、よっ-つ、よん	four	59G
駟	シ	four horses	駟
泗	シ、なみだ	name of a Chinese river; snivel	泗

60A 患 RECTIFICATION

🔖	患者 家族	2
60A	かんじゃかぞく	*

Pierced heart, afflicted 患

60B 喝 RECTIFICATION

🔖	喝さい	7C13
60B	かっさい	*

Chinese only range of interrogatives, say, encircle, surround and person: ask and/or threaten 喝

喝	カツ	shout, scold	60B
藹	アイ	flourishing; luxuriant; harmonize; graceful; noble; refined	藹
靄	アイ、もや	mist; haze; fog	靄
遏	アツ、とど.める、と.める	stop; suppress	遏
鞨	カツ、ガチ、セツ、ゼチ、かわぐつ	musical instrument	鞨
羯	カツ、ケツ	barbarian	羯
蠍	カツ、さそり	scorpion	蠍
蝎	カツ、さそり、すくもむし	scorpion	蝎
曷	カツ、なんぞ、いつ、いずくんぞ、なに	why; how; when	曷
偈	ゲ、ケツ、ケイ、いこ.う	verse in praise of Buddha; fast; healthy; rest	偈
碣	ケツ、いしぶみ	round stone; monument	碣
歇	ケツ、カイ、カツ、	exhausted; out of	歇

	や.める		
竭	ケツ、つく.す	end; exhaust	竭
臘	ロウ	year-end sacrifice; dried meat	臘

60C 懷 RECTIFICATION

🏳	壞滅	2B
60C	かいめつ	*

Wrap Chinese only conceal/carry in the sleeve, eye, variant of multitude 懷

60D 卸 RECTIFICATION

🏳	卸売	2–2
60D	おろしうり	*

Originally drive a cart 卸

卸	おろ-す、おろし	wholesale, grate	60D
啣	カン、くわ.える、くつわ	hold in mouth or between teeth	啣
禦	ギョ、ゴ、ふせ.ぐ	defend; protect; resist; ward off	禦

60E 喚 RECTIFICATION

🏳	叫喚	2–5
60E	きょうかん	*

Chinese only lively, women's genitals + spread thighs with hands, sex 喚

喚	カン	shout, yell	60E
奐	カン、あき.らか	clear; bright	奐
渙	カン、あきらか	scatter	渙
煥	カン、あきらか	shine	煥
夐	ケイ、ケン、はるか	far; distant	夐
瓊	ケイ、たま	red jewel; beautiful jewel	瓊

60F 融 RECTIFICATION

| 🖂 | 金融 | 2–3 |
| 60F | きんゆう | * |

Large pot on stand 隔

融	ユウ	dissolve, melt	60F
鬻	イク、シュク、かゆ、かい、ひさ.ぐ	sell; deal in	鬻
膈	カク	diaphragm	膈
鬲	カク、レキ、かなえ、へだ.てる	tripod	鬲

60G 兼 RECTIFICATION

| 🖂 | 兼用 | 5A5 |
| 60G | けんよう | 1\|1 |

Originally hand holding two rice plants, doing two things at once 兼
Original character expressing trader, items that are being traded 価

兼	ケン、か-ねる	combine, unable	60G
蒹	ケン、おぎ	type of reed	蒹
歉	ケン、カン、あきたりない	insufficiency; lack; shortage	歉
慊	ケン、キョウ、あきたりる、うら.む	satisfaction	慊
賺	タン、レン、すか.す	coax	賺
濂	レン	name of Chinese river	濂
価	カ、あたい	price, value, worth	60G
賈	コ、カ、あきな.い、あきな.う、う.る、か.う	buy; tradesman	賈

61A 挟 SAL-AMMONIAC

| ✻ | 板**挟**み | 4C10 |
| 61A | いたばさみ | * |

Non general use character insert, big person squeezed between two others 挾

挟	キョウ、はさ-む、はさ-まる	insert, pinch, squeeze between	61A
侠	キョウ、きゃん、おとこだて	tomboy; chivalry	侠
陝	キョウ、コウ、せま.い	narrow	陝
夾	キョウ、コウ、はさ.む	insert between	夾
筴	キョウ、サク、めどぎ	insert between; chopsticks; divining sticks; plan	筴
莢	キョウ、さや	pod; hull; husk;	莢

		shell; case	
挾	キョウ、ショウ、はさ.む、はさ.まる、わきばさ.む、さしはさ.む	put between; insert; jam; get caught; sandwich	挾
篋	キョウ、はこ	box	篋
鋏	キョウ、はさみ、はさ.む、つるぎ	scissors	鋏
浹	ショウ、あまねし	far and wide; cycle; period	浹
陝	セン	place name	陝

61B 巨 SAL-AMMONIAC

✳	巨人	3A5
61B	きょじん	*

Carpenter's square characterised by its large size 巨

巨	キョ	huge, giant	61B
渠	キョ、かれ、なんぞ、なに、みぞ、いずくんぞ	ditch; canal; lock	渠
秬	キョ、くろきび	a type of millet	秬
苣	キョ、ちしゃ	torch	苣
鉅	キョ、はがね	big; great	鉅
炬	コ、キョ	torch; signal fire	炬

61C 乙 SAL-AMMONIAC

✳	乙に	3A3
61C	おつに	*

Double bladed sword, unusual 乙

乙	オツ	odd, B, 2nd, stylish	61C
訖	キツ、お.える、お.わる、ついに	come to an end; reach; arrive at; finally	訖
屹	キツ、そばだ.つ	towering mountains	屹
吃	キツ、ども.る	stammer	吃

61D 仰 SAL-AMMONIAC

✻	信仰	3
61D	しんこう	*

Chinese only raise, bending person looking up respectfully 仰

61E 屈 SAL-AMMONIAC

✻	窮屈	4–2
61E	きゅうくつ	0|1

Originally tail/genitals, testes, put out/remove balls, castrate 屈
Formerly body and backbone, pregnant woman's body pulling against the backbone, discomfort 窮

屈	クツ	submit, crouch	61E
崛	クツ、そばだ.つ、たか.い	high & lofty (mountains)	崛
倔	クツ、つよ.い	stubborn	倔
窮	キュウ、きわ-める、きわ-まる	distress, extreme	61E
躬	キュウ、キョウ、み	body; self	躬

61F 缶 SAL-AMMONIAC

※	缶切り	3A7
61F	かんきり	*

Secure vessel for pouring liquid into 缶

缶	カン	can, boiler	61F
欝	ウツ、ウン、うっ.する、ふさ.ぐ、しげ.る	gloom; depression; melancholy	欝
罌	オウ、エイ、ヨウ、もたい、ほとぎ、かめ	vase	罌
掏	トウ、す.る、えら.ぶ	pickpocket	掏
綯	トウ、な.う、なわ、よ.る	twist; make rope	綯
淘	トウ、よな.げる	select	淘
寶	ホウ、たから	treasure; jewel; precious; rare	寶
寳	ホウ、たから	treasure; jewel; precious; rare	寳

61G 孤 SAL-AMMONIAC

※	孤立	2A6
61G	こりつ	*

Non general use character melon, phonetic alone 孤

孤	コ	orphan, lonely	61G
呱	コ	cry	呱
觚	コ、カ、く	corner; spire; goblet; wine cup	觚
瓠	コ、カク、ひさご	gourd	瓠
狐	コ、きつね	fox	狐

| 菰 | コ、こも、まこも | reed used for matting | 菰 |
| 觚 | コ、さかずき | cup | 觚 |

62A 偶 SILVER

⌂	偶然	4A4
62A	ぐうぜん	*

Chinese only begin, not clear/open, scorpion with twisting tail 偶

偶	グウ	by chance, spouse, doll	62A
禺	ウ	name of a Chinese emperor	禺
禺	グ、グウ、おながざる	long-tailed monkey	禺
嵎	グウ、グ、くま	mountain recesses	嵎
藕	グウ、グ、ゴウ、はすのね	lotus; lotus root; arrowroot	藕

62B 堅 SILVER

⌂	堅固	3–3
62B	けんご	*

Chinese only hard and wise, hand presses the eye? 堅

堅	ケン、かた-い	firm, solid, hard	62B
鰹	ケン、かつお	bonito	鰹
慳	ケン、カン、おし.む	regret; stinginess	慳
鏗	コウ、つく	clinking sound	鏗

62C 傑 SILVER

亼	豪傑	5D7
62C	ごうけつ	1|1

Chinese only bird's roost, heroic 傑
Originally referring to pig with (tall) fearsome sword-like weapons, wild boar 豪

傑	ケツ	outstanding	62C
桀	ケツ、ます、はりつけ	measuring box	桀
蕣	シュン、むくげ、あさがお	rose of Sharon; althea	蕣
磔	タク、チャク、さ.く、はりつけ、ひらく	crucifixion	磔
舛	ブ、セン、まい、そむ.く	dancing radical	舛
桝	ます	measuring box	桝
燐	リン	phosphorus	燐
鄰	リン、とな.る、となり	neighbour; neighbourhood	鄰
豪	ゴウ	strength, splendour, Australia	62C
濠	ゴウ、コウ、ほり	moat; ditch; canal; Australia	濠

62D 傘 SILVER

亼	相合傘	4A5
62D 並	あいあいがさ	*

Pictograph of a parasol 傘
Originally billowing vapours, later used to speak + rain 雲

雲	ウン、くも	cloud	62D
纃	ウン	a method of dyeing	纃

秐	ウン、くさぎ.る	weed	秐
紜	ウン、みだ.れる	disorder; confusion	紜
壜	ドン、タン、びん	bottle; vial; jar	壜
罎	ドン、タン、びん	bottle; vial; jar	罎

62E 華 SILVER

숲	慶弔	5–11
62E	けいちょう	2|03

Deer, love and goodness 慶
Originally showing a plant with many leaves coming into bud 華

慶	ケイ	joy	62E
麈	オウ、みなごろ.し	massacre; annihilation	麈
麌	グ、ゴ、おじか	stag; buck; hart	麌
灑	シャ、サイ、サ、セ、そそ.ぐ	sprinkle; wash; free and easy	灑
麈	シュ、ス、おおじか	moose; priest's horsehair flapper; elk	麈
麁	ソ、あら.い	rough; crude; coarse	麁
塵	チン、ジン、ちり、ごみ	dust; trash; garbage	塵
麋	ビ、なれしか	reindeer	麋
驪	リ、レイ	black horse	驪
儷	レイ、つれあい、ならぶ	companion	儷
漉	ロク、こ.し、こ.す、す.く	manufacture paper; spread out thin; strain; percolate	漉
轆	ロク、ころ	pulley; roller	轆
華	カ、ケ、はな	flower, showy, China	62E

崋	カ、ク	name of mountain	崋
譁	カ、ケ、かまびす.しい	noisy	譁
曄	ヨウ、かが.やく	shine; flourishing	曄

62F 需 SILVER

⛩	需要	4C15
62F	じゅよう	3‖05

Non general use character however, originally beard, beard soaked by the rain 需
Originally a pictograph of a pestle, borrowed to express middle of the day 午
Originally expressing a person, held in place (for a long time) 久

需	ジュ	need, demand	62F
揣	シ、スイ、タン、はか.る	conjecture	揣
臑	ジ、ドウ、ジュ、デイ、すね	leg; shin	臑
轜	ジ、ひつぎぐるま、じしゃ	hearse	轜
秫	ジ、メン、うるち	non-glutinous grain	秫
繻	シュ、うすぎぬ	satin	繻
孺	ジュ、おさない、ちのみご	child	孺
襦	ジュ、したぎ、はだぎ	underwear	襦
嬬	ジュ、よわ.い	mistress; weak	嬬
惴	ズイ、スイ、おそ.れる	fear; be afraid	惴
喘	ゼン、セン、あえ.ぐ、せき	pant; gasp; breathe hard	喘
蠕	ゼン、ダ、ネン、ジュ、ニュ、うごめ.く	crawling of a worm	蠕

懦	ダ、ジュ、ゼン、よわ.い	weakness; cowardice	懦
糯	ダ、ナ、もちごめ	glutinous rice	糯
猯	タン、いのしし、まみ	wild boar	猯
湍	タン、はや.い、はやせ	rapids	湍
午	ゴ	noon	62F
忤	ゴ、さから.う、もと.る	insubordinate; stubborn; wrong	忤
滸	コ、ほとり	vicinity	滸
久	キュウ、ク、ひさ-しい	long time	62F
柩	キュウ、グ、ひちぎ、ひつぎ	bier; coffin	柩
疚	キュウ、やま.しい、や.む	ashamed; painful; guilty conscious	疚
粂	くめ	used in proper names	粂

62G 雇 SILVER

全	回顧	2
62G	かいこ	*

Bird + door, ungainly flapping of a quail 雇

63A 頃 TIN

⽮	日頃	2–3
63A	ひごろ	*

Character indicates slumped head, person fallen to one side 頃

潁	エイ	name of a Chinese river	潁
穎	エイ、ほさき、のぎ	heads of grain; cleverness	穎

| 頴 | エイ、ほさき、のぎ | heads of grain; cleverness | 頴 |

63B 執 TIN

執		執着	2–3
63B		しゅうちゃく	*

Old form shows shackles + kneeling person, shackle a prisoner, seize 執

執	シツ、シュウ、と-る	take, grasp, execute	63B
鷙	ゴウ、シ、チツ	flying fish; vicious as a hawk; ferocious bird of prey	鷙
贄	シ、にえ	offering; sacrifice	贄
蟄	チツ、チュウ、ちっ.する、かく.れる	hibernation of insects	蟄

63C 舟 TIN

舟		渡し舟	6A14
63C		わたしぶね	*

Boat 舟

舟	シュウ、ふね、ふな	boat	63C
鍮	チュウ、トウ	brass	鍮
偸	ツ、トウ、チュウ、ぬす.む	steal	偸
俞	ツ、トウ、ユ、しかり	steal	俞
瘢	ハン、きず	scar	瘢
槃	ハン、たら.い	tub	槃
瑜	ユ	jewel	瑜

蝓	ユ	slug; snail	蝓
瘉	ユ、い.える、いや.す	get well; recover	瘉
逾	ユ、いよいよ、こ.える	pass; go beyond	逾
渝	ユ、かわ.る	change; be transformed	渝
榆	ユ、にれ	elm	榆
覦	ユ、ねが.う	coveting high rank	覦
踰	ユ、ヨウ、こ.える	go beyond	踰
揄	ヨウ、ユウ、ユ	pull; tease; play with	揄

63D 薫 TIN

♨	薫香	2B4
63D	くんこう	*

Pleasant smelling smoke 薫

薫	クン、かお-る	aroma, fragrance, aura	63D
燻	クン、くす.べる、ふす.べる、いぶ.す、いぶ.る、くす.ぶる、くゆ.らす	smoke; fog; vapor; smoke; cure	燻
燻	クン、くす.べる、ふす.べる、いぶ.す、いぶ.る、くす.ぶる、くゆ.らす	smoulder; fume; oxidize	燻
醺	クン、よう	hunger	醺
黥	ケイ、ゲイ、いれずみ	tattooing	黥

63E 渓 TIN

♨	渓谷	2A4

63E	けいこく	*

Originally valley + Chinese only 'doubt' twisting threads 渓

渓	ケイ	valley, gorge	63E
渓	ケイ、たに、たにがわ	valley	渓
谿	ケイ、たに、たにがわ	valley	谿
奚	ケイ、なんぞ	servant; what; why	奚
蹊	ケイ、みち、わた.る	path	蹊

63F 譲 TIN

	互譲	4E7
63F	ごじょう	0|3

Originally people accusing each other 譲
Formerly a pictograph showing a special spool used for evenly cross winding thread, mutual 互

譲	ジョウ、ゆず-る	hand over, yield	63F
驤	ジョウ、ショウ、あ.がる	lift one's head	驤
攘	ジョウ、ショウ、はら.う	rise; raise	攘
壤	ジョウ、つち	soil; loam; earth; rich	壤
攘	ジョウ、ぬす.む、はら.う	chase away; steal	攘
禳	ジョウ、はら.う	exorcise; drive away	禳
曩	ノウ、ドウ、さき.に	point	曩
嚢	ノウ、ドウ、ふくろ	pouch; purse; bag	嚢
互	ゴ、たが-い	mutual, reciprocal, together	63F
彑	ケイ、けいがしら	pig's head radical variant	彑

| 冱 | ゴ、コ、さ.える、こお.る、ひ.える | close up; freeze over; congeal | 冱 |
| 冴 | ゴ、コ、さ.える、こお.る、ひ.える | freeze; be cold; be clear; attain skill | 冴 |

63G 企 TIN

𠂉	企て	2A
63G	くわだて	*

Person + foot, phonetic precarious, standing on tiptoe 企

Chapter 10 Capricorn

64A 荒 VITRIOL

⌇	荒れ 狂う	2–3
64A	あれくるう	*

Chinese only vast watery waste, (river + death) 荒

荒	コウ、あら-い、あ-れる、あ-らす	rough, wild, waste	64A
贏	エイ、あまり	victory; surplus	贏
瀛	エイ、うみ	ocean; swamp	瀛
羸	ルイ、つか.れる、よわ.い	thin; weak	羸

64B 膝 VITRIOL

⌇	諸膝	2
64B	もろひざ	*

Tree + drops of moisture, resin, sap of the lacquer-tree 漆

64C 竜 VITRIOL

⌇	竜巻	4C9
64C	たつまき	*

Dragon, fearsome, flying 竜

竜	リュウ、たつ	dragon	64C
龕	カン、ガン、れい	alcove for an image	龕

槞	ロウ	cage	槞
蘢	ロウ	dragon grass	蘢
瓏	ロウ	clarity; sound of jewels	瓏
朧	ロウ、おぼろ	haziness; dreaminess; gloom	朧
隴	ロウ、リョウ、おか	hill; mound	隴
壠	ロウ、リョウ、おか、うね、つか	mound; grave; rice field dike	壠
篭	ロウ、ル、かご、こ.める、こも.る、こ.む	seclude oneself; cage; coop; implied	篭
聾	ロウ、ろう.する、つんぼ、みみしい	deafness; deaf person; deafen	聾

64D 顕 VITRIOL

0──	顕微鏡	2B1
64D	けんびきょう	*

Chinese only motes, small particles of dust, sunlight + double thread 顕

顕	ケン	manifest, visible	64D
隰	シツ、シュウ、さわ	be moist; be wet	隰

64E 秀 VITRIOL

0──	誘惑	3–7
64E	ゆうわく	*

Rice plant + bending person, rice plant bent (heavy head), excellent 秀

誘	ユウ、さそ-う	invite, tempt, lead	64E
楹	エイ、はしら	pillar	楹
盈	エイ、み.たす、み.ちる	fullness; enough; pride; satisfy	盈
銹	シュ、シュウ、さび	rust; tarnish	銹
綉	シュウ、ツ、トウ	embroidery	綉
仍	ジョウ、ニョウ、よ.って、しきりに、なお、よる	therefore; consequently	仍
莠	ユウ、はぐさ	appears good but is bad; type of weed which resembles rice	莠
孕	ヨウ、はら.む	become pregnant	孕

64F 珍 VITRIOL

⌐		珍奇	5–9
64F 並		ちんき	*

Jewel and person + hair, phonetic pure/unblemished: rare 珍
Originally pictograph of the roots of a tree, essence/origin 本

珍	チン、めずら-しい	rare, curious	64F
袗	シン	thin kimono; embroidery	袗
畛	シン、あぜ	boundary between paddies	畛
疹	シン、チン、はしか	measles; sickness	疹
軫	シン、よこぎ	sad; revolve	軫
趁	チン、お.う	go to; follow	趁

Kanji Alchemy III

饕	テツ、むさぼ.る	voracious; gluttonous	饕
殄	テン、た.つ、つき.る、つく.す	all; completely	殄
本	ホン、もと	root, true, book, this	64F
軆	タイ、テイ、からだ、かたち	the body; substance; object; reality	軆
笨	ホン、あら.い	coarse	笨

64G 升 VITRIOL

⌾	升目	3–2
64G	ますめ	*

Ladle 升

升	ショウ、ます	liquid measure	64G
陞	ショウ、のぼ.る	go up; climb	陞
枡	ます	measuring box; (kokuji)	枡

65A 寿 WATER

▽	寿命	2D11
65A	じゅみょう	*

Originally old man who has lived a long time 寿

寿	ジュ、ことぶき	long life, congratulation	65A
疇	チュウ、うね、たぐい、ひと.しい	farmland; arable land; category	疇
儔	チュウ、うね、たぐい、ひと.しい	before; companion; same kind	儔
籌	チュウ、かずとり、はかりごと	plan	籌

儔	チュウ、ジュ、ともがら	companion; similar kind	儔
躊	チュウ、チュ、シュウ、ジュ、ためら.う	hesitate	躊
椿	トウ	block of wood; blockhead; stupid	椿
樁	トウ	stump; foolish; ignorant	樁
擣	トウ、う.つ、つ.く	pound	擣
隯	トウ、チョウ、しま	island	隯
涛	トウ、なみ	waves; billows	涛
濤	トウ、なみ	waves; billows	濤

65B 叔 WATER

▽	叔父	5–5
65B	おじ	*

Originally hand pulling up a potato 叔

叔	シュク	uncle, young brother	65B
戚	シュク、セキ、せ.まる	a tight place; scowl; approaching	戚
俶	シュク、テキ、はじめ、よい	beginning; good; excel	俶
菽	シュク、まめ	beans	菽
椒	ショウ、はじかみ	mountain ash	椒
槭	セキ、シュク、かえで	maple tree	槭

65C 盾 WATER

	後盾	2B1
65C	うしろだて	0|1

Eye + shield and possibly piercing/intently 盾
Road, inverted foot + version of thread, phonetic expressing little, slow progress, delay 後

盾	ジュン、たて	shield, pretext	65C
質	シツ、シチ、チ、たち、ただ.す、もと、わりふ	matter; material; substance	質
後	ゴ、コウ、のち、うし-ろ、あと、おく-れる	behind, after, delay	65C
彳	テキ、たた.ずむ、ぎょうにんべん	stop; linger; loiter; going man radical	彳

65D 雌 WATER

	雌牛	2D8
65D	めうし	*

Non general use character this/here, foot/stop + sitting person 雌

雌	シ、め、めす	female	65D
疵	シ、きず	crack; flaw; scratch; speck	疵
觜	シ、くちばし、はし	beak; bill	觜
呰	シ、サ	blame; censure; damage; this	呰
觜	シ、スイ、くちばし、はし	beak; bill	觜
貲	シ、たから	treasure; assets; pay a fine	貲
髭	シ、ひげ、くちひげ	beard; moustache	髭

眥	セ、イシ、サイ、シ、セイ、まなじり、めじり	outside the corner of the eye	眥
眦	セ、イシ、サイ、シ、セイ、まなじり、めじり	corner of the eyes; eye sockets	眦

65E 崩 WATER

▽	山崩れ	2B4
65E	やまくずれ	*

String of matching jewels, matching join 崩

崩	ホウ、くず-れる、くず-す	crumble, collapse	65E
堋	ホウ	bury; archery target mound	堋
硼	ホウ	sound of stones struck together; boron	硼
弸	ホウ	strong bow; full	弸
繃	ホウ、ヒョウ、まく、たば.ねる	wrap	繃

65F 瀬 WATER

▽	瀬戸	2C6
65F	せと	*

Originally bundle, money, slash/cut, profit financially 瀬

| 瀬 | せ | shallows, rapids | 65F |
| | | | |

嗽	ソウ、シュウ、ソク、すす.ぐ、ゆす.ぐ、くちすす.ぐ、うがい	rinse; wash; gargle	嗽
藾	ライ	type of mugwort; cover; hide	藾
癩	ライ	leprosy	癩
籟	ライ、ふえ	rattling of the wind	籟
嬾	ラン、おこた.る、ものうい	lazy; languid	嬾
懶	ラン、ライ、ものうい、おこたる	languid; be lazy; be negligent	懶

65G 隻 WATER

▽	三隻	2–5
65G	さんせき	0|1

Bird and hand, one of a pair, as opposed to a pair 隻
Three extended fingers 三

隻	セキ	one of a pair, ship counter	65G
矍	カク	surprise & confusion	矍
钁	カク、キャク	hoe	钁
攫	カク、さら.う、つか.む	abduct	攫
雙	ソウ、たぐい、ならぶ、ふたつ、ふた	pair; set; comparison; counter for pairs	雙
蠖	ワク、カク	inchworm; geometer	蠖
三	サン、み、み-つ、みっ-つ	three	65G

| 彡 | サン、セン、さんづくり、かみかざり | three; hair ornament; short hair or fur radical | 彡 |

66A 帝 WHITE LEAD

ss	帝国	3A5
66A	ていこく	0|1

Two-tier table + cross-struts and item, variant of altar 帝

帝	テイ	emperor	66A
啻	シ、ただ.ならぬ、ただ.に	incomparable; merely	啻
梯	テイ	ornamental hairpin	梯
蒂	テイ、タイ、へた	peduncle; stem of plants	蒂
蔕	テイ、タイ、へた	calyx; stem	蔕
啼	テイ、な.く	bark; chirp; cry	啼

66B 卓 WHITE LEAD

ss	食卓	4–12
66B 並	しょくたく	*

Core meaning high/excellent 卓
Sun and one line cutting another representing cutting/opening, sun breaking through 早

卓	タク	table, excel, high	66B
綽	シャク、あだ、しな.やか、ゆる.やか	loose; lenient	綽
倬	タク	large; clear; remarkable	倬

啅	タク、トウ	noisy; peck at; chirping; twittering	啅
罩	トウ、こめ.る	fish basket kept in water	罩
棹	トウ、タク、さお、こ.ぐ	pole a boat	棹
掉	トウ、チョウ、ふる.う	shake & move	掉
早	ソウ、サッ、はや-い、はや-まる、はや-める	early, fast, prompt	66B
蕈	ジン、シン、きのこ、たけ	mushroom; toadstool; fungus	蕈
覃	タン、エン	extend; deep; large	覃
鐔	タン、シン、つば	sword guard; hilt	鐔
潭	タン、ジン、ふち、ふか.い	deep water; deep	潭
簟	タン、テン、たかむしろ	a type of bamboo; round bamboo lunchbox	簟
譚	タン、はなし	talk	譚

66C 逮 WHITE LEAD

≤	逮捕	2B9
66C	たいほ	*

Originally seizing an animal by the tail 逮

逮	タイ	chase, seize	66C
鱇	コウ	anglerfish	鱇
慷	コウ、なげ.く	weep; grieve	慷
糠	コウ、ぬか	rice bran	糠
繍	シュウ、ぬいとり	sew; figured cloth	繍
靆	タイ	cloud cover	靆
隶	タイ、	extend; give; cast; slave radical	隶

	れいづくり		
棣	テイ、タイ、にわざくら	flowering almond	棣
秉	ヘイ、と.る	take; cherish; sheaf; unit of volume (10 koku; 1,800 l)	秉
隷	レイ、したが.う、しもべ	servant; prisoner; criminal; follower	隷

66D 庶 WHITE LEAD

∽	庶民	2A4
66D	しょみん	*

Originally put things on a fire, many things 庶

庶	ショ	multitude, various, illegitimate	66D
廾	キョウ、ク、にじゅう、にじゅうあし	twenty; 20; twenty or letter H radical	廾
鷓	シャ	partridge	鷓
蔗	シャ、ショ、さとうきび	sugar cane	蔗
蹠	セキ、あしうら、あしのうら	sole of foot	蹠

66E 尼 WHITE LEAD

∽	尼寺	6A5
66E	あまでら	*

Two slumped figures, phonetically 'ni' of 'bikuni', Sanskrit nun
尼

尼	ニ、あま	nun, priestess	66E
睨	ケイ、ダイ、てい、い	glance at; gaze at	睨
怩	ジ	shame	怩
尸	シ、かたしろ、しかばね、しかばねかんむり	corpse; remains; flag radical	尸
屎	シ、キ、くそ	shit; excrement	屎
昵	ジツ、ショク、ちかづ.く	reconcile; become intimate	昵

66F 円 WHITE LEAD

≋	両**替**え	2–2
66F	りょうがえ	1|2

Two persons speaking, having an 'exchange' 替
Old form indicates roundness + round kettle, circle 円

替	タイ、か-える、か-わる	exchange, swap	66F
潸	サン	flowing of tears	潸
輦	レン、たごし、てぐるま	palanquin	輦
円	エン、まる-い	round, yen	66F
栴	セイ、セン、もみじ	maple tree; colourful autumn foliage	栴
旃	セン、はた	woollen cloth	旃

66G 捜 WHITE LEAD

∽	捜索隊	2B6
66G	そうさくたい	*

Originally searching for something by torchlight in a building 捜

捜	ソウ、さが-す	investigate	66G
溲	シュ、シュウ、ソウ、いばり、ひた.す	urine	溲
艘	ショウ、シュウ、ソウ、ふね	counter for small boats	艘
嫂	ソウ、あによめ	elder brother's wife	嫂
歃	ソウ、コウ、ショウ、すす.る	sip; slurp; suck	歃
插	ソウ、さ.す、はさ.む	insert; stick into; plant	插
叟	ソウ、シュウ、おきな	old person	叟

67A 縄 WINE

⩔	縄目	3B18
67A	なわめ	*

Thread and pictograph of a tadpole 縄

縄	ジョウ、なわ	rope, cord	67A
訛	イ、タ、ダ、わ.びる、わ.び、あざむ.く	deceive; delude	訛
龜	キ、キュウ、キン、かめ	turtle; tortoise	龜
鬮	キュウ、くじ	lottery; lot; raffle	鬮
鉈	シャ、なた、ほこ	hatchet	鉈

穐	シュウ、あき、とき	autumn	穐
穐	シュウ、あき、とき	autumn	穐
繩	ジョウ、なわ、ただ.す	rope; cord	繩
竈	ソウ、かまど、かま、へっつい	kitchen stove; furnace; oven; hearth	竈
竈	ソウ、かまど、かま、へっつい	hearth; kitchen stove	竈
佗	タ、イ、わび.しい、わび、ほか、わ.びる	proud; lonely	佗
沱	タ、ダ	flowing of tears	沱
鴕	ダ、タ	Chinese ostrich	鴕
柁	ダ、タ、かじ	rudder; helm; wheel	柁
駝	ダ、タ、せむし	hunchback; load	駝
它	タ、へび	other	它
黽	ボウ、ビン、ベン、ミン、メン、あおが.える、つと.める	green frog; industry	黽
蠅	ヨウ、はえ、はい	fly	蠅
蠅	ヨウ、はえ、はい	fly	蠅

67B 棟 WINE

ⓥ	病棟	3
67B	びょうとう	*

Originally raised earthen path around a field, raised, exposed 棟

67C 伐 WINE

Ⓥ	征伐	2A5
67C	せいばつ	*

Halberd cutting down 伐

伐	バツ	attack, cut down	67C
找	ソウ	look for; seek; make change	找
筏	バツ、ハツ、ボチ、いかだ	raft	筏
垡	ハツ、ボチ、ぬた	plough; cultivate; swamp; wetlands; (kokuji)	垡
弋	ヨク、いぐるみ、しきがまえ	piling; ceremony radical	弋
杙	ヨク、くい	stake; post; picket; piling	杙

67D 焦 WINE

Ⓥ	黒焦げ	2A2
67D	くろこげ	*

Bird roasting over a fire, scorching, charring, fretting 焦

焦	ショウ、こ-げる、こ-がす、こ-がれる、あせ-る	scorch, fret	67D
樵	ショウ、きこ.る、こ.る、きこり	woodcutting; lumberjack	樵
憔	ショウ、セウ、ソウ、やつ.れる、やせ.る	get thin	憔

67E 苗 WINE

⚗	苗字	3–1
67E	みょうじ	*

Plants still in the field, not ready yet for cropping 苗

苗	ビョウ、なえ、なわ	seedling, offspring	67E
錨	ビョウ、ミョウ、いかり	anchor; grapnel	錨

67F 苗 WINE

⚗	特徴	3C3
67F	とくちょう	*

Core meaning small, secretive 徴

徴	チョウ、しるし	sign, summon, levy	67F
澂	チョウ、すま.す、す.む	clear and still water	澂
黴	バイ、ビ、マイ、ミ、かび、か.びる	mould; mildew	黴
薇	ラ、ビ、ぜんまい	an edible fern	薇

67G 沈 WINE

⚗	消沈	2A4
67G	しょうちん	*

Originally hanging down in water, to sink 沈

沈	チン、しず-む、しず-める	sink	67G
忱	シン、まこと	sincere	忱

酖	タン、チン、ふ.ける	addiction; poison	酖
眈	タン、にら.む	watch intently	眈
鴆	チン	a poisonous Chinese bird	鴆

68A 幣 YEAR

| ～ | 弊害 | 3A5 |
| 68A | へいがい | * |

Cutting up by hand of small bits of cloth, offerings to gods 幣

幣	ヘイ	offering, money	68A
斃	ヘイ、たお.れる、たお.す	kill; die violent death	斃
幣	ヘイ、ぬさ	Shinto zigzag paper offerings; bad habit; humble prefix; gift	幣
敝	ヘイ、やぶ.れる	be worn-out; be dilapidated; be defeated	敝
瞥	ヘツ、ヘチ	setting sun	瞥
鼈	ベツ、ヘツ、すっぽん	snapping turtle	鼈

68B 凡 YEAR

| ～ | 平凡 | 3–2 |
| 68B | へいぼん | * |

Wind cloth, sail 凡

| 凡 | ボン、ハン | mediocre, common, toughly, in general | 68B |
| 丶 | チュ | dot; tick or dot radical | 丶 |

| 梵 | ボン、フウ | Sanskrit; purity; Buddhist | | 梵 |

68C 峰 YEAR

～	主峰	3D3
68C	しゅほう	*

Chinese only butt, gore, in Chinese only compounds sharp 峰

峰	ホウ、みね	peak, top	68C
篷	ホウ、とま	woven rush awning	篷
烽	ホウ、のろし、とぶひ	signal fire	烽
蚌	ボウ、ホウ、ビョウ、はまぐり、どぶが.い	clam	蚌

68D 曹 YEAR

～	軍曹	3A1
68D	ぐんそう	*

Originally two well matched people, (doubling of east/sack) 曹

曹	ソウ	official, companion	68D
艚	ソウ	boat	艚

68E 某 YEAR

～	媒介	3A1
68E	ばいかい	*

Sweet produce of certain trees 某

某	ボウ	a certain-, some-	68E
楳	バイ、うめ	plum	楳

68F 卑 YEAR

～	卑劣	2B10
68F	ひれつ	*

Originally hand holding a wine-pressing basket, the last drops 卑

卑	ヒ、いや-しい、いや-しむ、いや-しめる	lowly, mean, despise	68F
牌	ハイ、ぱい、ふだ	label; signboard; medal; mahjong tiles	牌
稗	ハイ、ヒ、ひえ	humble; deccan grass	稗
脾	ヒ	spleen	脾
裨	ヒ、おぎな.う、たす.ける、ます	help	裨
痺	ヒ、しび.れる	palsy; become numb; paralysed	痺
婢	ヒ、はしため	maidservant	婢
鵯	ヒ、ヒツ、ひよどり	brown eared bulbul	鵯
髀	ヒ、ヘイ、もも	thigh	髀
俾	フ、ヒ、ヘイ、かしずく、しむ	tutor	俾
睥	ヘイ、ながしめ、み.る	glare at	睥

68G 徹 YEAR

~	徹夜	2–1
68G	てつや	*

Originally remove pot from a stand, remove clear 徹

徹	テツ		go through, clear, remove	68G
轍	テツ、わだちい、わだち		rut; wheel track	轍

69A 僕 YELLOW AMBER

ぉ	公僕	3–4
69A	こうぼく	*

Originally slave carrying chamber-pot and turds, rough 僕

僕	ボク		manservant, I	69A
璞	ハク、あらたま		uncut gem; unpolished gem	璞
樸	ボク、ハク、ホク、こはだ、きじ		bark of a tree	樸
濮	ボク、ホク		name of Chinese river	濮
蹼	ボク、ホク、みずかき		webfoot; web	蹼

69B 揺 YELLOW AMBER

ぉ	揺りいす	2E4
69B	ゆりいす	*

Unclear swaying meat vessel 揺

揺	ヨウ、ゆ-れる、ゆ-る、ゆ-らぐ、	shake, swing, rock	69B

	ゆ-るぐ、ゆ-する、ゆ-さぶる、ゆ-すぶる		
徭	ヨウ、エウ、えだち、ふぞろ.い、つかい	compulsory service to the state; corvee	徭
窰	ヨウ、かま	brick kiln; furnace; coal mine pit	窰
瑤	ヨウ、たま	beautiful (as a jewel)	瑤
鷂	ヨウ、はいたか	sparrow hawk	鷂

69C 冒 YELLOW AMBER

ろ	冒険	2–4
69C	ぼうけん	*

Protective helmet worn over the eyes, fighting man 冒

冒	ボウ、おか-す	defy, risk, attack	69C
胄	チュウ、かぶと、ちすじ、よつぎ	lineage; bloodline	胄
冑	チュウ、かぶと、よろい	helmet	冑
冒	ボウ、おか.す	risk; brave; dare; face; defy; (diseases) attack; damage; desecrate; assume (a name)	冒
瑁	マイ、バイ、ボウ、モウ	ancient Chinese imperial jewels	瑁

69D 慢 YELLOW AMBER

ろ	腕自慢	4C15
69D 並	うでじまん	*

Kanji Alchemy III

Non general use character full/expansive 慢
Old form shows pot for steaming rice and lid, come together 会

慢	マン	lazy, rude, boastful	69D
蔓	かつら	surname	蔓
鬘	バン、マン、かつら	wig; hairpiece	鬘
饅	マン	bean-jam dumpling; manjuu	饅
鏝	マン、こて	soldering iron; trowel; curling iron; flat iron	鏝
縵	マン、バン	unpatterned silk; loose	縵
謾	マン、バン、あざむ.く、あなど.る	despise	謾
鰻	マン、バン、うなぎ	eel	鰻
曼	マン、バン、なが.い	wide; beautiful	曼
幔	マン、バン、まく	curtain	幔
会	カイ、エ、あ-う	meet	69D
繪	カイ、エ	picture; drawing; painting; sketch	繪
會	カイ、エ、あ.う、あ.わせる、あつ.まる	meet; party; association; interview; join	會
鱠	カイ、ケ、えそ、なます	lizard fish	鱠
膾	カイ、ケ、なま.す	raw fish salad	膾
薈	カイ、ワイ	luxuriant vegetation	薈
獪	カイ、わるがしこ.い	crafty	獪

69E 避 YELLOW AMBER

ひ	避妊	4–16
69E	ひにん	*

Buttocks, opening, needle, anal penetration 避

避	ヒ、さ-ける	avoid	69E
蘖	ゲツ、ひこばえ	sprout	蘖
檗	ハク、ビャク、きはだ、きわだ	Amur or Chinese cork tree	檗
蘗	ハク、ビャク、きはだ、きわだ	stump; sprout	蘗
擘	ハク、ヒャク、ヘキ、さ.く	tear up	擘
譬	ヒ、たと.える、たと.え	illustrate	譬
臂	ヒ、ひじ	elbow	臂
薜	ヘイ	type of vine	薜
嬖	ヘイ、きにいり	agreeable person	嬖
躄	ヘキ、いざ.る、いざ.り	crawl; cripple	躄
辟	ヘキ、ヒ、きみ、ひら.く、め.す	false; punish; crime; law	辟
僻	ヘキ、ヒ、ヘイ、へき.する、ひが.む	prejudice; bias; rural area	僻
霹	ヘキ、ヒャク	thunder	霹
甓	ヘキ、ビャク、かわら	floor tiles	甓
劈	ヘキ、ヒャク、つんざ.く、さく	break; tear; split	劈
襞	ヘキ、ヒャク、ひだ、しわ	pleat; fold; tuck; crease	襞
闢	ヘキ、ビャク、ひら.く	open	闢

69F 噴 YELLOW AMBER

る	噴水	3–2
69F	ふんすい	*

Make a 'pon' sound with the mouth 噴

噴	フン、ふ-く	emit, spout, gush	69F
賁	フン、ヒ、ホン	decorate	賁
濆	フン、ホン、ほとり、わ.く	gush forth; also	濆

69G 抜 YELLOW AMBER

る	手抜かり	2B7
69G	てぬうかり	1|2

Obscure element dog, phonetic extract 抜
Originally beat hemp with sticks to make clothes, pulverise 散

抜	バツ、ぬ-く、ぬ-ける、ぬ-かす、ぬ-かる	pluck, extract, miss	69G
黹	チ、ぬう、ぬいとり、ふつ	sewing radical	黹
秡	ハツ、バチ	damaged grain	秡
魃	ハツ、バツ	(god of) drought	魃
跋	ハツ、バツ、おくがき、ふ.む	epilogue; postscript	跋
髟	ヒュウ、ヒョウ、かみがしら、かみかんむり	hair hanging long; mane; long hair radical	髟
黻	フツ、あや	lap robe; embroidery pattern	黻
祓	フツ、ハイ、はら.う	exorcise	祓
散	サン、ち-る、ち-らす、	scatter	69G

	ち-らかす、ち-らかる		
繖	サン	parasol; umbrella	繖
霰	セン、サン、あられ	hail; hailstones; small cubes	霰

70A 寮 ZINC

彡	寮生	4B6
70A	りょうせい	*

Chinese only fuel used in sacrifices 尞

寮	リョウ	hostel, dormitory	寮
鷯	リョウ	wren	鷯
瞭	リョウ、あきらか	clear	瞭
鐐	リョウ、あしかせ	silver; platinum; chains	鐐
繚	リョウ、まと.う、めぐ.る	put on; twist around	繚
撩	リョウ、ロウ	disorder	撩
潦	ロウ、にわたずみ	heavy rainfall; runoff	潦

70B 累 ZINC

彡	累計	2B8
70B	るいけい	*

Originally three fields suggesting build up, accumulation 累

累	ルイ	accumulate, involve	70B
疊	ジョウ、チョウ、たた.む、たたみ、かさ.なる	repeat; duplicate; repetitious	疊

疊	ジョウ、チョウ、たた.む、たたみ、かさ.なる、かさ.ねる	counter for tatami mats; fold	疊
騾	ラ	mule	騾
儡	ライ	defeat	儡
櫑	ライ、さか.だる	decorated wine cask; decorated sword hilt	櫑
罍	ライ、さかだる	liquor jar	罍
縲	ルイ	tie	縲
瘰	ルイ、ラ、ライ	swollen neck glands	瘰

70C 腕 ZINC

夗	手腕家	3C5
70C	しゅわんか	*

Originally straighten a bent body, display of strength 腕

腕	ワン、うで	arm, skill	70C
婉	エン、うつく.しい、したが.う	graceful	婉
鴛	エン、オン、おし、おしどり	male mandarin duck	鴛
鋺	エン、かなまり	metal bowl	鋺
蜿	エン、ワン	meandering	蜿
豌	エン、ワン	pea	豌

70D 励 ZINC

夗	策励	2–8

70D	さくれい	*

Formerly showing a scorpion, phonetically expressing to strive 励

励	レイ、はげ-む、はげ-ます	encourage, strive	70D
枥	とち	type of oak; stable	枥
砺	レイ、あらと、みが.く	whetstone; polish	砺
礪	レイ、あらと、みが.く	whetstone; polish	礪
蛎	レイ、かき	oyster	蛎
蠣	レイ、かき	oyster	蠣
勵	レイ、はげ.む、はげ.ます	strive; encourage	勵
癘	レイ、ライ、えやみ	contagious disease; leprosy	癘
糲	レイ、ラツ、あら.い、くろごめ	unpolished rice	糲

70E 并 ZINC

幵	併用	5–11
70E	へいよう	*

Non general character put together, two persons and matching stakes 併

併	ヘイ、あわ-せる	unite, join	70E
甕	オウ、かめ、みか	jar; jug; vat	甕
罋	オウ、もたい	jar; jug; container	罋
剏	ソウ、ショウ、はじ.める	begin; be damaged; break; fall	剏
垪	ハ	used in proper names	垪

并	ヘイ、ヒョウ、あわ.せる、なら.ぶ	put together	并
屏	ヘイ、ビョウ、おお.う、しりぞ.く、びょう.ぶ	wall; fence	屏
餅	ヘイ、ヒョウ、もち、もちい	rice cake	餅
胼	ヘン	callus; corn	胼
駢	ヘン、なら.ぶ	two-horse carriage	駢
絣	ホウ、かすり	splashed pattern (on cloth)	絣
迸	ホウ、ヒョウ、ほとば.しる、は.しる	gush out; spurt	迸

70F 麻 ZINC

乇		麻薬	4A7
70F		まやく	*

Originally cloth plant, hemp, flax 麻

麻	マ、あさ	hemp, flax, numb	70F
麾	キ、さしまね.く、さしずばた	beckon to; command	麾
糜	ビ、ただ.れる	be inflamed	糜
靡	ヒ、ビ、ミ、なび.く、ない、わ.ける	flutter; wave; bow to; obey; seduce	靡
縻	ビ、ミ、きずな	rope	縻
麽	ビ、ミ、バ、マ、モ	rope	麽
嘛	マ	wheat	嘛
痲	マ、バ、しび.れる	measles; paralysis	痲

70G 戻 ZINC

孑	空涙	2A3
70G	そらなみだ	*

Originally crouching dog and door, semantically unclear 戻

戻	レイ、もど-す、もど-る	return, bring back, rebel, bend, vomit	70G
綟	レイ、もじ	yellowish green; coarse mesh linen	綟
唳	レイ、れつ	cry; honking of birds; droning of cicadas	唳
捩	レイ、レツ、よじ.る、ね.じる、ねじ.れる、も.じる	screw; twist; wrench; distort	捩

Index & Definitions of Alchemical Symbols

⌂	1	AIR	Equals breath, breeze, spirit, wind, weather
♏	2	ALEMBIC	Or capitellum (helmet) is a vessel set over the retort to receive and collect vapours
✤	3	ALUM	Grows as hair on fire-resistant salamanders; asbestos
⚹	4	AMALGAM	A composition of gold or silver and quick silver
♁	5	ANTIMONY	Also mineral or chemical wolf. Could be used as universal medicine making all other medicine redundant
₿	6	ARMENIAN BOLE	Red clay, cure against the bite of poisonous snakes
A	7	ATHANOR	An oven that is adapted for composing the stone of the philosophers

♃	8	BALM	A preserver of all bodies from destruction and putrefaction
♆	9	BATH OF VAPOURS	A furnace in which the distillatory vase is suspended only over the steam of water in such a manner that the waters do not touch the body
♭	10	BISMUTH	Weissmuth or white substance, bright metal of white colour
⚓	11	BLACK BRIMSTONE	Also horse brimstone, used externally by veterinary surgeons
⊂	12	BLOOD STONE	Synonym for gold
⚭	13	BORAX	Also atincar or rock borax, mineral salt used in foldering, brazing and calling gold
▥	14	BRICK	The plural (Latin lateres) refers to iron tiles

℞	15	CALCINATION	Calcination of bodies is combustion which takes place in a strong heat
ⅩO	16	CAMPHOR	Can be used for medicinal or cullinary purposes
℔	17	CAPUT MORTUUM	Residue in the retort from which the phlegmatic part has been extracted
☿	18	CINNABAR	Used by Venetian painters because of its blood-colour, also used as an antidote in medicine
♀	19	COPPER, VENUS	A metallic body of bluish colour with a dark ruddy tinge, igneous and fusible
⚕	20	CORAL	A substance that originated from the head of the Medusa
♉	21	CRUCIBLE	A melting vessel made of some earth which can absolutely withstand fire
✧	22	DAY	To be distinguished from Nycthemeron which is night & day: 24 hours

♆	23	DECOCTION	Thick juice made by boiling grain or animal/vegetables
	24	DIGEST	To slowly draw out effective ingredients from drugs by using solvents whilst subjected to stable temperatures
	25	DISSOLUTION	The vaporising of matter and the capture of the condensed moisture thereof in another vessel
	26	DISTILLATION	A process in which the essence is extracted in the form of a liquid
	27	DRAGON'S BLOOD	Synonym for cinnabar, also used as medicine against scratches and the french disease
	28	DRAM	A weight of 3,373 gramm
	29	EARTH	Red earth from lemnos was famous for protecting against poison and plague

⚗	30	EBULLITION	The act, process, or state of boiling or bubbling up
EF	31	EFFERVESCENCE	To escape from a liquid as bubbles; bubble up
⚗	32	ELEMENT	The elements are the matrices of substances: fire, air, water, and earth are the four universal matrices
dP	33	EQUAL PARTS	From all parts the same quantity
⚗	34	ESSENCE	Essence is a simple extract which contains the whole nature and perfecton of the substances from which it is derived
⇌	35	EXTRACTION	Extraction is the separation of the essential part from the body
⚗	36	FERMENTATION	The incorporation of a fermenting substance with a substance which is to be fermented

♃	37	FILTRATION	Subduction by filtration in a colander; but this process in the chymical filter may also be called straining, or percolation
△	38	FIRE	Fire for the stone of the philosophers
☿	39	FIRST MATTER	Soul and heaven of the elements
♃	40	FIXATION	To make firm, to solidify
♄	41	FLOWERS OF SATURN	Lead oxide, the red form is known as litharge and the yellow form as massicot
⊟	42	FURNACE	A furnace or oven
♁	43	GLASS	Glass, sieve, riddle for distillation, grave, churchyard, because the stone lies hidden therein, and is driven up / down
♋	44	GLUE OF THE WISE	Special sticky substances used for sealing off the apparatus for distillation

☉	45	GOLD, SUN	Called sol by the chemists, and dedicated to the sun, is the most tempered of all the metals
	46	GRADE OF FIRE	There are four different grades of fire ranging from tepid to the highest possible level of heat
	47	GRANATE	It is a transparent, ruby-coloured gem, like the blossom of the pomegranate, and is more dusky than the carbuncle
	48	GUM	A transforming substance on account of its adhesive quality. The "glue of the world" (glutinum mundi) is the medium between mind and body
♀	49	GYPSUM	Its use is chiefly in external application, on account of its extremely drying and destroying nature
⧖	50	HOUR	Time measured by an hourglass

♁	51	IRON, MARS	This metal is attributed to mars by the chemist, and is so called, because of its many uses in war
♃	52	JUNIPER	Juniper berries are a spice used in a wide variety of culinary dishes and best known for flavouring in gin
♄	53	LEAD, SATURN	Lead with a heavy metallic body, very little whiteness and much of earthy nature
ℳ	54	MAGNESIA	Magnesia is produced when silver and quicksilver are united so as to form a heavy fluid metal. It is also the matter of the philospher's stone
✕	55	NIGHT	Period of time between sunset and sunrise
♄	56	OIL OF SATURN	Also liquor saturni, lead acetate
♛	57	PHILOSOPHICAL STONE	Universal medicine by which age is renewed in youth, metals are transmuted, and all diseases are cured

☿	58	QUICKSILVER, MERCURY	Primary matter of metals, incorporates volatility
✥	59	QUINTESSENCE	A concoction that contains all the powers and qualities of substances in the purest form
✍	60	RECTIFICATION	Concentration of a fluid through distillation
✵	61	SAL-AMMONIAC	Salmiac, corrosive and desiccating, best from a camel's discharge
⌂	62	SILVER, MOON	The luna of chemists, the metal ranked next after gold
♃	63	TIN, JUPITER	Tin, white metallic substance, not pure, livid
⚚	64	VITRIOL	Also roman vitriol, green atrament, a mixture of salt and sulfates
▽	65	WATER	A dry mineral first substance, a catholic water which dissolves all metals
⚹	66	WHITE LEAD	Synonym for tin

	67	WINE	Medicinal drugs used to be mixed with wine
	68	YEAR	The annus chymicus or annus philosophicus lasts for 30 days and 30 nights
	69	YELLOW AMBER	Once thought to have derived from the seed of wales and worn around the neck as an amulet
	70	ZINC	Element: term first used by Paracelsus (c. 1526) due to the form of the crystals after smelting

Index Signature Characters

亜	ア	next, sub-, Asia	20A
愛	アイ	love	39E
哀	アイ、あわ-れ、あわ-れむ	sorrow, pity	57A
委	イ	committee; entrust to; leave to; devote; discard	26G
医	イ	doctor; medicine	28C
以	イ	start.point, means, use, through, because	38B
胃	イ	stomach	42G
為	イ	do, purpose	56G
尉	イ	military rank	59B
偉	イ、えら-い	great, grand	48C
異	イ、こと	differ, strange	51A
域	イキ	area, limits	51C
員	イン	member, official	25B
隠	イン、かく-す、かく-れる	hide	59D
因	イン、よ-る	cause, be based on, depend on	48A
宇	ウ	eaves, roof, heaven	51D
羽	ウ、は、はね	wing, feather, bird counter	11G
永	エイ、なが-い	long, lasting	30E
易	エキ、イ、やさ-しい	easy, change, divination	43D
園	エン、その	garden, park	6C
鉛	エン、なまり	lead	13F
延	エン、の-びる、の-べる、の-ばす	extend, postpone	53G

炎	エン、ほのお	inflammation, flame, blaze	24D
王	オウ	king	6B
央	オウ	center	32A
桜	オウ、さくら	cherry	9A
乙	オツ	odd, b, 2nd, stylish	61C
卸	おろ-す、おろし	wholesale, grate	60D
音	オン、イン、おと、ね	sound	3G
可	カ	approve, can, should	16E
佳	カ	beautiful, good	42E
渦	カ、うず	whirlpool, eddy	46E
加	カ、くわ-える、くわ-わる	add, join	42F
家	カ、ケ、いえ、や	house, specialist	9D
化	カ、ケ、ば-ける、ば-かす	change, bewitch	2A
果	カ、は-たす、は-てる、は-て	fruit, result, carryout	42B
貝	かい	shellfish	3F
介	カイ	mediate, shell	18C
拐	カイ	deceive, kidnap, bend	40A
戒	カイ、いまし-める	command, admonish	36C
快	カイ、こころよ-い	pleasant, cheerful	24E
壊	カイ、こわ-す、こわ-れる	break, destroy, ruin	60C
灰	カイ、はい	ashes	27C
各	カク、おのおの	each	28D
角	カク、かど、つの	horn, angle	18G
革	カク、かわ	leather, reform	55F
且	か-つ	furthermore, besides	18A
喝	カツ	shout, scold	60B

滑	カツ、すべ-る、なめ-らか	slide, slip, smooth	56E
感	カン	feeling	17C
官	カン	government, official	30D
漢	カン	Han China, man	34F
観	カン	watch, observe	36G
監	カン	supervise, watch	51G
敢	カン	daring, tragic	52C
喚	カン	shout, yell	60E
缶	カン	can, boiler	61F
甘	カン、あま-い、あま-える、-あま-やかす	sweet, presume upon	59G
寒	カン、さむ-い	cold, midwinter	33A
貫	カン、つらぬ-く	pierce	45F
干	カン、ほ-す、ひ-る	dry, defence	23C
巻	カン、ま-く、ま-き	roll, reel, volume	50G
患	カン、わずら-う	disease, afflicted	60A
牙	ガ、ゲ、きば	tusk; fang	41A
我	ガ、われわ、わが	I, self, my	53C
害	ガイ	harm, damage	34A
慨	ガイ	lament, deplore	59A
楽	ガク、ラク、たの-しい、たの-しむ	pleasure, music	12B
眼	ガン、ゲン、まなこ	eye	22D
幾	キ、いく	how many, how much	34C
鬼	キ、おに	devil, demon, ghost	58A
企	キ、くわだ-てる	plan, undertake	63G

貴	キ、たっと-い、とうと-い、たっと-ぶ、とうと-ぶ	precious, revered	51F
机	キ、つくえ	desk, table	54B
基	キ、もと、もとい	base	30A
旧	キュウ	old, past	39F
丘	キュウ、おか	hill	58G
及	キュウ、およ-ぶ、およ-び、およ-ぼす	reach, extend, and	31G
九	キュウ、ク、ここの、ここの-つ	nine	4E
球	キュウ、たま	sphere, ball	23F
弓	キュウ、ゆみ	bow	40F
巨	キョ	huge, giant	61B
居	キョ、い-る	be, reside	43A
虚	キョ、コ	empty, hollow, dip	55C
去	キョ、コ、さ-る	go, leave, past	28A
協	キョウ	cooperate	44C
享	キョウ	receive, have	57C
凶	キョウ	bad luck, disaster	57D
鏡	キョウ、がかみ	mirror	36D
京	キョウ、ケイ	capital	16B
郷	キョウ、ゴウ	village, rural	55E
挟	キョウ、はさ-む、はさ-まる	insert, pinch, squeeze between	61A
橋	キョウ、はし	bridge	24C
斤	キン	ax, weight	15C
禁	キン	ban, forbid	47A

義	ギ	righteousness	37C
疑	ギ、うたが-う	doubt, suspect	56A
暁	ギョウ、あかつき	dawn, light, event	35E
仰	ギョウ、コウ、あお-ぐ、おお-せ	look up, state, respect	61D
玉	ギョク、たま	ball, sphere, coin	1F
吟	ギン	recite	5F
区	ク	ward, section	31F
句	ク	phrase, clause	48F
空	クウ、そら、あ-く、あ-ける、から	sky, empty	4B
屈	クツ	submit, crouch	61E
薫	クン、かお-る	aroma, fragrance, aura	63D
君	クン、きみ	lord, you Mr	32B
具	グ	equip, means	31B
偶	グウ	by chance, spouse, doll	62A
軍	グン	military, army	21C
慶	ケイ	joy	62E
系	ケイ	lineage, connection	6G
径	ケイ	path, direct	26E
渓	ケイ	valley, gorge	63E
敬	ケイ、うやま-う	respect	57F
恵	ケイ、エ、めぐ-む	blessing, kindness	55D
形	ケイ、ギョウ、かた、かたち	shape, pattern	15E
頃	ケイ、ころ	time; about; toward	63A
契	ケイ、ちぎ-る	pledge, join	49B

傑	ケツ	outstanding	62C
穴	ケツ、あな	hole	27A
欠	ケツ、か-ける、か-く	lack	29D
結	ケツ、むす-ぶ、ゆ-う、ゆ-わえる	bind, join, end	40D
県	ケン	prefecture	31A
倹	ケン	thrifty, frugal	41F
顕	ケン	manifest, visible	64D
犬	ケン、いぬ	dog	53D
兼	ケン、か-ねる	combine, unable	60G
堅	ケン、かた-い	firm, solid, hard	62B
拳	ケン、こぶし	fist	49C
建	ケン、コン、た-てる、た-つ	build, erect	33B
見	ケン、み-る、み-える、み-せる	look, see, show	4D
激	ゲキ、はげ-しい	violent, fierce, strong, intense	59E
玄	ゲン	occult, black	50A
元	ゲン、ガン、もと	originally, source	18B
言	ゲン、ゴン、い-う、こと	word, say, speak	19F
原	ゲン、はら	plain, origin	9E
孤	コ	orphan, lonely	61G
顧	コ、かえり-みる	lookback	62G
己	コ、キ、おのれ	I, me, you, self	7E
戸	コ、と	door	9G
古	コ、ふる-い、ふる-す	old	15A
孝	コウ	filia lpiety	13A
洪	コウ	flood, vast	25E

康	コウ	peace, health	34E
航	コウ	sail, voyage	38G
侯	コウ	marquis, lord	41C
講	コウ	lecture	49F
荒	コウ、あら-い、あ-れる、あ-らす	rough, wild, waste	64A
岡	コウ、おか	hill; height; knoll; rising ground	58D
黄	コウ、オウ、き、こ	yellow	9C
考	コウ、かんが-える	consider	19A
甲	コウ、カン	shell, armour, high, 1st, a	57G
行	コウ、ギョウ、アン、い-く、ゆ-く、おこな-う	go, conduct, column	11F
工	コウ、ク	work	7B
幸	コウ、さいわ-い、さち、しあわ-せ	happiness, luck	25D
更	コウ、さら、ふ-ける、ふ-かす	anew, change, again, grow late	32C
高	コウ、たか-い、たか、たか-まる、たか-める	tall, high, sum	16C
耕	コウ、たがや-す	till, plough	48B
広	コウ、ひろ-い、ひろ-まる、ひろ-める、ひろ-がる、ひろ-げる	wide, spacious	8B
交	コウ、まじ-わる、まじ-える、ま-じる、ま-る、ま-ぜる、か-う、か-わす	mix, exchange	4F
刻	コク、きざ-む	chop, mince, engrave	50D
黒	コク、くろ、くろ-い	black	13D

谷	コク、たに	valley, gorge	15G
告	コク、つ-げる	proclaim, inform	37E
護	ゴ	defend, protect	50F
誤	ゴ、あやま-る	mistake, mis-	58F
号	ゴウ	number, call, sign	29F
合	ゴウ、ガッ、カッ、あ-う、あ-わす、あ-わせる	meet, join, fit	7F
左	サ、ひだり	left	3B
才	サイ	talent, year of age	11B
債	サイ	debt, loan	44F
栽	サイ	planting	54C
砕	サイ、くだ-く、くだ-ける	break, smash	38C
妻	サイ、つま	wife	14E
采	サイ、と-る	dice; form; appearance; take; colouring; general's baton	39G
最	サイ、もっと-も	most, -est	40C
作	サク、サ、つく-る	make	10B
察	サツ	judge, surmise, realise	29A
皿	さら	dish, bowl, plate	22F
傘	サン、かさ	umbrella, parasol	62D
参	サン、まい-る	attend, go, be in love, be at a loss, 3	40E
山	サン、やま	mountain	1A
座	ザ、すわ-る	seat, sit, gather	54D
司	シ	administer, official	41E
至	シ、いた-る	go, reach, peak	11C
市	シ、いち	city, market	15D

氏	シ、うじ	clan, family, mr	13B
志	シ、こころざ-す、こころざし	will, intent	42D
刺	シ、さ-す、さ-さる	pierce, stab, thorn	58B
支	シ、ささ-える	branch, support	53B
死	シ、し-ぬ	death	21A
子	シ、ス、こ	child	1G
止	シ、と-まる、と-める	stop	11D
旨	シ、むね	tasty, good, gist	22E
紫	シ、むらさき	purple, violet	65D
式	シキ	ceremony, form	23B
識	シキ	knowledge	47F
七	シチ、なな、なな-つ、なの	seven	4A
膝	シツ、ひざ	knee; lap	64B
失	シツ、うしな-う	lose	37F
執	シツ、シュウ、と-る	take, grasp, execute	63B
舎	シャ	house, quarters	47E
車	シャ、くるま	vehicle, chariot	2C
者	シャ、もの	person	23D
尺	シャク	measure, foot	52D
朱	シュ	vermilion, red	54F
首	シュ、くび	head, neck, chief	8E
主	シュ、ス、ぬし、おも	master, owner, main	20B
秋	シュウ、あき	autumn	20D
収	シュウ、おさ-める、おさ-まる	obtain, store, supply	56F
宗	シュウ、ソウ	religion, main	46A

舟	シュウ、ふね、ふな	boat	63C
周	シュウ、まわ-り	circumference, around	12D
叔	シュク	uncle, young brother	65B
宿	シュク、やど、やど-る、やど-す	lodge, shelter, house	32E
出	シュツ、スイ、で-る、だ-す	emerge, put out	23G
俊	シュン	excellence, genius	44G
処	ショ	dealwith, place	56C
庶	ショ	multitude, various, illegitimate	66D
章	ショウ	badge, chapter	26B
尚	ショウ	furthermore, esteem	43F
将	ショウ	command, aboutto	52E
焦	ショウ、こ-げる、こ-がす、こ-がれる、あせ-る	scorch, fret	67D
象	ショウ、ゾウ	elephant, image	31C
升	ショウ、ます	liquid measure	64G
詔	ショウ、みことのり	imperial edict	33F
宵	ショウ、よい	evening	25G
色	ショク、シキ、いろ	colour, sensuality	7E
娠	シン	pregnancy	28G
辛	シン、から-い	sharp, bitter	14A
心	シン、こころ	heart, feelings	11E
臣	シン、ジン	retainer, subject	43B

進	シン、すす-む、すす-める	advance	22G
真	シン、ま	true, quintessence	22A
身	シン、み	body	20C
申	シン、もう-す	say, expound	10A
字	ジ、あざ	letter, symbol	2F
侍	ジ、さむらい	attend (upon)	10E
自	ジ、シ、みずか-ら	self	17G
事	ジ、ズ、こと	thing, matter, act	15F
耳	ジ、みみ	ear	4C
弱	ジャク、よわ-い、よわ-る、よわ-まる、よわ-める	weak	10C
需	ジュ	need, demand	62F
受	ジュ、う-ける、う-かる	receive	21E
寿	ジュ、ことぶき	longlife, congratulation	65A
充	ジュウ、あ-てる	full, fill, provide	23E
従	ジュウ、ショウ、ジュ、したが-う、したが-える	follow, comply	54E
十	ジュウ、ジッ、とお、と	ten	3C
重	ジュウ、チョウ、え、おも-い、かさ-ねる、かさ-なる	heavy, pile, -fold	25A
述	ジュツ、の-べる	state, relate	41D
盾	ジュン、たて	shield, pretext	65C
縄	ジョウ、なわ	rope, cord	67A
乗	ジョウ、の-る、の-せる	ride, mount, load	21B
譲	ジョウ、ゆず-る	hand over, yield	63F

須	ス、あごひげ、すべからく…べ-し	ought; by all means; necessarily	12G
垂	スイ、た-れる、た-らす	suspend, hang down	50E
寸	スン	measure, inch	7D
瀬	せ	shallows, rapids	65F
制	セイ	system, control	47B
斉	セイ	equal, similar	55A
勢	セイ、いきお-い	power, force	35B
西	セイ、サイ、にし	west	14F
青	セイ、ショウ、あお、あお-い	blue, green, young	3E
井	セイ、ショウ、い	well	33G
正	セイ、ショウ、ただ-しい、ただ-す、まさ	correct	5B
星	セイ、ショウ、ほし	star	26F
成	セイ、ジョウ、な-る、な-す	become, make, consist	30C
隻	セキ	one of a pair, ship counter	65G
赤	セキ、シャク、あか、あか-い、あか-らむ、あか-らめる	red	5D
石	セキ、シャク、コク、いし	stone, rock	2E
昔	セキ、シャク、むかし	olden times, past	32D
夕	セキ、ゆう	evening	4G
折	セツ、お-る、おり、お-れる	bend, break, occasion	41B
説	セツ、ゼイ、と-く	preach, explain	16F
宣	セン	promulgate, state	56B
泉	セン、いずみ	spring	17E
先	セン、さき	previous, precede, tip	3A

外	セン、し-める、うらな-う	divine, occupy	12A
銭	セン、ぜに	sen, coin, money	35C
是	ゼ	proper, this	30G
舌	ゼツ、した	tongue	12C
然	ゼン、ネン	duly, thus, so, but	29C
前	ゼン、まえ	before, front	14B
全	ゼン、まった-く	whole, completely	32F
善	ゼン、よ-い	good, virtuous	53F
遡	ソ、さかのぼ-る	goupstream; retrace the past	48G
壮	ソウ	manly, strong, grand, fertile	33E
創	ソウ	start, wound	41G
僧	ソウ	priest	48D
曹	ソウ	official, companion	68D
争	ソウ、あらそ-う	conflict, vie	38A
送	ソウ、おく-る	send	24B
捜	ソウ、さが-す	investigate	66G
相	ソウ、ショウ、あい	mutual, minister, aspect	21G
走	ソウ、はし-る	run	19G
窓	ソウ、まど	window	43G
操	ソウ、みさお、あやつ-る	handle, chastity	55B
即	ソク	immediate, namely, accession	35D
則	ソク	rule, model, standard	39B
足	ソク、あし、た-りる、た-る、た-す	leg, foot, sufficient	3D
息	ソク、いき	breath, rest, child	27E
束	ソク、たば	bundle, manage	31D

尊	ソン、たっと-い、とうと-い、たっと-ぶ、とうと-ぶ	value, esteem, your	53E
蔵	ゾウ、くら	storehouse, harbour	53A
族	ゾク	clan, family	26C
属	ゾク	belong, genus	44D
逮	タイ	chase, seize	66C
帯	タイ、お-びる、おび	wear, zone	33D
替	タイ、か-える、か-わる	exchange, swap	66F
択	タク	choose, select	27B
宅	タク	house, home	52G
卓	タク	table, excel, high	66B
単	タン	simple, single, unit	33C
旦	タン	daybreak; dawn; morning	56D
探	タン、さぐ-る、さが-す	search, probe	26A
台	ダイ、タイ	platform, stand	14C
大	ダイ、タイ、おお、おお-きい、おお-いに	big	1B
代	ダイ、タイ、か-わる、か-える、よ、しろ	replace, world, generation, fee	28F
暖	ダン、あたた-か、あたた-かい、あたた-まる、あたた-める	warm	58C
池	チ、いけ	pond, lake	8G
知	チ、しる	know	17F
築	チク、きず-く	build	46B
中	チュウ、なか	middle, inside, China	1C
虫	チュウ、むし	insect, worm	5G
朝	チョウ、あさ	court, morning	16D

兆	チョウ、きざ-す、きざ-し	sign, omen, trillion	36A
調	チョウ、しら-べる、ととの-う、ととの-える	adjust, investigate, tone, tune	10F
徴	チョウ、しるし	sign, summon, levy	67F
丁	チョウ、テイ	block, exact	2B
鳥	チョウ、とり	bird	46D
長	チョウ、なが-い	long, senior	16A
直	チョク、ジキ、ただ-ちに、なお-す、なお-る	direct, upright, fix	16G
沈	チン、しず-む、しず-める	sink	67G
珍	チン、めずら-しい	rare, curious	64F
追	ツイ、お-う	chase, pursue	28E
通	ツウ、ツ、とお-る、とお-す、かよ-う	pass, way, commute	13E
廷	テイ	court, government office	30B
亭	テイ	pavilion, inn	44B
帝	テイ	emperor	66A
弟	テイ、ダイ、デ、おとうと	youngerbrother	14D
適	テキ	suitable, fit, go	52B
的	テキ、まと	target, like, adjectival suffix	35G
徹	テツ	go through, clear, remove	68G
田	デン、た	rice field	7A
斗	ト	dipper, measure	9F
刀	トウ、かたな	sword	13C
唐	トウ、から	(T'ang) China	59F
豆	トウ、ズ、まめ	beans, miniature	19D

棟	トウ、むね、むな	ridgepole, building	67B
匿	トク	conceal	54A
屯	トン	barracks, camp, post	47G
豚	トン、ぶた	pig, pork	40G
奴	ド	slave, servant, guy	38E
度	ド、ト、タク、たび	degree, times	22B
土	ド、ト、つち	earth	6A
銅	ドウ	copper	6F
童	ドウ、わらべ	child	24G
那	ナ	what?	45C
内	ナイ、ダイ、うち	inside	8A
南	ナン、ナ、みなみ	south	18E
尼	ニ、あま	nun, priestess	66E
日	ニチ、ジツ、ひ、か	sun, day	1D
乳	ニュウ、ちち、ち	breasts, milk	57E
妊	ニン	pregnant, swollen	45G
忍	ニン、しの-ぶ、しの-ばせる	endure, stealth	50C
能	ノウ	ability, can, Noh	46G
脳	ノウ	brain	54G
派	ハ	faction, send	35F
波	ハ、なみ	wave	27F
博	ハク、バク	extensive, spread, gain, gamble	38D
白	ハク、ビャク、しろ、しら、しろ-い	white	6D
発	ハツ、ホツ	discharge, start, leave	19C
犯	ハン、おか-す	crime, violate, commit, assault	45A

半	ハン、なか-ば	half, middle	19B
反	ハン、ホン、タン、そ-る、そ-らす	oppose, anti, reverse, bend, cloth, measure	21F
煩	ハン、ボン、わずら-う、わずら-わす	trouble, pain, torment	51E
馬	バ、うま、ま	horse	8C
倍	バイ	double, -fold	29B
媒	バイ	intermediary	68E
売	バイ、う-る、う-れる	sell	8F
爆	バク	burst, explode	45D
伐	バツ	attack, cutdown	67C
抜	バツ、ぬ-く、ぬ-ける、ぬ-かす、ぬ-かる	pluck, extract, miss	69G
番	バン	turn, number, guard	15B
非	ヒ	not, un-, fault	27G
卑	ヒ、いや-しい、いや-しむ、いや-しめる	lowly, mean, despise	68F
比	ヒ、くら-べる	compare, ratio	29E
避	ヒ、さ-ける	avoid	69E
必	ヒツ、かなら-ず	necessarily	42C
筆	ヒツ、ふで	writingbrush	12F
票	ヒョウ	vote, label, sign	39D
表	ヒョウ、おもて、あらわ-す、あらわ-れる	show, surface, list	20E
苗	ビョウ、なえ、なわ	seedling, offspring	67E
父	フ、ちち	father	17B
付	フ、つ-ける、つ-く	attach, apply	34D
布	フ、ぬの	cloth, spread	37D

夫	フ、フウ、おっと	husband, man	39A
不	フ、ブ	not, un-, dis-	32G
風	フウ、フ、かぜ、かざ	wind, style	17D
副	フク	deputy, vice-, sub-	24A
復	フク	again, repeat	42A
噴	フン、ふ-く	emit, spout, gush	69F
武	ブ、ム	military, warrior	47C
仏	ブツ、ほとけ	Buddha, France	11A
生	セイ、ショウ、い-きる、い-かす、い-ける、う-まれる、う-む、お-う、は-える、は-やす、き-なま	life, birth, grow	1E
分	ブン、フン、ブ、わ-ける、わ-かれる、わ-かる、わ-かつ	divide, minute, understand	5C
丙	ヘイ	c, 3rd	23A
弊	ヘイ	my (humble), evil, exhaustion	68A
併	ヘイ、あわ-せる	unite, join	70E
並	ヘイ、なみ、なら-べる、なら-ぶ、なら-びに	row, line, rank with, ordinary	49G
兵	ヘイ、ヒョウ	soldier	39C
平	ヘイ、ビョウ、たい-ら、ひら	flat, even, calm	19E
編	ヘン、あ-む	edit, knit, book	51B
変	ヘン、か-わる、か-える	change, strange	37G
片	ヘン、かた	one side, piece	45B
米	ベイ、マイ、こめ	rice, America	20F

補	ホ、おぎな-う	make good, stopgap	57B
保	ホ、たも-つ	preserve, maintain	44E
歩	ホ、ブ、フ、ある-く、あゆ-む	walk	18D
方	ホウ、かた	side, way, square, direction, person	10G
崩	ホウ、くず-れる、くず-す	crumble, collapse	65E
包	ホウ、つつ-む	wrap, envelop	36E
峰	ホウ、みね	peak, top	68C
豊	ホウ、ゆたか	abundant, rich	49E
北	ホク、きた	north, flee	7G
墓	ボ、はか	grave	44A
棒	ボウ	pole, bar, club	58E
冒	ボウ、おか-す	defy, risk, attack	69C
僕	ボク	manservant, I	69A
没	ボツ	sink, disappear, die, lack, not	55G
凡	ボン、ハン	mediocre, common, toughly, in general	68B
麻	マ、あさ	hemp, flax, numb	70F
毎	マイ	each, every	12E
妹	マイ、いもうと	younger sister	5E
末	マツ、バツ、すえ	end, tip	34B
慢	マン	lazy, rude, boastful	69D
妙	ミョウ	exquisite, strange, mystery	14G
民	ミン、たみ	people, populace	35A
矛	ム、ほこ	halberd, lance, spear	46C

明	メイ、ミョウ、あ-り、あか-るい、あか-るむ、あか-らむ、あき-らか、あ-ける、あ-く、あ-くる、	clear, open, bright	7C
面	メン、おも、おもて、つら	face, aspect, mask	27D
免	メン、まぬか-れる	escape, avoid	31E
綿	メン、わた	cotton, cotton wool	48E
茂	モ、しげ-る	grow thickly	59C
盲	モウ	blind	52F
目	モク、ボク、め、ま	eye, ordinal, suffix	2G
門	モン、かど	gate, door	17A
夜	ヤ、よ、よる	night	13G
厄	ヤク	misfortune, disaster	49A
役	ヤク、エキ	role, service, duty	25C
輸	ユ	transport, send	46F
由	ユ、ユウ、ユイ、よし	reason, means, way	30F
悠	ユウ	compose, distant, long time, ample	45E
融	ユウ	dissolve, melt	60F
勇	ユウ、いさ-む	courage; cheer up; bein high spirits; bravery; heroism	43C
憂	ユウ、うれ-える、うれ-い、う-い	grief, sorrow	52A
有	ユウ、ウ、ある	have, exist	29G
雄	ユウ、お、おす	male, powerful	49D
誘	ユウ、さそ-う	invite, tempt, lead	64E
予	ヨ	already, prior, I	18F
与	ヨ、あた-える	give, convey, impart, involvement	21D

余	ヨ、あま-る、あま-す	excess, ample, I	47D
陽	ヨウ	sunny, male, positive (yang)	8D
曜	ヨウ	day of the week	10D
妖	ヨウ、あや-しい、なまめ-く	attractive	43E
要	ヨウ、い-る	need, vital, pivot	34G
羊	ヨウ、ひつじ	sheep	26D
揺	ヨウ、ゆ-れる、ゆ-る、ゆ-らぐ、ゆ-るぐ、ゆ-する、ゆ-さぶる、ゆ-すぶる	shake, swing, rock	69B
利	リ、き-く	profit, gain, effect	36F
里	リ、さと	village, league	9B
陸	リク	land	36B
立	リツ、リュウ、た-つ、た-てる	stand, rise, leave	2D
竜	リュウ、たつ	dragon	64C
留	リュウ、ル、と-める、と-まる	stop, fasten	50B
呂	リョ、ロ	spine; backbone	20G
寮	リョウ	hostel, dormitory	70A
量	リョウ、はか-る	measure, quantity	37A
良	リョウ、よ-い	good	38F
倫	リン	principles, ethics	37B
林	リン、はやし	woods, forest	40B
累	ルイ	accumulate, involve	70B
涙	ルイ、なみだ	tear	70G
令	レイ	order, rule	28B
励	レイ、はげ-む、はげ-ます	encourage, strive	70D

列	レツ	row, line	22C
錬	レン	refine, train, drill	25F
録	ロク	record, inscribe	24F
六	ロク、む、む-つ、むっ-つ、むい	six	5A
腕	ワン、うで	arm, skill	70C

Bibliography

Coulmas, Florian (1981), Ueber Schrift, Suhrkamp Taschenbuch Wissenschaft
DeFrancis, John (1984), Chinese Language: Fact and Fantasy, University of Hawaii Press
Henshall, Kenneth G. (1995), A Guide to Remembering Japanese Characters, Tuttle
Jim Breen's WWWJDIC [Online] Available http://www.csse.monash.edu.au/ (2014)
Nozaki Kanji Frequency List: [Online] Available http://web.archive.org/web/20080320143000/http://nozaki-lab.ics.aichi-edu.ac.jp/nozaki/asahi/kanji.html (2014)
Ostler, Nicolas (2006), Empires of the Word, Harper Perennial
Rick Harbaugh's Zhongwen Chinese Character Genealogy: [Online] Available http://zhongwen.com/ (2014)
Seeley, Christopher (2000), A History of Writing in Japan, Ateneo de Manilla University Press
Shirakawa, Shizuka (2003), 常用漢字解, Heibonsha
Shirakawa, Shizuka (2006), 人名字解, Heibonsha
Toyoda, Etsuko: 'Enhancing Autonomous L2 Vocabulary Learning Focusing on the Development of Word-Level Processing Skills' 2007 [Online] Available www.readingmatrix.com/articles/etsuko_toyoda/article.pdf (2014)

Alchemy and Astrology

Bobrick, Benson (2006), The Fated Sky: Astrology in History, Simon & Schuster
De Sphaera Mundi [Online] Available 1230
Eliade, Mircea (1979), The Forge and the Crucible: The Origins and Structure of Alchemy, The University of Chicago Press
Gettings, Fred (1981), Dictionary of Occult, Hermetic and Alchemical Sigils, Routledge & Kegan Paul Ltd
Klibansky, Raymond, Panofsky, Erwin, Saxl, Fritz (1992), Saturn und Melancholie: Studien zur Geschichte der

Naturphilosophie und Medizin, der Religion und der Kunst, Suhrkamp Taschenbuch Wissenschaft
Maier, Michael: 'Atalanta Fugiens' 1617 [Online] Available
Poisson, Albert: 'Theories et Symboles des Alchimistes Le Grand Oeuvre' 1891 [Online] Available
http://chrysopee.url.ph/_ouvrages/377.pdf (2014)
Rulandus, Martin: 'A Lexicon of Alchemy or Alchemical Dictionary' 1612 [Online] Available
http://www.rexresearch.com/rulandus/rulxa.htm (2014)
Splendor Solis 1532 [Online] Available

Mnemonics

Carruthers, Mary (2008), The Book of Memory: A Study of Memory in Medieval Culture, Cambridge Studies in Medieval Literature
Higbee, Kenneth L. (2001), Your Memory: How It Works and How to Improve It, Da Capo Press
Rossi, Paolo (2000), Logic and the Art of Memory: The Quest for a Universal Language, University of Chicago Press
Yates, Frances (2014), The Art of Memory, Random House UK

www.ingramcontent.com/pod-product-compliance
Lightning Source LLC
Chambersburg PA
CBHW070527010526
44118CB00012B/1072